An Appetite for Art

Recipes and Art from the
North Carolina Museum of Art

Compiled and Edited by
Elizabeth K. Norfleet
Editor-In-Chief, Taste·Full *Publications*

Featuring paintings and objects
from the collection of
the North Carolina Museum of Art
Raleigh, North Carolina

TASTE·FULL
PUBLICATIONS

PUBLISHER
EDITOR-IN-CHIEF
Elizabeth K. Norfleet

CONTRIBUTING WRITERS
Gale Duque
Paul Gilster
Constance Nelson

RECIPE COORDINATOR
Trent Colbert

RECIPE CONSULTANTS
Janet Grennes
Betty Rusher

DESIGN AND ART DIRECTION

ART DIRECTOR
Elizabeth K. Norfleet

GRAPHIC DESIGN
Larry Bellamy
Faye Edwards

FOOD STYLIST
Janet Grennes

PROP STYLIST
Susann Hodges

FOOD PHOTOGRAPHY
Scott LeVoyer
Lara Richardson, Assistant

ADDITIONAL PHOTOGRAPHY
Jerry Blow
Melva Calder

PRINTER
PBM Graphics

ISBN: 0-9704345-1-0

Taste•Full Publications
P.O. Box 426
Pinehurst, NC 28370
Toll Free (888) 499-6283
www.taste-full.com
editor@taste-full.com

The North Carolina Museum of Art
wishes to acknowledge and thank The Fresh Market, Inc.
for their generous support of this publication.

FOR THEIR CONTRIBUTIONS to this cookbook,
grateful acknowledgement is made to the Museum committee —
Emily S. Rosen, Judith Dickey, Bill Blaauw and Art Taylor —
and to curators John Coffey, Rebecca Martin Nagy,
David Steel and Dennis Weller.

ASSISTING IN THE PRODUCTION AS WELL WERE
Carrie Hedrick, Noelle Ocon, David Findley, Ruby Bennett and
Museum Housekeeping, Ken Smith and Museum Security,
Karen Malinofski, Christopher Ciccone, Michael Klauke,
Marcia Erickson, Huston Paschal, Georganne Bingham, Mary Blake,
Karen Cochran and William Holloman.

NORTH CAROLINA
Museum of Art

2110 Blue Ridge Road • Raleigh, NC
(919) 839-6262
www.ncartmuseum.org

COVER: *Three Trees, Two Clouds,* a painting by John Beerman (page 71) provides the setting for this North Carolina picnic and spurs an appetite for art. This simple repast features a delightful stuffed vegetable sandwich (page 69), and a rustic apple tart (page 194).

PAGE 1: Lucas Cranach the Elder (German), *Madonna and Child in a Landscape* (detail), c. 1518.

PAGE 2: A savory tart inspired by *The Feast of Esther,* Jan Lievens, c. 1625-26.

Dedication

*T*o Beth Paschal
a devoted volunteer, supporter
and friend to
the North Carolina Museum of Art
and editor of the NCMA's first cookbook,
A Celebration of Art and Cookery.

AN APPETITE FOR ART

EMBRACING THE ARTS

The North Carolina Museum of Art celebrates artistic vision and accomplishment in all manners of expression. Our galleries span over 5,000 years of art history, from a marble Cycladic figure several millennia old through the myriad treasures of our European, American and African collections to provocative works by modern masters. Our outdoor concert season and indoor concert series present diverse and dynamic musicians from across the country and around the world. And the art of the cinema is explored both in our summer "movies on the lawn" and through our winter film programs.

But the full impact of our commitment to the arts would be incomplete without a similar celebration of the culinary arts, surely an integral part of the Museum's identity and reputation.

The elegance and inventiveness of chefs Andy and Jennifer Hicks are well known to anyone who has visited Blue Ridge, the Museum Restaurant, for a weekday lunch or a Sunday brunch or who has savored the cuisine at one of our major exhibition openings. Not so regularly apparent, however, are the culinary skills of other members of the Museum family. The opportunity to showcase their favorites and spotlight several creations by our chefs at Blue Ridge makes the cookbook in your hands—a treasury of both the visual and culinary arts—an important addition to the roster of publications related to the NCMA.

As many of you know, this is not the first cookbook created in conjunction with the NCMA. A quarter of a century ago, Beth Paschal—one of the Museum's dearest friends and staunchest supporters, an asset to the Museum even before its opening—led a tireless staff of volunteers, including Harriett Poole, Louise Talley and Barbara Worth, in compiling and creating the first Museum cookbook,

A Celebration of Art and Cookery. Those recipes have graced untold dining room tables throughout the state of North Carolina, and Beth has said the success of that cookbook was more than she dared hope. Certainly well deserved, that success has not only proven a testament to her fine work but has also given our staff and supporters today the encouragement to embark on this exciting new volume, aptly titled *An Appetite for Art.*

I don't need to enumerate here the delicious recipes and wonderful artwork you'll find throughout this handsomely produced collection. Even the most cursory glance will reveal enchanting entrées, succulent side dishes and delectable desserts.

I would, however, like to call attention to the wide range of contributors whose enthusiasm ensured the quality of this compilation. Special mention must be made of a handful of people at the Museum who helped spearhead this project: Emily S. Rosen, assistant director for marketing; Bill Blaauw, director of special events; Judith Dickey, book buyer and product development assistant; and Museum docents Evie Durbin and Nancy Gregg. The expertise of editor Elizabeth Norfleet should also be recognized for guiding the project from start to finish. But this volume represents a collaboration on a much larger scale. *An Appetite for Art* includes recipes and write-ups by staff members from our curatorial and development departments, from our Museum Store and from our security personnel, among others. The Museum's docents and volunteers, in particular, have gone beyond the call of duty with their involvement in this book, and I'm pleased to see strong support here from our members, our boards and our colleagues at the Department of Cultural Resources. A special section features selections from the repertoire of Blue Ridge's Andy and Jennifer Hicks, including a menu they prepared for the Princess de Latour D'Auvergne, whose family once owned the *Latour D'Auvergne Triptych,* one of the jewels of our European collection. I'm also honored to have my own contributions

included as well, and take my word for it: My Aunt Pauline's White Chocolate Coconut Cake is truly a work of art from first glance to last bite.

Just as this generosity of time and of recipes speaks to the commitment of the Museum's friends, supporters and staff, the diversity of the artwork and recipes also serves as a reminder of the various pleasures to be found at our Museum. In saying this, I refer not just to the images reproduced in these pages, not just to the tart which complements *The Feast of Esther* or to the juxtaposition of freshly baked scones against the backdrop of *Beulah's Baby.* Instead, something more subtle is at play, a resonance between the contents of this cookbook, the contents of our collection and the overall mission of the Museum.

When I read about Salade Niçoise with Fresh Tuna and other Mediterranean recipes, I picture the majestic artwork from the region that visitors can find in our galleries: the Greek vases, the Italian masters, the Spanish still lifes. The Mexican soup Caldo Xochitl sends my imagination into our Ancient American Gallery, where a Vera Cruz deity stands watch over cherished relics of New World art. The brisket recipe "A Gahntze Tzimmes" (Yiddish for "A Grand Production") reminds me with great pride of the Museum's Judaic Gallery, a rarity among American art museums, one of the highpoints of our collection and a "grand production" all its own. The mention of Cedar Island Shrimp conjures up images of the North Carolina coast as vivid as a Claude Howell painting— just one of the North Carolina artists whose works the Museum is grateful to own. And the chapter on "Picnic Fare" certainly provides the promise of a relaxing afternoon or enchanting evening in the Museum Park.

To everyone who contributed to the production of this cookbook, I offer my hearty thanks. And on behalf of everyone at the Museum, I also extend our appreciation to you, the reader, for your interest in the North Carolina Museum of Art and for your "appetite for art" in all its forms.

— *Lawrence J. Wheeler, Director*

ON FAMILIAR GROUND

Just as a painter or sculptor, I am a dreamer. I dream of concepts and projects that incorporate the culinary arts with other art forms. Having grown up in a family of good cooks, my appreciation for good food was developed at an early age. By the same token, early exposure to fine art and other cultural explorations helped shape a lifelong interest in the arts. Being an art enthusiast has helped cultivate my visual imagination in spite of the fact that, much to my dismay, I am not particularly gifted with a paintbrush.

The North Carolina Museum of Art (NCMA) has been a part of my life since elementary school. On family trips to visit my grandparents in Edenton, oftentimes my mother would break the journey from Winston-Salem with a welcome detour to the NCMA for an hour or two of culture. We'd stretch our legs and stroll the Museum's pastoral grounds and vast galleries.

Recent years have allowed me the opportunity to become reacquainted with the NCMA. On frequent trips to Raleigh for photo shoots I would navigate the capital city using the NCMA's location as a geographic point of orientation. The Museum is that familiar; the drive as automatic as one to your alma mater for a college football game.

Last February I contacted Larry Wheeler, the NCMA's energetic and talented director, about my interest in collaborating with the Museum on a cookbook. I remembered from an interview in 1996 that Dr. Wheeler had a keen interest in cooking and good food, and I hoped to spur his interest in a book that would celebrate both the arts and our contemporary Southern cuisine. Imagine my excitement upon receiving a quick handwritten note expressing his interest — the first step in realizing my dream for a Museum cookbook. What an honor it has been to be a part of the delicious and stimulating process of creating *An Appetite for Art.*

Emily S. Rosen, assistant director for marketing at the NCMA, has been my main point person in developing the project, with assistance from Judith Dickey, book buyer and product development assistant of the Museum Store; Bill Blaauw, director of special events (and an accomplished chef in his own right); and Art Taylor, assistant director of communications. A group of active Museum docents — Evie Durbin, Nancy Gregg, Barbara Allen and Betty Ginn — also helped spearhead efforts to develop a cookbook for a new generation of museum supporters. Had it not been for their enthusiasm in such an undertaking, the idea may have been put on hold. Herein lies the bounty of this team effort.

In different yet infinitesimal ways both art and good food can nurture one's soul. An hour's visit to a wing or two of the NCMA can renourish your appreciation of beauty, and refocus attention to life's finer details. One look at Claude Monet's *The Cliff, Etretat, Sunset* (page 12) compels a person to seek out that peaceful time of day in a special spot of his own. The sheer simplicity yet utter goodness of a dish such as the Backfin Crabmeat on Cornmeal-Crusted Tomatoes (page 108) can be as inspirational in a different way. The taste of summer's juicy tomatoes with lightly dressed crabmeat serves to remind us that, even for the short term, some meals should remain a celebration in an often hectic life. These experiences rejuvenate the spirit.

An Appetite for Art celebrates the fine and ever-evolving collection of paintings, sculpture and objects at the NCMA. When conceptualizing the cookbook, my vision was that the reproductions of the Museum's collection would extend beyond a mere coexistence with the food photography. It was my hope that the food and the art would wed, creating a perfect union exemplified in exceptional photographs. The visual accompaniment for the Backfin Crabmeat recipe is one example. Another appears on the cookbook's introductory pages: The Hearty Middle Eastern Tart photographed with Jan Lievens' *The Feast of Esther*

demonstrates the remarkable experience of how specific NCMA paintings became the source of inspiration for delightful cuisine. I applaud everyone at the Museum who played a role in forging this unique relationship between the Museum's collection and the recipes within *An Appetite for Art*. The result is a stunning and original cookbook that pays homage to the Museum's collection — precisely my intent.

A professional and personal crossroads led me to approach Dr. Wheeler about his interest in a new Museum cookbook. I had recently made the difficult decision to cease publication of *Taste•Full*, a statewide food and travel publication, after 10 years as publisher. The decision was made with family in mind, particularly my three-year-old son and 18-month-old daughter. It was my desire to continue working although with less frequent deadlines, as well as to devote my creative energy to projects I believe in — especially those that serve institutions and organizations that have influenced my life and will my children's lives. The Museum clearly fits the new criteria. The multi-faceted environment at the NCMA is one that will continue to be a big part of our lives. Our home is now in Pinehurst, so chances are that my children will also learn to navigate Raleigh in relation to the Museum's location. I certainly hope so.

Early in the production of *An Appetite for Art*, the Museum made the decision to dedicate the cookbook to Beth Paschal, the editor of *A Celebration of Art and Cookery*, the NCMA's first collection of recipes. Upon first meeting Beth, I recognized a kindred spirit who understood what an undertaking this new cookbook was. A copy of *A Celebration of Art and Cookery* has been close at hand during the entire production process, alongside the memory of Beth's soft spoken words of encouragement. As you peruse the recipes, you will notice the sign 📖, signifying recipes from the earlier book making an encore appearance that were particular favorites of Beth's. Enjoy!

— *Elizabeth K. Norfleet, Editor*

OPENINGS

At the North Carolina Museum of Art there are no humble beginnings — only spectacular openings. Great openings set the stage for the Museum's most successful exhibitions. Appetizers can do the same for a well-planned menu. Carefully chosen to enhance the main course, appetizers provide a sneak peek of foods to come and set the stage for a memorable meal.

MOTHER'S BUFFET CRAB MEAT

A popular way to bring a taste of the coast to a crowd of people, this recipe was handed down by Scotty Steele's mother.

1   pound crab meat
1   can cream of celery soup
1   tablespoon grated onion
1½ teaspoons mace or ½ teaspoon nutmeg
• salt and pepper
• dash of hot sauce

Carefully pick through crab for shells.

Place crab and soup in top of a double boiler. Add onion, mace or nutmeg, salt, pepper and hot sauce. Cook over medium heat until heated through. Serve warm in chafing dish with crackers or toast rounds. Serves 8-10.

SCOTTY STEELE
RALEIGH, NC

CRAB AND SWISS ON SOURDOUGH

An enticing hors d'oeuvre. Prepare ahead and assemble at party time. This combination would also make a great open-faced crab melt sandwich. The use of canned or frozen crabmeat is perfect for winter months when fresh crabmeat is scarce.

1   6-ounce can crabmeat or 6-ounce package frozen crabmeat
1   cup grated Swiss cheese
½ cup sour cream
2   tablespoons minced green onions
3   tablespoons lemon juice
½ teaspoon Worcestershire sauce
¼ teaspoon salt
¼ teaspoon white pepper
2   dashes Tabasco sauce
1   small can water chestnuts, drained
3   7-inch sourdough rolls

Drain and flake crabmeat (thaw frozen crab first). Combine in a small bowl with cheese, sour cream, green onions, lemon juice, Worcestershire, salt, pepper and Tabasco. Set aside. Slice 10 water chestnuts in thirds and set aside. Chop remaining drained water chestnuts finely and mix into crabmeat.

Preheat oven to 400°. Slice each sourdough roll crosswise into 10 slices. Spoon 2 tablespoons crabmeat mixture evenly on top of each. Garnish each slice with 1 piece water chestnut. Arrange on an ungreased baking sheet. Bake 10-15 minutes until bubbly and slightly browned. Serve hot. Makes 30 pieces.

JUANITA B. WILSON
RALEIGH, NC

PREVIOUS PAGES: **CLAUDE MONET** (French), *THE CLIFF, ETRETAT, SUNSET* (detail), 1883

Versatile Latin Seviche can be a perfect appetizer at your next dinner party.

LATIN SEVICHE

The full richness of seafood emerges in this marinated salad of fresh fish, tomatoes and avocado. Serve on a bed of lettuce as an appetizer with toasted pita triangles on the side.

½   pound small-to-medium shrimp

½   pound fresh fish, grouper

½   pound bay scallops

•   juice of 3 limes

1   teaspoon salt

¼   cup olive oil

1   large tomato, peeled and seeded

½   small can green chilies

1   tablespoon chopped cilantro

½   cup red onion, thinly sliced

1   avocado, ripe

•   fresh ground pepper

•   Tabasco sauce

Cook shrimp in boiling water until slightly pink. Do not cook completely. Cool and peel. Combine shrimp in a large bowl with bite-size pieces of fish. Stir in scallops. Add lime juice to cover. Refrigerate at least 5 hours or overnight.

An hour or two before serving, stir in salt, olive oil, tomato cubes, chilies, cilantro, onion, diced avocado, pepper and Tabasco sauce to taste. Cover and refrigerate until serving time. Drain liquid from seviche and spoon into a bowl lined with lettuce leaves. Serves 6.

NANCY GREGG
RALEIGH, NC

JANS JANSZ. DEN UYL (Dutch), *VANITAS BANQUET PIECE*, c. 1635

SMOKED TROUT AND MACKEREL PATÉ

A cherished recipe from a British friend of Dorothy O'Connor. If smoked mackerel or smoked trout are not available, substitute with other smoked fish.

⅓-½ pound smoked trout fillets

½   pound peppered mackerel fillets

6   tablespoons unsalted butter, at room temperature

•   juice of one lemon

1   cup sour cream

•   freshly ground pepper

•   pinch cayenne

Remove skin and bones from fish. Break into small pieces. Place in food processor with butter, lemon juice and sour cream. Mix until smooth. Season to taste with black pepper and cayenne. Spoon into a crock.

Cover with foil and freeze or refrigerate until needed. Chill at least an hour before using. Serve with crackers. Refrigerate for up to 4 days. Makes 2 cups.

DOROTHY O'CONNER
CARY, NC

TANGY SHRIMP MOLD

Creamy, tangy and bursting with shrimp, this molded dish tempts the taste buds as an appetizer or pacifies the palate as a luncheon entrée. Make in a fish or shell mold for added appeal.

1	envelope gelatin
1	10-ounce can tomato soup
1	8-ounce cream cheese
1	pound small shrimp
1	cup diced celery
¼	cup chopped scallions
1	tablespoon Worcestershire sauce
⅛	teaspoon garlic powder
⅛	teaspoon white pepper

Dissolve gelatin in ½ cup hot water. In a small saucepan heat tomato soup and cream cheese together on low. Add gelatin mixture and stir until well-blended. In a medium saucepan, cook shrimp; cool and peel. Stir into tomato base with celery, scallions, Worcestershire, garlic powder and white pepper.

Place mixture in an oiled 1-quart mold, cover with plastic wrap and refrigerate at least 4 hours. Unmold onto a plate lined with lettuce leaves. Garnish with parsley and cherry tomatoes. Serve with crackers or bread rounds. Serves 8-10.

JOAN NEWMAN COHEN
CHAPEL HILL, NC

BARBECUED SHRIMP & VIDALIAS

No need to fire up the grill for these delicious shrimp marinated in a delightful homemade barbecue sauce. Serve cold as an appetizer or over salad for a light lunch.

2	pounds shrimp
2	medium Vidalia onions

HOMEMADE BARBECUE SAUCE:

1	cup vegetable oil
¼	cup cider vinegar
¼	cup ketchup
4	bay leaves
2	tablespoons Worcestershire sauce
1	teaspoon salt
½	teaspoon dry mustard
•	dash of Tabasco sauce

Cook and peel shrimp. Slice onions into thin rings.

For Homemade Barbecue Sauce: In a medium bowl, whisk together remaining ingredients. Pour over shrimp and onions in a large resealable plastic bag and refrigerate at least 24 hours. Turn often.

Drain off sauce and place shrimp and onions in serving dish, discarding bay leaves. Serves 6-8.

MARTHA MICHAELS
RALEIGH, NC

GENOA SHRIMP OVER FOCACCIA

Shrimp and cured olives are seasoned with Mediterranean flavors. Spoon over the fresh focaccia on page 164.

1	pound shrimp
1	teaspoon Old Bay Seasoning
2	tablespoons fresh parsley
2	tablespoons fresh basil
1	cup Niçoise olives
2	teaspoons capers
¼	cup minced red onion
2	cloves garlic, minced
½	cup olive oil
2	tablespoons red wine vinegar
1	tablespoon lemon juice
•	freshly ground pepper

Drop shrimp into 1½ quarts boiling water seasoned with Old Bay. When water returns to boil, drain shrimp, cool and peel. Cut into ¾-inch pieces.

Chop parsley and basil. Remove pits from olives, chop coarsely and combine in a medium bowl with shrimp, capers, onions, garlic, parsley and basil.

In a separate small bowl whisk together olive oil, vinegar, lemon juice and pepper. Add to shrimp mixture. Cover and refrigerate at least 2 hours, stirring once or twice. Serves 6.

PÂTÉ GIBIER

This recipe for venison pâté was included with those favored by Rene Verdon, White House Chef during the Kennedy years. Ground veal may be substituted for the venison, and sausage with sage can replace the pork. Slice pâté thinly and serve on toast points or with crackers and a good French mustard.

2	pounds ground venison
3	tablespoons cognac
¼	teaspoon salt
¼	teaspoon white pepper
1	teaspoon sage
½	teaspoon allspice
½	pound ground pork
2	eggs
½	cup chopped pistachio nuts or 12 truffles
½	pound thinly sliced Smithfield or country ham

In a medium bowl, marinate venison with cognac for 15 minutes. Combine salt, pepper, sage and allspice and sprinkle 2-3 pinches of seasoning over venison. In another bowl, mix together pork, eggs, pistachios, if used, and remaining spices. Stir in venison and mix well.

Preheat oven to 350°.

Line a 6½-inch x 2½-inch mold with thin slices of ham. Layer venison mixture with ham in 3 parts all the way to top of mold ending with ham. If truffles are used instead of nuts, they should be arranged to form the center layer of the paté. Cover with foil and bake for 1½ hours, until a sharp knife inserted in center comes out clean. Let cool slightly, then pour off excess fat and cool completely. Turn out of mold and slice thinly. Serves 10-12.

PEGGY JO KIRBY
PITTSBORO, NC

STILTON TART WITH CARAMELIZED WALNUTS

This pleasing tart combines two of port's best food pairings — walnuts and a blue cheese such as Stilton.

CREAM CHEESE PASTRY:

1	cup flour
1	teaspoon sugar
½	teaspoon salt
4	ounces cold cream cheese
4	tablespoons cold butter

FILLING:

1	8-ounce cream cheese
½	pound Stilton blue cheese
3	tablespoons whipping cream
¼	cup port
2	eggs
1	cup chopped walnuts
¼	cup brown sugar

CARAMELIZED WALNUT TOPPING:

½	cup sugar
36	whole walnuts

Make Cream Cheese Pastry: In a food processor put flour, sugar and salt. Process briefly to combine. Cut cream cheese and butter into pieces and add to processor. Pulse until mixture resembles coarse meal. Bring together into a ball; wrap in plastic wrap and chill 15 minutes.

Preheat oven to 400°. Roll dough between 2 sheets of wax paper, then press into 9-inch tart pan with removable bottom. Prick bottom and chill 15 minutes. Bake 15-20 minutes, pricking bottom again every 5 minutes. Remove and reduce oven temperature to 375°.

For filling: Combine cream cheese, Stilton and whipping cream in food processor and process until smooth. Add port and eggs; process again until smooth and fluffy. Pour into hot pastry shell. In separate small bowl combine chopped walnuts and brown sugar. Sprinkle over tart. (Put tart pan on larger pan for easier handling.) Return to 375° oven and bake 25-30 minutes until set. Cool on rack. Store in refrigerator, if desired, for a day or two.

Make Caramelized Walnut Topping while tart is baking. Serves 6-8.

CARAMELIZED WALNUT TOPPING: Melt sugar in a heavy skillet over medium heat, swirling pan until liquefied and golden brown. Add walnuts and toss quickly to coat well. Pour out onto marble or a wax paper-lined pan and separate with a fork or knife for individual nuts. Cool. Place walnuts around edge of tart and save remaining for garnish.

Sometimes heavy hors d'oeuvres are destined for more intimate gatherings. For an evening of quiet conversation with good friends, forego the dining room table and serve a delicious spread of toothsome appetizers in a comfortable living room. Such a sampling could include Polenta Stars with Wilted Spinach & Gorgonzola (page 21), a Stilton Tart with Carmelized Walnuts, Zucchini & Red Pepper Toasts (page 21) and Pâté Gibier.

DAVID TENIERS THE YOUNGER (Flemish), *DANCERS AT A VILLAGE INN*, c. 1650

David Teniers the Younger excelled in depictions of outdoor merrymakers of the type seen in *Dancers at a Village Inn*. Against a backdrop of the flat Flemish countryside, Teniers painted a group of villagers engaged in an outdoor celebration alive with eating and drinking, music and dancing. The results of overindulgence have not escaped the eye of the artist; to the right people stagger as they make their way home. The inclusion of these figures likely provided a moralizing message to the contemporary viewer.

Zucchini & Red Pepper Toasts

A sassy toast cup filled with a tangy vegetable marinade. These bite-size morsels feature thin slices of zucchini, red pepper and carrot resting in an Italian marinade. Vegetable trays — move over!

2 small zucchini

¾ pound carrots, see note

1-2 large red bell peppers

··

MARINADE:

⅓ cup vegetable oil

⅓ cup olive oil

¼ cup red wine vinegar

1 teaspoon Italian seasoning

2 tablespoons fresh chopped parsley

½ teaspoon salt

1 teaspoon black pepper

··

TOAST CUPS:

1 loaf whole wheat bread

Make Toast Cups.

Peel carrots if needed and slice into very thin rounds. Quarter zucchini lengthwise and slice thinly. Remove seeds and stems from red peppers. Cut pepper into thin strips, cut again into ½-inch pieces. Make sure there is an equal amount of each vegetable.

For marinade: In a large bowl combine all marinade ingredients. Add the sliced vegetables to the marinade; refrigerate at least 2 hours before serving. Toss occasionally.

Just prior to serving, fill toast cups with marinated vegetables. Makes 40-50 pieces; allow 2 per person. Serves 20-25.

NOTE: You may need to buy carrots with a small diameter so they slice into thin rounds. Try to buy the already peeled, snack carrots available in your supermarket's produce section.

TOAST CUPS: With a rolling pin, flatten each piece of bread to about 1⁄16 inch. Cut each flattened piece into 4 equal squares or cut with a cookie cutter. Gently press square into lightly greased cups of a mini-muffin tin. Bake at 350° for 15 minutes or until crisp. Remove from muffin tins and let cool. These can be made up to 3 days ahead. Store in tight container.

Polenta Stars with Wilted Spinach & Gorgonzola

This treat will be the "star" of your party. Sautéed spinach with garlic and pine nuts enhanced with melted gorgonzola combine in this tantalizing delicacy. Prepare polenta a day ahead when you have time to stir.

SUN-DRIED TOMATO POLENTA:

1 cup sun-dried tomatoes (dry)

6 cups water

2 cups yellow cornmeal

2 teaspoons salt

··

SPINACH TOPPING:

¼ cup olive oil

6 cloves garlic, minced

½ cup pine nuts

8 cups baby spinach leaves, large stems removed

4 ounces Gorgonzola cheese, crumbled

Prepare polenta the day before. Oil two 10-inch x 14-inch baking dishes.

Cover sun-dried tomatoes with boiling water for 2 minutes to soften. Drain water and chop tomatoes. Set aside. Bring 6 cups of water to boil in a heavy-bottomed saucepan. Whisk in cornmeal, a little at a time. Add salt. Continually stir and cook mixture for 20-30 minutes, until it begins to pull away from sides of the pan. Fold in reserved tomatoes. Divide mixture between prepared baking pans. Smooth mixture carefully with a spatula. Cool and refrigerate, covered for at least 4 hours or overnight.

Preheat oven to 425°. Oil two baking sheets. Using a cookie cutter, cut polenta into 2½-inch star shapes and place on baking sheets. Bake for 15-20 minutes, until firm and slightly browned.

Meanwhile, prepare spinach topping. In a large sauté pan, heat oil. Add garlic and pine nuts and sauté until slightly browned. Add spinach and cook just until wilted with a bright green color.

With a slotted spoon, place spinach mixture on polenta stars, dividing evenly. Top each with crumbled Gorgonzola. Place under broiler until cheese is bubbly and starting to melt. Serve immediately. Makes 35.

MARINATED GOAT CHEESE WITH SMOKED SALMON AND CRACKERS

Only an artist's canvas could match the vivid colors presented in this outstanding yet easily assembled appetizer.

12	ounces plain mild goat cheese
1	red bell pepper
1	green bell pepper
1	yellow bell pepper
½	cup extra virgin olive oil
1	shallot, finely chopped
¼	cup chopped fresh parsley
1	teaspoon oregano
1	teaspoon basil
2	teaspoons freshly ground black pepper
½	pound smoked salmon, cut in thin strips

BAGUETTE CRACKERS:

1	baguette, cut into ¼-inch pieces
½	cup olive oil
4	tablespoons butter, melted

Place goat cheese logs in a shallow glass baking dish and refrigerate.

Seed peppers and cut into a fine dice. Heat oil in a skillet, on medium heat. Add shallot and peppers and cook until softened but not browned, about 10 minutes. Add parsley, oregano, basil and pepper to the pan, and cook for 2 more minutes. Remove from heat and cool mixture for 15 minutes. Pour over goat cheese and refrigerate up to 2 days, tightly covered.

Make Baguette Crackers.

About 30 minutes before serving, arrange cheese, with pepper marinade on top, in the middle of a large serving platter. The pepper marinade will begin releasing some of its oil and juices and the platter will need to be cleaned up after 20 minutes. Arrange baguette crackers on one side of the cheese and smoked salmon on the other. Spread goat cheese with marinade on cracker with a decorative cheese or paté knife; dollop cheese with a strip of smoked salmon using a small decorative fork. Let guests assemble their own bites. Serves 12.

BAGUETTE CRACKERS: Preheat broiler. Arrange bread on a sheet pan. Combine butter and olive oil and heavily brush each piece with the butter mixture. Broil until deep golden, about 1-2 minutes. Turn over and toast the other side for 1-2 minutes as well. Remove from oven and cool. Crackers will keep in airtight container for 2 days.

SAVORY BLUE CHEESE & VIDALIAS ON PUMPERNICKEL TOASTS

A great party hors d'oeuvre. The longer the blue cheese and Vidalias marinate, the tastier it becomes.

2	cups sliced Vidalias or any sweet onions
½	cup light olive oil
1	teaspoon salt
1	teaspoon sugar
2	tablespoons lemon juice
•	freshly ground black pepper
•	dash Tabasco sauce
•	dash paprika
1	cup crumbled blue cheese
•	pumpernickel cocktail rounds, buttered

Place onions in bottom of 9-inch x 13-inch glass baking dish; the shallow depth aids in marinating the onions.

Whisk together oil, salt, sugar, lemon juice and seasonings. Pour over onions. Stir in blue cheese. Cover and refrigerate 2-5 days. Stir occasionally. Pour into a decorative dish and serve with buttered toast rounds. Serves 10-12.

CAROLYN HERGENROTHER
DURHAM, NC

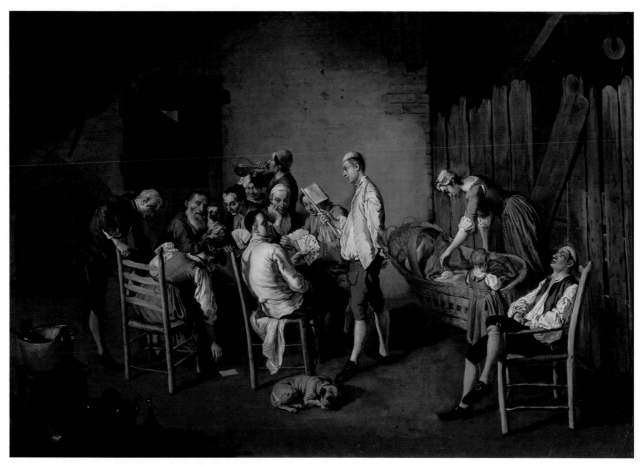

GIACOMO ANTONIO MELCHIORRE CERUTI (Italian), *THE CARD GAME*, c. 1738-50

SMOKED TURKEY IN CURRANT MINI-MUFFINS

Mini sandwiches for that time of day when it's not quite lunch or dinner. Make muffins, cut in half, spread with chutney butter and fill with smoked turkey or ham. Just watch them disappear.

TURKEY FILLING:

½ pound unsalted butter, softened

3 tablespoons chutney

1 pound smoked turkey (or ½ pound ham and ½ pound turkey), sliced

. . . .

CURRANT MINI MUFFINS:

1 cup butter, softened

2 cups sugar

1 teaspoon orange extract

4 eggs

1 cup buttermilk

4 cups flour

2 teaspoons baking soda

1 teaspoon salt

1 cup currants

TURKEY FILLING: Make filling by mixing together unsalted butter and chutney. Spread on muffin half and fill with thin slices of smoked turkey or ham.

CURRANT MINI-MUFFINS: Preheat oven to 375°. Grease mini-muffin pans.

In a large bowl, with a mixer cream butter and sugar. Add extract and eggs and beat well. In a separarte bowl combine flour, baking soda and salt. Blend in buttermilk alternating with mixed dry ingredients. Stir in currants. Fill mini-muffin cups ⅔ full and bake 15-20 minutes until golden brown on top.

Cool muffins, then split in half. Makes 72 mini-muffins.

Spicy Marinated Olive Mix

A big hit at a party, these olives will zing your tastebuds. Recipe doubles easily. Serve olives at room temperature with frilled toothpicks. If desired, 1-1½ pounds cubed cheese such as Swiss or jalapeño havarti may be tossed with olives before serving.

1	pound large pitted black olives
1	pound large pitted green olives
¾	cup olive oil
1	tablespoon lemon juice
1	tablespoon minced garlic
1	tablespoon Jerk Seasoning
½	tablespoon crushed red pepper flakes
2	bay leaves, crumbled
1½	teaspoons pepper

JERK SEASONING:

1	tablespoon allspice
1	teaspoon salt
1	teaspoon pepper
1	teaspoon ground thyme
1	teaspoon cinnamon
½	teaspoon nutmeg
¼	teaspoon cayenne pepper

Drain olives. Whisk together olive oil with lemon juice, garlic and jerk seasoning, red pepper, bay leaves and pepper. Pour over olives, cover and marinate 24-48 hours. Serves 30.

JERK SEASONING: Mix ingredients together. Makes ¼ cup.

EGYPTIAN, LATE PERIOD, DYNASTY XXII-XXXIII, *MUMMY CASE OF AMONRED,* c. 945-712 BC

MUSHROOM CROUSTADES

Bite-size tartlets featuring mushrooms mixed with spring onions and fresh herbs. The bread shells, called croustades, and the filling can be made ahead, then assembled and baked at cocktail time.

24	slices thin-sliced white bread
½	cup butter, divided
½	pound mushrooms
3	tablespoons green onions
2	tablespoons flour
1	cup milk
½	teaspoon salt
¼	teaspoon red pepper
1	tablespoon chopped fresh parsley
½	tablespoon chopped fresh chives
1	teaspoon lemon juice
•	Parmesan cheese

To make croustades: Preheat oven to 400°. Grease mini-muffin tins.

Cut 3-inch rounds from each slice of bread. Melt 4 tablespoons butter and brush both sides of bread. Press into tins and bake for 10 minutes. Set aside to cool.

Finely chop mushrooms and green onions. In a large sauté pan melt remaining 4 tablespoons butter. Cook mushrooms and onions 5-8 minutes. Add flour, stirring well. Add milk and cook, stirring, until slightly thickened. Mix in salt, red pepper, parsley, chives and lemon juice. Cool before filling croustades.

Preheat oven to 400°. Fill toast cups with mushroom mixture. Sprinkle Parmesan on top. Bake until hot and bubbly. Serve warm. Makes 24.

GEORGANNE BINGHAM
RALEIGH, NC

BAKED CHEDDAR DELIGHTS

Baked cheese straws with the added surprise of tangy olive inside.

½	pound sharp cheddar cheese, grated
1	cup butter or margarine, softened
2½	cups flour
¼	teaspoon cayenne pepper
¼	teaspoon salt
1	6-ounce jar small Spanish olives (58 olives)

Preheat oven to 375°. Blend cheese and butter together using your hands if necessary to obtain a smooth mixture. Sift flour with pepper and salt and stir into cheese. Drain olives and dry on pepper towels. Mold the dough around each olive to make ½-inch cheese balls. Arrange balls evenly on a baking sheet. Bake 20 minutes. Serve immediately. Makes 58.

To freeze: Arrange balls on a baking sheet 1-inch apart and freeze. Once frozen, store in a resealable plastic bag and refreeze. Take out 1-hour before serving, then bake as above.

MRS. ZOË S. WEBSTER
RALEIGH, NC

PEGGY'S SPICY SALMON SPREAD

An attractive party dish that can be made ahead. Serve with good water crackers or Baguette Crackers on page 22.

1	15½-ounce can red sockeye or coho salmon
1	8-ounce cream cheese, softened
1	tablespoon lemon juice
1	tablespoon grated onion
2	teaspoons horseradish
¼	teaspoon salt
¼	teaspoon Tabasco sauce
•	dash Worcestershire sauce
½	cup chopped or sliced almonds
¼	cup chopped fresh parsley

Drain salmon; remove any dark skin and bones. Combine thoroughly with cream cheese, lemon juice, onion, horseradish, salt, Tabasco and Worcestershire. Cover and chill at least 2 hours.

Shape mixture into a ball or log and roll in a mixture of almonds and parsley covering all sides. Refrigerate until time to serve. Serves 20.

PEGGY ALLGOOD
CARY, NC

CUCUMBER DIP

A refreshing dip to serve with crackers or raw vegetables.

2 medium cucumbers
1 8-ounce cream cheese, softened
¼ cup mayonnaise
¼ cup chopped onion
½ teaspoon garlic salt

Peel and dice cucumbers. In a small bowl, mix together cream cheese, mayonnaise and garlic salt. Fold in cucumbers and onions and mix well. Refrigerate 1 hour. Yields 2 cups, serving 10-12.

RITA ELLIOTT
APEX, NC

SALMON CARPACCIO

Thinly sliced fresh fish, exploding with essence of lemon. When served over tender chive tossed potatoes, this dish turns a casual patio supper into something elegant and exciting.

¼ cup extra virgin olive oil
• zest of 3 lemons
½ cup vegetable oil
¼ cup chopped chives
2 sprigs fresh thyme
2 sprigs fresh rosemary
8-10 fingerling potatoes
½ teaspoon black peppercorns
8-10 ounces fresh salmon fillet
¼ cup heavy cream
• salt and pepper
• lemon wedges

To make a lemon oil: In a small bowl, combine olive oil and lemon zest and let steep in the refrigerator 1 hour. To make a chive oil: Puree vegetable oil and chives in a blender. Strain and chill.

In a large pot, put thyme, rosemary, potatoes and peppercorns. Cover with water and boil until tender. Let cool. Peel potatoes; cut into ¼-inch thick slices.

Slice salmon as thin as possible. Divide slices into 4 portions. Place each portion in a circular pattern between 2 large sheets of plastic wrap. Using a mallet, carefully pound salmon as thin as possible.

In a large saucepan, warm potato slices with heavy cream and chive oil. Bring to a simmer and add salt and pepper to taste. Spoon potatoes into center of each plate. Remove plastic wrap from one side of salmon and invert over potatoes. Remove second plastic sheet.

Brush salmon with lemon oil. Season with kosher salt and freshly ground black pepper. Garnish with lemon wedges and fresh chives. Serves 4.

MICHAEL HAYNES
RALEIGH, NC

TOFU-PESTO DIP

For this recipe from her aunt, Karen Sorensen Whitney, Heather Looney recommends the Nanna's brand of corn chips, available at specialty grocers, for the ultimate flavor punch with this zesty dip. Pluto's spice line is available at most specialty stores.

1 12.3 ounce package tofu
2 cups prepared pesto
• salt
• dash of Pluto's Jamaican Jerk Spice
1 package corn chips

Open package of tofu and drain water. Rinse under cold water. Pat dry with paper towels (this enables the tofu to absorb more flavor).

Break tofu into pieces and place in blender or food processor. Pour in most of the pesto, and turn machine on low speed. (If using blender, frequently pause and press the dip back down because of thickness.) Mix until completely blended and a light green color. Add salt to taste. Add a bit more pesto and salt at intervals to get the perfect balance of flavor. For a little more "umph", add a couple dashes of Pluto Jerk spice. Serve with corn chips. Serves 10-12.

HEATHER LOONEY
RALEIGH, NC

HIGH ROLLERS

These appetizers are best made a day or two ahead. Lahvash is a Syrian bread found in specialty food stores. You can substitute Hye-Roller pre-moistened cracker bread. Be sure and note that the lahvash needs to be softened ahead of time.

1	large disk of Valley Lahvash cracker bread
1	8-ounce cream cheese
4	ounces feta cheese
¼	cup basil pesto
1	teaspoon minced garlic
1	7-ounce jar roasted red peppers
1	4-ounce jar artichoke hearts
2	green onions, minced
⅔	cup shredded fresh spinach leaves

Soften cracker bread between two very damp terry cloth towels according to package directions. This will take at least 1 hour.

Bring cream cheese to room temperature, and crumble feta cheese. With electric mixer, blend cream cheese and feta together. Add pesto and garlic; beat until smooth. Spread mixture evenly over surface of cracker bread. Lay red peppers and artichoke pieces on top of cheese, pizza fashion. Sprinkle with onions and shredded spinach. Cut disk in half and roll up each side tightly from rounded edge to straight edge, forming two long rolls. Place seam side down on plastic wrap and wrap tightly. Chill overnight or up to two days. These may also be frozen. Slice rolls into ¼" slices and serve on a platter. Makes 36 pieces.

CAROLYN BOOTH
RALEIGH, NC

SPINACH FETA BITES

Wilted spinach seasoned with feta cheese and bacon is spooned into hard-boiled egg halves. These bites are attractive and easy, and they add variety to an hors d'oeuvres menu by being non-bread.

10	eggs
6	slices bacon
4	cups chopped spinach leaves
3	tablespoons bacon grease, reserved
1	tablespoon red wine vinegar
½	cup crumbled feta cheese
•	salt and pepper

Hard boil eggs, stirring frequently to keep yolks centered. Cool under cold water, then peel and cut in half widthwise. Remove yolks, and cut a small slice off bottom of each white so each will sit squarely on a serving plate.

Cook bacon in a sauté pan until crisp. Drain and reserve pan with bacon drippings. Crumble 3 pieces and set aside 3 slices for garnish.

In reserved pan, sauté spinach until just wilted. Remove from heat. Stir in vinegar, feta cheese and crumbled bacon. Season with salt and pepper.

Fill each egg half with spinach mixture and top with a small piece of crisp bacon. Makes 20 bites.

QUICK BLACK BEAN AND CORN SALSA

A recipe adapted from a cookbook from the Junior League of Birmingham, Alabama. Easily doubled. Keep the provisions on hand for instant entertaining.

2	15-ounce cans black beans, drained
1	16-ounce can corn, drained
½	cup chopped fresh cilantro
⅓	cup lime juice
⅓	cup vegetable oil
½	cup finely chopped red onion
1	tablespoon ground cumin
2	14.5-ounce cans diced tomatoes with mild green chilies
1	8-ounce jar medium or hot picante sauce
•	salt and pepper

Combine black beans, corn, cilantro, lime juice, oil, red onion, cumin, diced tomatoes with green chilies and picante sauce. in a large bowl. Season with salt and pepper. Cover and refrigerate 24 hours, stirring occasionally.

Serve with chips or as a side dish. Makes 1 quart.

MARY M. BLAKE
RALEIGH, NC

FROM
BREAKFAST TO
BRUNCH

BLUEBERRY-STUFFED FRENCH TOAST

These delightfully easy bread pockets are stuffed with spring's blueberries. A little Grand Marnier gives the blueberry orange sauce extra zest, but the addition is strictly optional.

- • cooking spray
- 6 eggs
- 1 teaspoon grated orange peel
- ⅔ cup orange juice
- 3 tablespoons sugar, divided
- • pinch salt
- 1 cup fresh or frozen blueberries (not necessary to thaw)
- 8 slices thick Italian bread
- ⅓ cup sliced almonds

....

BLUEBERRY ORANGE SAUCE:

- 3 tablespoons sugar
- 1 tablespoon cornstarch
- ⅛ teaspoon salt
- ¼ cup orange juice
- ¼ cup water
- 1 cup blueberries
- 1 cup orange sections (about 2 oranges)
- 2 tablespoons Grand Marnier, optional

Preheat oven to 400°. Spray a large baking sheet with cooking spray.

In a medium bowl, beat eggs, orange peel, juice, 2 tablespoons sugar and salt until well blended. Pour into a separate 9-inch x 13-inch x 2-inch baking pan. In a bowl, mix blueberries with remaining 1 tablespoon sugar.

With tip of sharp knife make a pocket in each slice of bread by slicing it 1½-inches lengthwise along the bottom edge, creating an opening. Stuff each pocket with sugared blueberries, dividing berries between 8 slices of bread.

Place filled slices in egg mixture on one side about 5 minutes, the turn over on the other side. Arrange slices on prepared pan, sprinkle with almonds. Bake about 15 minutes until golden brown. Serve with Blueberry Orange Sauce. Serves 4.

BLUEBERRY ORANGE SAUCE: In a small bowl combine sugar, cornstarch and salt; set aside. In a small saucepan bring orange juice and ¼ cup water to a boil. Add blueberries and orange sections. Return to a boil; cook about 2 minutes. Stir in sugar mixture and Grand Marnier, if desired. Cook, stirring constantly, until sauce thickens. Makes 2 cups.

RUSSIAN BLINCIS

Blincis (or blintzes) are really like crepes. Filled with cottage cheese, they are a delightful change of pace for a weekend breakfast.

- 4 eggs, separated
- 3 teaspoons oil
- ½ teaspoon sugar
- ½ teaspoon salt
- ½ teaspoon vanilla extract
- 2 cups milk (whole or cream)
- 1 cup water
- 2 cups flour

....

COTTAGE CHEESE FILLING:

- 1 pint cottage cheese
- 2 teaspoons sugar
- 1 teaspoon vanilla extract

In a large bowl, beat together egg yolks, oil, sugar, salt, and vanilla. Add milk and water. Add flour a little at a time, beating until smooth. Let stand 20 minutes.

In a separate bowl, beat egg whites until they form stiff peaks. Fold into batter.

Heat crepe pan or 7-inch omelet pan over moderate heat. Brush pan lightly with oil. Pour 2½ teaspoons of batter into pan tilt to spread. Cook until lightly browned. Then flip and cook 30 seconds on other side. Stir batter occasionally. A little water may be needed to thin.

Serve with cottage cheese filling, fresh fruit or other desired condiments. Makes about 18, serving 6.

COTTAGE CHEESE FILLING: Mix all ingredients in a small bowl.

Dean Wasil Klemushin, Sr.
Micro, NC

For a family breakfast or an elegant brunch, serve Everyone's Favorite Fluffy Pancakes.

EVERYONE'S FAVORITE FLUFFY PANCAKES

Pancakes are a popular homemade treat for breakfast company. The yogurt adds extra flavor and fluff.

2	cups flour
2	teaspoon baking powder
1	teaspoon baking soda
1	tablespoon sugar
1	8-ounce fat-free yogurt, plain or flavored
1¼	cups milk, skim or whole
2	eggs, beaten
2	tablespoons melted butter or margarine

Sift flour, baking powder, baking soda and sugar into a large bowl.

In a separate bowl, mix together yogurt, milk, eggs and butter. Pour liquid into dry ingredients and mix until just dampened.

Ladle batter onto hot, greased griddle or skillet and then cook until done on both sides. Makes 12 pancakes.

KRISTA DOROSHENKO
KERNERSVILLE, NC

OVERNIGHT APPLE FRENCH TOAST

Prepare the night before and bake the next morning. This is a scrumptious combination of fruit and French bread topped with homemade apple syrup.

1 cup packed light brown sugar
½ cup butter
2 tablespoons light corn syrup
2 large apples
4 eggs
1½ cups milk
1 teaspoon vanilla extract
9 thick slices French bread

....

HOMEMADE APPLE SYRUP:

1 cup applesauce
½ cup apple jelly
½ teaspoon cinnamon
⅛ teaspoon ground cloves

In a saucepan cook brown sugar, butter and corn syrup until thick, about 5-7 minutes. Pour into an ungreased 9-inch x 13-inch x 2-inch baking pan.

Peel and slice apples ¼-inch thick and arrange on top of sugar sauce.

In a mixing bowl beat eggs with milk and vanilla. Soak each bread slice in egg mixture for 1 minute then place over apples in baking pan. Pour remaining egg mixture over bread slices. Cover and refrigerate overnight.

Preheat oven to 350°. Remove pan from refrigerator 30 minutes before baking. Bake uncovered 30-40 minutes.

While French toast bakes make Homemade Apple Syrup.

HOMEMADE APPLE SYRUP: Combine applesauce, jelly, cinnamon and cloves in a small saucepan. Cook, stirring until blended and warm. Serve warm with Apple French Toast. Serves 4-6.

HEYWARD H. McKINNEY, JR.
RALEIGH, NC

GRAND MARNIER PUFFED PANCAKE

This big puffed pancake bakes in a hot oven in a shallow ovenproof pan. Cut into wedges and serve with fruit and our Orange-Honey Syrup.

½ cup butter
¼ cup Grand Marnier liqueur
¾ cup orange juice
• grated rind of 1 orange
½ cup plain yogurt
6 eggs
1½ cups flour
3 cups fresh fruit, such as strawberries, raspberries or blueberries

....

ORANGE-HONEY SYRUP:

½ cup honey
¼ cup orange juice
1 tablespoon Grand Marnier
• grated rind of 1 orange

Choose a shallow ovenproof pan that will hold 4½-5 quarts. Check volume by filling with water. A big iron frying pan or a large glass baking dish will do.

Preheat oven to 425°. Place butter in pan and set in oven. While butter melts, prepare batter.

Combine Grand Marnier, orange juice and rind and yogurt in a measuring cup. Place eggs in a blender and blend for 1 minute. With motor running, pour in orange juice mixture. Gradually add flour and continue to mix for 30 seconds.

Remove pan from oven and pour in batter. Return pan to oven and bake until pancake is puffy and well browned, 20-25 minutes. Cut pancake in squares or wedges and serve at once. Spoon fresh fruit over pancake and pour Orange-Honey Syrup over the top. Serves 4-6.

ORANGE-HONEY SYRUP: Heat all ingredients in a saucepan for a few minutes; serve over pancake.

ENGLISH MORNING PUFF

This delicious egg casserole has the body to withstand being made ahead. This can be doubled. It also freezes well after baking. Just thaw completely and reheat in the microwave.

4	tablespoons butter, divided
½	pound mushrooms
2	tablespoons fresh sage
5	eggs, beaten
¼	cup flour
½	teaspoon baking powder
¼	teaspoon salt
1	cup small curd cottage cheese
½	pound shredded English Sage Derby cheese
1	4-ounce jar chopped pimientos, drained
•	Dash of cayenne

Preheat oven to 350°. Grease an 8-inch x 8-inch glass baking dish.

Heat 2 tablespoons of the butter in large, heavy skillet over medium-high heat. Add mushrooms and sauté until they release their liquid and it evaporates, about 5 minutes.

Chop sage. Beat eggs with flour, baking powder and salt. Stir in cottage cheese, Sage Derby cheese, sautéed mushrooms, pimiento, fresh sage and cayenne. Pour into a baking dish. Bake for 40-45 minutes. Cut into squares. Serves 4-6.

INDIAN SUMMER FRITTATA

Fresh fall vegetables fortify a frittata to overflowing. A hint of balsamic vinegar highlights the blend of egg and cheese.

3	small white potatoes
6	slices bacon (optional)
1	leek
1	red bell pepper
1	medium zucchini
2	tablespoons olive oil
6	eggs, lightly beaten
2	tablespoons fresh chopped basil
¼	cup Parmesan cheese
2	tablespoons balsamic vinegar

Preheat oven to 425°. Peel potatoes and slice thinly. Blanch potatoes 2 minutes in boiling water; drain and set aside. Fry bacon until crisp; drain, cool and crumble. Thinly slice leek, red bell pepper and zucchini and sauté in a 9-inch ovenproof skillet in olive oil. Remove vegetables. In the same skillet add eggs, stirring to scramble slightly. When the bottom begins to set, spread basil, vegetables, potatoes and bacon over the top. Sprinkle with Parmesan.

Bake in oven 10-12 minutes until a knife inserted in the center comes out clean. Drizzle balsamic vinegar over the frittata. Serve immediately. Serves 4-6.

*A*s a family affair or a late morning gathering with friends, brunch says, "This is a special day!" Set the table with grandmother's handmade, lace cloth and embroidered napkins. Serve coffee in the silver pot. The main course can be as easy as English Morning Puff, as spicy as Salsa Poached Eggs (page 36), as elegant as a Bombay Omelet (page 35), or as homespun as Everyone's Favorite Fluffy Pancakes (page 30). Now you have all afternoon to savor a visit to the art museum.

An English Morning Puff inspired by John Singleton Copley's painting is served with Canadian bacon and a Cherry Coffee Cake, page 159, for a memorable Sunday brunch.

JOHN SINGLETON COPLEY (American), *SIR WILLIAM PEPPERRELL AND HIS FAMILY*, 1778

After achieving fame as the preeminent portrait painter in the American colonies, John Singleton Copley moved to England with the intent of proving himself against the best of London's painters. It was there that he painted the extravagant portrait of fellow American Sir William Pepperrell with his wife and children. This work, with its sumptuously rendered fabrics and skillfully composed elements, was exhibited at the Royal Academy in 1778 and demonstrated to the British public Copley's considerable talents.

BOMBAY OMELET

A delicious combination of chutney and cream cheese fills this omelet. A non-stick pan is a worthwhile investment if you really want to make a good omelet.

For each omelet:

- 2 tablespoons cream cheese, softened
- 2 tablespoons chutney
- 1 teaspoon butter
- 2 eggs or ½ cup egg substitute

Cut cream cheese into small pieces so it melts easily. Prepare omelet as directed below. Place cream cheese on omelet in a single layer and spoon chutney on top. Fold the omelet over, cook 30 seconds more, and turn out onto a plate.

TECHNIQUE FOR THE PERFECT OMELET: Prepare filling first. Have all ingredients ready and at hand.

For each omelet, beat 2 eggs or ½ cup egg substitute in a small bowl with a whisk or fork.

Melt 1 teaspoon butter in omelet pan over medium high heat. When the butter begins to sizzle, pour in beaten egg. With one hand move the pan back and forth across burner while making a circular motion in the middle of eggs with a rubber spatula in the other hand. (This can be accomplished easily with a little practice.) This action will make the omelet light and fluffy. When the bottom of the omelet begins to set, lift its edge with the spatula to let any uncooked egg run under the cooked part.

Put desired filling on the half of the omelet away from pan's handle. Fold the other half over top of filling and cook 30 seconds more. Remove pan from heat and slide folded omelet right to edge of pan.

Grab pan handle with your palm facing up and tilt the pan's edge to a warm plate. Flip the omelet over and out by turning the pan over. It is easier to do this if the plate is empty and can be tilted up to meet pan.

Hold prepared omelets in 175° oven while cooking remaining omelets.

OMELET DEL GIORNO

An Italian twist to the Western omelet by featuring prosciutto.

For each omelet:

- 3 tablespoons diced prosciutto
- 2 teaspoons butter, divided
- 1 small plum tomato, peeled and diced
- 2 tablespoons grated mozzarella cheese
- 2 eggs or ½ cup egg substitute
- 1 tablespoon fresh chopped parsley

Sauté prosciutto pieces in 1 teaspoon butter until crisp. Add chopped tomato and heat through. Set aside.

Prepare omelet according to directions above. Sprinkle mozzarella cheese before adding tomato and prosciutto. Fold the omelet over and cook 30 seconds more. Turn out onto a plate and garnish with chopped parsley.

SALSA POACHED EGGS over CORNMEAL MADELEINES

A delightful hint of salsa adds zest to poached eggs. The cornmeal madeleines are baked with a hint of jalapeño. Having an egg poacher insert for your pan is necessary in this recipe. Madeleines also require a special pan with shell-shaped molds or simply slice cornmeal muffins in two.

1½ cups mild salsa, divided, see note

8 eggs

CORNMEAL MADELEINES:

½ cup flour

½ cup yellow cornmeal

¼ teaspoon salt

1 teaspoon sugar

1½ teaspoons baking powder

1 egg, lightly beaten

½ cup milk

2 tablespoons melted butter

2 tablespoons chopped green chilies

Bring ½-inch water to boil in a large sauté pan. Heat salsa on low or in the microwave.

Spread 1 tablespoon salsa evenly into each section of the egg poacher insert and then break an egg on top. Lower heat in the sauté pan so the water stops bubbling; place the insert over the water. Cover and poach eggs approximately 3 minutes.

Carefully remove egg with a plastic spoon and place 2 eggs on each warm plate at the center of 3 fanned madeleines. Spoon 2 more tablespoons warm salsa over the eggs and serve hot. Repeat, poaching the eggs until all guests are served.

NOTE: If using a bottled salsa, add 2 tablespoons chopped fresh cilantro and 1 tablespoon lime juice to "refresh" the taste. Serves 4.

CORNMEAL MADELEINES: Preheat oven 425°. Grease madeleine pans or spray with vegetable oil. In a medium bowl combine flour, cornmeal, salt, sugar and baking powder. In another bowl mix egg, milk and butter. Stir wet ingredients into dry until just blended; do not over mix. Drain chilies and puree in food processor until smooth; fold gently into batter. Spoon batter by the teaspoonful into each shell and bake for 10 minutes. Cool in pans 5 minutes, remove and serve warm. If made ahead, store in an airtight container and reheat in a 300° oven before serving.

CALIFORNIA BREAKFAST CASSEROLE

This delectable breakfast casserole has a subtly spicy taste with hints of California.

1 9-ounce package frozen artichoke hearts

½ cup butter

2 cups sliced mushrooms

10 eggs

2 cups cottage cheese

1 pound Monterey Jack cheese, grated

½ cup flour

1 teaspoon baking powder

½ teaspoon salt

2 4-ounce cans diced green chilies, drained

• salsa, optional

Preheat oven to 350°. Lightly butter a 9-inch x 13-inch glass baking dish.

Thaw artichoke hearts, drain off any excess water and dice. Melt butter in a medium pan and sauté mushrooms with artichoke hearts for 3 minutes.

In a large bowl, beat eggs until well-blended. Stir in cottage cheese. Grate Monterey Jack cheese; fold it into egg mixture along with flour, baking powder, salt, artichoke hearts, butter and mushrooms. Add green chilies.

Pour mixture into prepared pan and bake for 35 minutes or until lightly browned. Serve immediately with salsa on side. Serves 10-12.

SALMON SCRAMBLED EGGS IN PORTOBELLO MUSHROOMS

Deceptively easy, this is an attractive scramble of "eggs"travagance. Look for the smoked salmon bits at the deli counter or buy by the slice and cut into small pieces. Have the plates already composed with fresh fruit as the eggs should be served quickly after cooking.

4 medium portobello mushrooms (about 4-inch diameter)

• olive oil

2 tablespoons butter

⅓ pound smoked salmon pieces

8 eggs, well-beaten

2 tablespoons chopped parsley

Preheat oven to 400°. Remove stems from mushrooms and brush off any visible dirt. Place on a baking sheet and brush both sides with olive oil. Bake for 8-10 minutes, or preheat the broiler and cook 3-4 minutes per side. Set aside and keep warm.

In a large non-stick sauté pan, heat butter on medium high. Add salmon pieces and toss to heat through. Pour in beaten eggs and scramble, cooking almost to desired doneness. The eggs will continue to cook as you assemble the plates. Remove pan from heat.

To serve: Place a mushroom cap on each plate and fill the caps with a mound of eggs, dividing evenly among them. Sprinkle a little parsley on top of each and serve immediately. Serves 4.

The Jewish Sabbath commences in the home on Friday evening when the mother pronounces the prescribed benediction, lights the candles and confers her blessing on her children. It ends on Saturday night with a ceremony (havdalah) that incorporates the senses: the lighting of candles, the sipping of wine and the inhaling of the fragrance of sweet herbs from a spice container — this to carry the sweetness of the Sabbath into the week ahead.

EUROPEAN, CENTRAL, *SPICE CONTAINER IN THE FORM OF AN EGG,* 19th Century

JALAPEÑO GOAT CHEESE QUESADILLAS

This sumptuous combination rolled into tortillas is a colorful way to bring Tex-Mex to a casual brunch.

1 tablespoon garlic, minced

½ red pepper, julienned

½ cup shredded zucchini

3 teaspoons olive oil, divided

4 14-inch flour tortillas, whole wheat or regular

¼ pound jalapeño goat cheese, divided in two portions, see note

5 ounces Monterey Jack cheese, shredded

• prepared salsa

• chopped fresh cilantro

In a medium nonstick skillet over medium high heat sauté garlic, red pepper and zucchini in 1½ teaspoons olive oil until crisp and tender, 3-4 minutes. Spread each half of the jalapeño goat cheese on each of 2 tortillas. Top this with sautéed vegetables and shredded Monterey Jack. Cover with 2 remaining 2 tortillas.

In the same nonstick skillet heat the remaining 1½ teaspoons olive oil over medium high heat. Brown quesadillas 2-3 minutes per side.

Allow to cool slightly before cutting in wedges. Serve with salsa and chopped cilantro if desired. Serves 6 as an appetizer or 2 as an entrée.

NOTE: If jalapeño goat cheese is unavailable, use regular goat cheese and sprinkle 1-2 teaspoons minced jalapeño pepper on each quesadilla.

PHYLLO CHÈVRE TART

An unusual combination of goat cheese, wild mushrooms, turkey and pepperoni is baked in phyllo dough. Delicious!

1 tablespoon butter of margarine

½ cup julienned turkey, uncooked

10 slices pepperoni, chopped

½ cup scallions, chopped

1 cup chopped shiitake or oyster mushrooms

½ pound chèvre or soft goat cheese

1-2 tablespoons light sour cream or nonfat yogurt

2 eggs, beaten

½ cup fresh basil, chopped

....

PHYLLO CRUST:

½ cup unsalted butter, melted

5 sheets phyllo dough

⅓ cup toasted pine nuts, finely chopped

⅓ cup toasted bread crumbs

½ teaspoon red pepper, crushed

Prepare Phyllo crust, recipe below.

In a 10-inch nonstick skillet, melt butter over medium heat. Add turkey, pepperoni, scallions, and mushrooms and sauté until onions are translucent.

Place goat cheese, eggs and sour cream or yogurt in a mixing bowl and whisk until well-combined. Add fresh basil and sautéed ingredients. Pour into phyllo crust and bake for 30-40 minutes at 350° or until lightly browned and puffy. Serve warm. Serves 6.

PHYLLO CRUST: Preheat oven to 425°. Melt butter. Combine pine nuts, bread crumbs and red pepper. Brush 1 sheet of phyllo with melted butter. Sprinkle with ¼ of the nut/crumb mixture. Add another phyllo sheet, brush with butter and sprinkle with ¼ of the nut mixture. Continue with the other sheets ending with the fifth and brush it with butter.

Line an 8-inch round glass baking dish, tucking in corners as needed, but laying carefully over edge. Bake 5-10 minutes.

ITALIAN ZUCCHINI CRESCENT PIE

This delectable dish baked in a crescent roll crust is passed down from John Turner's grandmother, Frankie Temple.

2	large zucchini
1	cup chopped onion
4	tablespoons butter
½	cup chopped parsley
½	teaspoon salt
½	teaspoon pepper
¼	teaspoon garlic powder
¼	teaspoon basil
¼	teaspoon oregano
2	eggs
2	cups grated mozzarella cheese (8 ounces)
1	8-ounce can crescent dinner rolls
2	teaspoons Dijon mustard

Thinly slice zucchini to yield 4 cups. Sauté with onion in butter in a large pan over medium heat for 10 minutes. Stir in parsley, salt, pepper, garlic, basil and oregano.

In a medium bowl, beat eggs lightly; stir in cheese. Add zucchini to egg mixture and stir to blend.

Preheat oven to 375°. Open crescent roll can and separate dough into 8 triangles. Arrange triangles in an ungreased 10-inch pie pan to cover bottom, and up the sides. Press edges together to create a pie crust. Spread mustard over bottom of crust.

Fill with zucchini mixture. Bake for 18-20 minutes until center is set. During the last 10 minutes of baking, cover crust with foil to prevent over-browning. Let pie stand 10 minutes before serving. Serves 6.

JOHN TURNER
RALEIGH, NC

BETTY'S FAMOUS TOMATO PIE

A wonderful luncheon dish or light evening meal using the best of summer's ripe tomatoes. Shared by Dellaine Risley's daughter-in-law's mother, Betty, this is perfect when served with salad and bread.

3	large, ripe tomatoes
1	9-inch pie shell
½	teaspoon salt
¼	teaspoon pepper
½	teaspoon Italian seasoning
¼	cup chopped onion
½	cup mayonnaise
2	cups shredded cheddar cheese

Slice tomatoes ½-inch thick and drain on paper towels. Bake pie shell at 425° for 10 minutes and cool.

Preheat oven to 350°. Arrange tomato slices on baked pie shell. Combine salt, pepper, Italian seasoning and onion and sprinkle over tomatoes. Mix mayonnaise and cheese together and spread over top to cover completely to edges of pie shell. Bake for 35 minutes. Let rest 15 minutes before slicing to serve. Serves 4.

DELLAINE RISLEY
RALEIGH, NC

SYMPHONY BEEF

A twist on traditional creamed chipped beef, this dish is excellent for brunch or a light supper ... before or after the symphony.

2	tablespoons butter
8	ounces chipped beef, cut in strips
1	tablespoon flour
2	cups sour cream
½	cup dry vermouth
1	14-ounce can artichoke hearts
2	tablespoons Parmesan cheese
•	paprika

In a large skillet, melt butter over low heat. Add chipped beef and cook until frizzled. Sprinkle flour over beef, then mix in sour cream and vermouth. Stir well and cook until smooth.

Drain artichoke hearts and cut in half. Stir into creamed beef with Parmesan cheese. Heat through and serve over toasted English muffins with a dash of paprika on top of each. Serves 4.

IRENE LEJMAN
RALEIGH, NC

Soups & Stews

COLD CUCUMBER SOUP

Mazie Froelich first had this soup at Pawley's Island for lunch in the early 1970s at her friend Libba Beerman's creek house. She thought it was so good she felt sure it was a lot of trouble to make. When her friend shared the recipe, she could hardly believe how simple it was. It has since been served every summer during the Froelich's sojourns at the beach.

2	medium cucumbers
1	cup sour cream or plain yogurt
1	small onion, chopped
1	can cream of chicken soup
2	tablespoons red wine vinegar
•	salt
•	white pepper

Score cucumbers, cut in half lengthwise and remove seeds. Coarsely chop. Put cucumber in blender or food processor with sour cream or yogurt, onion, soup and vinegar. Process until smooth. Season to taste with salt and white pepper. Refrigerate at least 2 hours before serving. Serves 4.

Mazie Froelich
High Point, NC

CHILLED AVOCADO SOUP

This creamy avocado soup is a delightful addition to a luncheon or a summer supper. It is very rich so a little goes a long way.

1	small onion
3	large ripe tomatoes
3	medium ripe avocados
2	tablespoons minced green pepper
½	cup dry sherry
2	tablespoons lime juice
1	teaspoon salt
½	teaspoon white pepper
2	cups chicken stock
1	cup sour cream
½	cup half-and-half
•	mint sprigs

Chop onion. Peel, seed and quarter tomatoes. Peel avocados, remove pits and mash pulp coarsely.

Place avocado, onion, tomato and green pepper in a blender or food processor. Add sherry, lime juice, salt and white pepper. Puree for 1 minute. Pour into a medium glass bowl. Add chicken stock, sour cream and half-and-half. Blend ingredients by hand until smooth. Adjust seasoning with more sherry, salt and pepper to your taste. Chill 1 hour before serving. Garnish with mint sprigs. Serves 8 as a first course.

SPRING FENNEL SOUP

The essence of anise breathes life into a basic potato leek soup. Serve warm or chill to serve as fennel vichyssoise.

2	small fennel bulbs
3	medium leeks
2	tablespoons butter
5	cups chicken stock
3	medium potatoes, peeled and diced
1	cup half-and-half
1	teaspoon salt
¼	teaspoon white pepper

Cut fennel stalks 1-inch above bulbs. Save a few leaves for garnish and thinly slice bulbs.

Slice white and green parts of leeks lengthwise. Rinse under cold water to remove dirt and slice into ¼-inch rounds.

In a soup pot, sauté leeks and fennel in butter over medium heat until they begin to brown. Add chicken stock and potatoes. Bring to a boil and simmer 10-15 minutes until potatoes are tender.

Purée soup in a food processor or blender and return to pot. Stir in half-and-half and season with salt and pepper. Serve warm or chilled. Ladle into bowls and garnish with chopped fennel leaves. Serves 4.

$\mathcal{S}$*ummer* **in the Southern** United States heralds an abundant

harvest of plump, lush tomatoes whose cheerful red color adds drama to the dinner table.

This unusual Cold Summer Tomato Soup is quick, delicious and can be made ahead —

perfect for a luncheon or as a starter for suppers during the hot "dog days" of August.

COLD SUMMER TOMATO SOUP

You must try this to believe it — the tomato lover's dream soup! You simply make it in a soup bowl, so the instructions are written for one serving only.

1-2   ripe tomatoes
  •   salt
1½   tablespoons mayonnaise
½   teaspoon mustard
  •   fresh chives, basil or dill, chopped

Chop tomatoes in chunks into soup bowl. Salt lightly and chill to almost crispy/icy, at least 2 hours. Mix mustard and mayonnaise together and dollop on top of tomatoes. Garnish with fresh herbs. Serves 1.

VERONESE ATKINS
SOUTHERN PINES, NC

CLAIRE'S MOM'S CORN POTATO CHOWDER

A filling chowder perfect for lunch with a green salad or as an appetizer for a casual Sunday supper. It would also make a good soup base for adding oysters.

3   medium red potatoes
4   cups chicken stock
3   strips thick-cut bacon, diced
1   medium onion, diced
1   cup heavy cream
1   14-ounce can golden corn, drained
1   14-ounce can creamed corn
  •   salt and pepper

Cut potatoes in ½-inch dice. Bring stock to boil in a large soup pot. Add potatoes, lower heat to medium and let simmer 10-15 minutes until they begin to soften.

In a sauté pan, fry bacon pieces until half-cooked, not crisp. Remove bacon and add onion to same pan. Cook until translucent. Add bacon and onions to potatoes. Lower heat and stir in cream, golden corn and creamed corn. Stir and cook another 15 minutes. Season with salt and pepper. Serves 6-8.

CLAIRE C. HESTER
RALEIGH, NC

AUNT MARTHA'S CABBAGE SOUP

Hearty and delicious, this family favorite will warm your bones and fortify your spirits on a cold day.

1   cabbage (2-3 pounds)
1   2-pound sirloin steak (choice sirloin tip)
2   tablespoons oil
2   15-ounce cans tomato sauce
1   28-ounce can whole tomatoes, crushed
1   onion, finely chopped
2   teaspoons salt
3   tablespoons sugar
3   tablespoons lemon juice

Shred cabbage and boil in salted water for 5 minutes.

Drain and rinse cabbage. In a large soup pot, sear whole sirloin in oil to brown both sides. Add cabbage, tomato sauce, crushed whole tomatoes, onion, salt, sugar and lemon juice. Bring to a boil, lower heat, cover and cook 1 hour on low. Taste and re-season if necessary and cook 1 more hour, stirring occasionally.

Remove meat before serving. Either shred into small pieces and add back into soup, or cut into large pieces and place in bowl before spooning soup over. Serves 10-12.

MARILYN WOLBERG
CARY, NC

30-Minute Black Bean Soup

A healthy, reduced fat, quick-and-easy soup. The turkey sausage gives basic black bean soup new dimension and extra flavor.

1 tablespoon olive oil

1 onion, chopped

1 red bell pepper, diced

6 ounces fat-free turkey sausage

1 15-ounce can black beans, not drained

2 cups chicken stock or broth

1 tablespoon dry sherry

½ teaspoon cumin

1 bay leaf

• juice of ½ lime

1 tablespoon chopped cilantro

• freshly ground pepper

In a soup pot, heat oil over medium high heat and sauté onion and red pepper 5-6 minutes. Add crumbled turkey sausage, and cook another 2 to 3 minutes. Add black beans, stock, sherry, cumin and bay leaf. Bring to a boil, reduce heat, simmer uncovered 10-15 minutes.

Remove bay leaf and add lime juice, cilantro and pepper to taste. Serves 4.

Jane Parker Smith
Goldsboro, NC

Bogota's Chicken and Potato Soup

Called Ajiaco Bogotano, *this is a Colombian-style meal in a bowl. Succulent chicken, tender potatoes and corn star in this homespun stew. A hint of capers is added to each soup bowl before the stew is ladled in.*

1 3-pound chicken, cut up

1 pound soup bone (found in frozen food section)

2 quarts water

1 large onion, peeled and halved

1 bay leaf

½ teaspoon ground cumin

½ teaspoon thyme

1 teaspoon salt

¼ teaspoon pepper

4 medium potatoes, peeled and cubed

1 pound small potatoes, peeled and halved

3 ears corn, cut in 2-inch rounds

1 cup plus 2 tablespoons heavy cream

2 tablespoons capers, drained and rinsed

1 avocado, peeled and thinly sliced

In a 5-quart soup pot place cut-up chicken, soup bone, water, onion, bay leaf, cumin, thyme, salt and pepper. Bring to a boil skimming, making certain to skim the surface of fat. Reduce heat, cover and cook until chicken is tender. Remove chicken, and cool. Discard skin and bones, and cut meat into strips.

Strain stock and return to pot. Add potatoes and cook until done. Mash cubes against side, but leave small potatoes whole. Add chicken and corn. Cook until corn is tender. Season with extra cumin and thyme, if desired.

To serve, add 3 tablespoons cream and 1 teaspoon capers into the bottom of 6 deep soup bowls. Ladle in soup. Garnish with avocado on top. Serves 6.

Gloria B. Perry
Morrisville, NC

JEAN SIMÉON CHARDIN (French), *STILL LIFE WITH RAY AND BASKET OF ONIONS*, 1731

Chardin's still lifes were unusual because he chose to paint ordinary objects. However, the artist did not include these common objects haphazardly. He selected items that appealed to his sense of material surfaces and his fondness for curved shapes, and he worked out his compositions with corresponding deliberation and care. The sensitive and unassuming quality of his work made Chardin the most influential French still-life painter of his day.

CALDO XOCHITL

Caldo Xochitl is a delicious Mexican chicken stew. Serve over El Mirador Rice and accompany with warm tortillas for a complete meal in a bowl.

5   cloves garlic
1   tablespoon dried oregano
¼   teaspoon ground cloves
2½ quarts water
1   2-3 pound chicken
1   tablespoon salt
1   teaspoon pepper
1   tablespoon chicken base
1   tablespoon cumin
3   bay leaves
3   fresh basil leaves
2   carrots
1   green bell pepper
2   stalks celery
1   medium onion
2   medium zucchini
1   17-ounce can garbanzo beans, drained
1   bunch green onions, chopped
1-2 jalapeño peppers, minced
2   tomatoes, cubed
1   avocado, peeled and diced

EL MIRADOR RICE:

¾   cup long grain rice
•   hot water
1   tablespoon lemon juice
2   tablespoons oil
2   medium tomatoes, chopped
2   cups chopped green pepper
1   clove garlic, minced
1   tablespoon chicken base
1¼ cup water
1   teaspoon cumin
¼   teaspoon salt
•   pepper

In a small bowl mix garlic, oregano and cloves to a paste; set aside.

In a large soup pot add water, chicken, salt and pepper. Bring to boil, reduce heat and simmer a few minutes. Skim foam and add chicken base, cumin, bay leaves, basil and garlic paste. Let chicken simmer until cooked 45 minutes-1 hour. Remove chicken and set aside to cool.

Peel, quarter and slice carrots. Cut green pepper and celery into small dice. Add with chopped onion to stock and bring back to boil. Reduce heat and simmer until vegetables are tender.

Meanwhile remove skin and bones from chicken. Return chicken meat to soup with sliced zucchini and garbanzo beans and heat through. To serve, place ¼ cup El Mirador Rice in soup bowl. Spoon soup over rice and garnish with any or all of green onions, jalapeños, tomato, avocado. Serves 8-10.

EL MIRADOR RICE: Measure out rice into a bowl and cover with hot water and lemon juice. Let soak 5 minutes and drain thoroughly. In a large skillet heat oil. Add rice and sauté until golden. Stir in tomatoes, peppers and garlic. Sauté 5 minutes. Add chicken base, water and seasonings. Boil, reduce heat, cover and simmer 20-30 minutes until fairly dry.

Liz Gottlieb
Durham, NC

CHICKEN TORTILLA SOUP

This easy soup tastes like you've worked for hours. Just prep the ingredients ahead and assemble to order. This soup is a quick fix for those Tex-Mex cravings which Carolyn Stidham, who grew up in San Antonio, may get occasionally.

1   whole chicken breast (bone in) or 2 boneless breast halves
1   tablespoon vegetable oil
1   cup chopped onion
4   cups chicken broth
2   tablespoons prepared salsa
4   cups tortilla chips
1   cup grated Monterey Jack cheese
¼   cup chopped cilantro
¼   cup sour cream

Cook chicken and cool. Remove skin and bones if necessary and shred meat.

Heat oil in a medium saucepan. Sauté onion until translucent. Add chicken meat, broth and salsa and heat through.

Divide crushed tortilla chips among 4 bowls. Put ¼ cup grated cheese in each. Spoon soup into bowls and garnish each with 1 tablespoon cilantro and 1 tablespoon sour cream. Serve immediately. Serves 4.

Carolyn Stidham
Raleigh, NC

POPEYE'S SPINACH SOUP

Red tomatoes and fresh spinach cooked in a savory broth make a refreshing start to a meal. The red and green color is delightful during the Christmas holidays.

2   vegetable bouillon cubes
8   cups boiling water
2   tablespoons olive oil
4   cloves garlic, minced
1   small onion, halved and thinly sliced
½   teaspoon oregano
2   14-ounce cans diced tomatoes
1   5-ounce package fresh baby spinach
⅓   cup fresh basil, chopped
•   salt and freshly ground pepper

Dissolve bouillon cubes in boiling water and reserve. Heat olive oil in a heavy-bottomed soup pan. Add garlic, onion and oregano. Sauté until garlic is golden but not burned. Add reserved vegetable broth. Bring to a boil. Simmer 15-30 minutes. Longer simmering will intensify the flavor. Add tomatoes and simmer for 5 minutes.

Coarsely chop spinach. Add spinach and basil. Cook for only 3-4 minutes to retain the spinach color. Adjust seasoning with salt and pepper, and serve immediately. Serves 4-6.

Earthy, **aromatic flavors make** Caldo Xochitl, a Mexican chicken stew, a wonderful choice for a soup supper with friends. This unusual recipe is brimming with vegetables and flavor.

COCONUT CURRY CHICKEN SOUP

The delightful essence of lemongrass and coconut envelop the chicken with flavors of the Pacific Rim. Lemongrass, fish sauce and rice noodles may be purchased in Asian markets or specialty stores. This spicy soup would be a delightful, edible adventure for a soup supper with friends.

2	tablespoons vegetable oil
3	cloves garlic, minced
3	tablespoons curry powder
3	cups chicken broth
2	14-ounce cans unsweetened coconut milk
1	cup water
2	stalks lemongrass
1	1½-inch piece ginger root
1	teaspoon black peppercorns
1	whole chicken breast (bone in)
⅓	cup fresh lime juice
⅓	cup fish sauce (nuoc man)
½-1	pound rice noodles (vermicelli style)
⅓	cup chopped cilantro

In a large pot or heavy saucepan heat oil over moderately low heat. Add garlic and sauté briefly. Stir and add curry powder. Cook 30 seconds and stir in broth, coconut milk and water.

Remove outer leaves from lemongrass, trim ends and mince tender inners. Peel ginger and cut into 10 slices ⅛-inch thick.

Add peppercorns to soup and bring to a boil. Add chicken, lemongrass and ginger. Reduce heat and poach at a bare simmer until chicken is cooked through, about 20 minutes. Remove with a slotted spoon and cool. Keep soup warm, but do not boil. Discard skin and bones from chicken when cool, shred meat and add chicken to soup with lime juice and fish sauce. Reheat soup over medium heat, stirring until hot.

Meanwhile, if rice noodles are dried, soak in warm water to cover for 5 minutes. Drain and cook in large pot of boiling, salted water for 5 minutes. Drain, rinse under cold water and drain again. Cook fresh noodles as directed.

Divide noodles among bowls, fill with soup and sprinkle chopped cilantro on top. Serves 4 as main course, 8 as an appetizer.

EMILY S. ROSEN
RALEIGH, NC

SHRIMP BISQUE

Sweet carrots and aromatic vegetables provide a delightful base for this delicious seafood bisque. The soup base may be made ahead and reheated at dinnertime with the shrimp being added closer to serving. Elegant and extremely rich, one cup per serving will suffice.

¼	cup butter
2	cups chopped onion
1	cup chopped celery
4	cups peeled sliced carrots
5	cups chicken stock or vegetable stock
1	cup heavy cream
1	teaspoon salt
½	teaspoon white pepper
2	tablespoons olive oil
2	tablespoons minced shallots
1	pound peeled shrimp, coarsely chopped
⅓	cup sherry
2	tablespoons fresh chopped dill

In a large pot, heat butter, sauté onion, celery and carrots for 3 minutes. Add stock, bring to boil and simmer 10-15 minutes until carrots are soft. Puree to a smooth soup in the food processor. Return to pot; add cream, salt and pepper. The bisque base may be refrigerated until time to reheat on low.

In a large sauté pan, heat olive oil and sauté shallots on medium-high. Add shrimp and stir to cook quickly, 1-2 minutes. When shrimp begin to turn pink, add sherry, deglaze pan and simmer shrimp 1 minute more. Add to hot bisque. Stir well to blend. Ladle into bowls and garnish with fresh dill. Serves 8.

PORTUGUESE KALE SOUP

The spicy chorizo or linguiça sausage seasons this hearty and wholesome soup. Serve with hot, peppered cornbread or a French baguette. A crowd-pleaser to serve on a wintry day.

1	tablespoon butter
2	medium onions, chopped
2	cloves garlic, minced
1	pound chorizo or linguiça sausage
2-3	medium potatoes
1	28-ounce can whole peeled tomatoes with juice
3	cups beef broth
2	cups water
¾	pound kale
1	16-ounce can kidney beans

In a large soup pot melt butter over medium heat and sauté onions and garlic for 3 minutes. Cut sausage into ½-inch slices and add to the pot. Continue to cook until sausage browns, about 10 minutes more.

Peel and dice potatoes and add to the pot with the tomatoes, beef broth and water. Wash kale, removing the large stems. Chop coarsely and add to the soup. Simmer soup 2 hours, stirring occasionally. Drain kidney beans and stir into soup; cook another 10 minutes and serve. Serves 6-8.

THREE APPLE SOUP

Three apple varieties give this soup a delicate, delightful taste. Bring several types of apples back from a fall foliage weekend.

2	tablespoons vegetable oil
1	cup chopped onion
3	large shallots, finely chopped
1½	pounds Granny Smith apples
1½	pounds Golden Delicious apples
1½	pounds Rome apples
1	bouquet garni
3	cloves garlic, minced
5-6	cups chicken stock or broth
1	teaspoon salt
6	tablespoons heavy cream
6	small sprigs fresh rosemary

BOUQUET GARNI:

1	bay leaf
1	teaspoon thyme,
1	teaspoon black peppercorns
1	tablespoon chopped parsley

Heat oil in a large, heavy-bottomed soup pot over medium heat. Add onion and shallots; cook until translucent but not browned, about 10 minutes.

Make Bouquet Garni. Peel, core and chop all apples. Add to soup pot and cook for 3 minutes, stirring continuously. Add bouquet garni, fresh garlic and chicken stock. The stock will not cover apples completely. Simmer for 20 minutes over medium heat. Remove bouquet garni.

Puree apple mixture in blender 1 cup at a time. Pour through a fine mesh strainer into a clean pot. Add salt. Return to low heat to keep warm.

To serve, divide among 6 warm bowls. Add 1 tablespoon cream to each bowl. Using tip of a sharp knife, make a circular pattern in each bowl making a swirling pattern with cream and soup. Garnish with rosemary. This soup may also be served cold. Serves 6.

BOUQUET GARNI: Tie spices in a piece of cheesecloth.

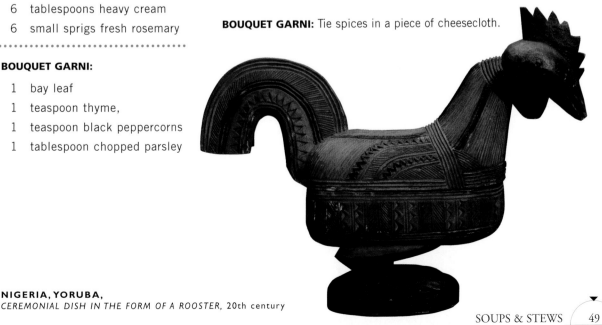

NIGERIA, YORUBA,
CEREMONIAL DISH IN THE FORM OF A ROOSTER, 20th century

CREAMY ZUCCHINI SOUP

A thick and smooth vegetable soup with subtle flavor.

1½ pounds zucchini, thinly sliced

2 celery stalks, thinly sliced

1 carrot, small dice

1 large or 2 small potatoes, small dice

1 onion, finely chopped

¾ cup water

4 cups vegetable or chicken broth

1 teaspoon basil

½ cup milk

• salt and white pepper

• low fat plain yogurt or sour cream

Place zucchini, celery, carrots, potatoes, onions, stock, water and basil in a large soup pot. Add enough liquid to almost cover vegetables. Bring to a boil. Reduce heat and simmer until carrots are tender, about 20 minutes. Remove from heat and add milk.

Puree soup with either a hand blender or food processor. Return to pot and season with salt and pepper.

Keep warm, but do not boil when reheating. Garnish each bowl with a dollop of yogurt or sour cream. Makes 2 quarts.

NANCY WAY
RALEIGH, NC

COYOTE CALL CHICKEN 'N' BLACK BEAN CHILI

This chicken and black bean chili will become a new favorite meal. It's something to howl about!

1 pound dry black beans

4 tablespoons vegetable oil, divided

1½ pounds boneless chicken breast

1 onion, diced

5 cloves garlic, minced

1 28-ounce can peeled tomatoes, roughly chopped

1 16-ounce can crushed tomatoes

1 jalapeño pepper, seeded and minced

2 tablespoons chili powder

2 tablespoons cumin

2 teaspoons salt

1 tablespoon pepper

1 cup chicken stock

¼ cup chopped fresh cilantro

2 tablespoons chopped fresh basil

• grated cheddar cheese, optional

• sour cream, optional

To cook black beans: Sift through beans and remove any stones. Rinse, drain and pour in a large pot. Cover beans with 1 quart water, bring to a simmer over high heat. Remove pot from heat immediately and let stand 1 hour. Drain beans into colander and rinse. Put back into large pot with 1 quart water. Cook over high heat until soft, about 1 hour, stirring occasionally. Add water as needed, ½ cup at a time. Drain beans, set aside.

Heat 2 tablespoons oil in a large skillet. Sauté chicken over medium high heat 4-5 minutes per side or until cooked through. Remove from pan and cut into ½-inch dice.

In a large soup pot or Dutch oven, sauté onion and garlic in remaining 2 tablespoons oil over medium high heat for about 5 minutes. Add both cans tomatoes and cook another 5 minutes. Stir in jalapeño, chili powder, cumin, salt, pepper and stock. Simmer 10 minutes more. Add diced chicken, cilantro and basil. Simmer another 10 minutes. Stir in beans, reduce heat to low, simmer 30 minutes more. Serve with grated cheese and/or sour cream. Serves 6-8.

TARBORO BRUNSWICK STEW

Making a pot of Brunswick Stew in the backyard was a family project when Betzy Nizich was growing up in Tarboro, NC. Her father would cook the stew in a huge iron pot over an oak fire, insisting that it be stirred with an oak paddle. The combination of the fire and paddle gave the stew a much desired smoky flavor. This would take a long afternoon during which family and friends took turns stirring the pot and turning it into a festive occasion. Many Southerners add rabbit or squirrel to the pot. Serve it with hot pepper vinegar, cole slaw and saltine crackers. This recipe has been adapted to cook on the stove, and may be doubled to accommodate large crowds. Betsy says to adjust this recipe as needed, that it's a "feel and taste thing".

1   5-6 pound plump chicken
2   slices thick cut bacon
1   medium onion, chopped
1   28-ounce can tomatoes
1   pound baby lima beans (fresh or frozen)
1-2 medium potatoes, ¼-inch diced
1   can creamed corn
2   teaspoons sugar
1   teaspoon oregano
½   teaspoon crushed red pepper
2-3 dashes liquid smoke
•   salt and pepper

Cook chicken in a large pot of simmering water until meat falls off the bones. (Chicken base or broth cubes may be added to enrich flavor). Remove chicken, saving broth, and discard skin and bones. Shred meat and set aside.

Cut bacon into small pieces. In a large heavy soup pot, cook bacon until browned. Sauté onion in drippings for 3-4 minutes. Add chicken meat and 2 cups reserved broth. Stir in tomatoes with juice and lima beans, and cook slowly over medium low heat for about 1 hour. Stir often adding broth as needed.

Add potatoes and cook 20 minutes more. Stew will become thickened so stir and be careful not to scorch. Add corn, sugar, oregano, red pepper and liquid smoke. Heat through about 10 minutes, stirring occasionally. Salt and pepper to taste. Serves 8-10.

BETSY A. NIZICH
CARY, NC

RUSSIAN BORSCH

This hearty beef soup boasts a rich beef stock. Dean Klemushin serves this special recipe with warm sourdough or pumpernickel bread.

8-10 beets
1   tablespoon vegetable oil
12-15 ounces stew beef (chuck steak, sirloin, etc.)
1   onion, chopped
1   carrot, diced small
1   tablespoon minced garlic
2   quarts rich beef stock
2-3 bay leaves
1   teaspoon salt
2   teaspoons pepper
¼   cup lemon juice or cider vinegar
1   teaspoon sugar
¼   cup chopped fresh parsley
•   sour cream, optional

Preheat oven to 375°.

Remove tops from beets, leaving about 1 inch of the stems intact, so they don't bleed while cooking. Bake in a roasting pan for 40 minutes or until beets are tender. Cool, remove skins and tops and cut into small cubes or julienne strips.

Cube beef. In a large 4-quart pot heat oil and brown beef cubes; remove and set aside. Sauté onion, carrot and garlic briefly in same pan. Return beef to pan and add beets, beef stock, bay leaves, salt, pepper, lemon juice and sugar. Bring to boil and reduce heat. Simmer 30-45 minutes.

To serve, ladle into bowls, garnish with chopped parsley and a dollop of sour cream, if desired. Serves 6-8.

DEAN WASIL KLEMUSHIN, SR.
MICRO, NC

GARDEN
SALADS

ASIAN NOODLE SALAD

Crisp and crunchy, featuring many of today's convenience foods such as broccoli slaw and shelled sunflower seeds.

1	package broccoli slaw
2	packages dry ramen noodles, beef flavor is best
1	cup toasted, shelled sunflower seeds
1	bunch scallions, chopped
⅓	cup cider vinegar
⅔	cup oil
1	tablespoon soy sauce
1½	tablespoons minced fresh ginger

Put broccoli slaw in a large bowl. Crumble in dry noodles; set aside seasoning packets. Mix in sunflower seeds and scallions. In a separate bowl whisk together vinegar, oil, soy sauce, ginger and 2 packets seasoning. Combine with salad and chill at least 30 minutes before serving. Serves 6-8.

NANCIE A. WAGNER
RALEIGH, NC

FAR EAST CUCUMBER SALAD

Crisp and lightly seasoned with hot pepper and sesame oil. These cukes are wonderful served with grilled chicken in a pita pocket.

4	cucumbers, peeled if waxed
1¼	teaspoons salt, divided
1	carrot, peeled and shredded
½	teaspoon crushed red pepper
¼	cup red wine vinegar
¼	cup sugar
2	tablespoons sesame oil

Cut cucumber in half lengthwise. Slice diagonally in bite-size pieces. Sprinkle 1 teaspoon salt over cucumbers and let stand 5 minutes. Rinse with cold water and drain. Add carrot and pepper to cucumber. Combine vinegar, sugar, remaining ¼ teaspoon salt and sesame oil and pour over cucumbers. Allow to marinate at least 40 minutes in refrigerator. Stir occasionally. Serves 6-8.

BETTY GINN
RALEIGH, NC

SANTA FE SALAD

The pineapple in this light and fresh salad adds just enough citrus to complement any spicy dish. Mixed lettuces are recommended: arugula, red leaf, Boston, beet greens, chicory, dandelion and/or radicchio.

6-8	cups mixed greens
1	orange bell pepper
1	ripe avocado
2	cups diced pineapple

BASIC BASALMIC DRESSING:

½	cup vegetable oil
¼	cup extra virgin olive oil
2	tablespoons balsamic vinegar
2	tablespoons lemon juice

Wash greens, pat dry and tear into bite-size pieces. Slice orange pepper into thin strips. Remove skin and pit from avocado and slice lengthwise. Combine ingredients in a medium salad bowl. Toss with dressing, and serve. Serves 6.

BASIC BASALMIC DRESSING: Whisk oils together with vinegar and lemon juice until well-blended.

SALMON COBB SALAD

Poached salmon replaces the chicken or turkey found in the traditional cobb salad, made famous by Hollywood's Brown Derby Restaurant. For easy assembly at serving time, you may prepare all the steps ahead.

1½ pounds salmon fillet
1 bay leaf
½ lemon, sliced
½ medium onion, sliced
8 black peppercorns
1 pound bacon
3 avocados, divided
3 medium tomatoes (or 1½ pounds cherry tomatoes)
7 cups mixed romaine and bibb lettuce, washed and drained
1 cup watercress, washed and drained
½ large red onion, thinly sliced
1½ cups shredded mozzarella

COBB DRESSING:

1 cup olive oil
½ cup vegetable oil
⅓ cup white wine vinegar
3 tablespoons minced shallots
1 teaspoon salt
½ teaspoon ground pepper

To poach salmon: In a deep sauté pan or soup pot, add bay leaf, lemon, onion and peppercorns to 6 cups water. Bring to boil and simmer 10 minutes. Place salmon carefully in water and poach 10-15 minutes, uncovered, depending on the thickness of fillet. To test for doneness, gently insert a knife into the center seam and separate; when the color has turned from orange to pink, remove salmon to cool.

Prepare Cobb Dressing. Cook bacon; drain and set aside. Leave at room temperature.

An hour before serving: Separate salmon into 1-inch chunky flakes and marinate with ¼ cup Cobb dressing, tossing to coat well; refrigerate for 30-40 minutes.

Remove pits and peel from 2 avocados and cut into 1½-inch pieces. Save the third avocado to slice for garnish. Dice tomatoes; if cherry tomatoes, cut in half. Break lettuce into bite-size pieces. In a large bowl, layer the lettuce, watercress, salmon, red onion, tomatoes, avocados, mozzarella and crumbled bacon. Toss carefully with remaining dressing. Plate salads and garnish with thin avocado slices. Serves 6.

COBB DRESSING: Whisk ingredients together in a small bowl or shake in a jar until well-blended.

SPRING VEGETABLE ORZO SALAD

A beautifully arranged salad using the best of spring's bounty. Crunchy cukes and asparagus blend well with feta and orzo to entice your palate.

3 cups cooked orzo pasta
1 medium red pepper, diced
1 pound asparagus tips, blanched and cooled
1 cup cucumbers, halved lengthwise and sliced
4 ounces feta cheese, crumbled
3 tablespoons white wine vinegar
½ cup olive oil
• salt and pepper
2 whole artichokes, optional
• chopped parsley, for garnish

Combine pasta with pepper, asparagus, cucumbers and feta cheese in a large, decorative bowl. In a separate small bowl whisk together vinegar, oil, salt and pepper. Toss with orzo mixture.

Quarter artichokes and scatter over salad. Garnish with chopped parsley. Allow to sit at room temperature 30 minutes prior to serving. Serves 6-8.

NOTE: To cook artichokes, trim stem and remove any bruised outer leaves. Using a sharp knife, cut each in half, then in half again. Use a spoon to remove the fuzzy interior of the choke, being careful to keep the quarter from falling apart. Rub all vegetable quarters with fresh lemon to prevent browning. Cook in boiling water for 10-15 minutes or until they are soft when pierced with a knife tip. Drain and refresh under cool water.

SAVORY SAGE SALAD

A mere sprinkling of fresh sage leaves highlights this simple salad. The basic dressing is one to file away in your memory — it's the perfect blend of very ordinary ingredients.

1   large head Bibb lettuce
⅓   cup fresh sage leaves
½   cup chopped scallions

RED WINE VINEGAR DRESSING:

1   cup olive oil
¼   cup red wine vinegar
2   cloves garlic, minced
1   teaspoon Dijon mustard
•   freshly ground pepper

Wash Bibb lettuce thoroughly and pat dry. Break leaves into bite-size pieces. In a large salad bowl combine lettuce with sage leaves and scallions. Toss with just enough dressing to wet the leaves. The salad should remain light and airy, not weighted down by dressing. Serves 6.

RED WINE VINEGAR DRESSING: In a small bowl, whisk oil and vinegar together with garlic, mustard and pepper until smooth. Yields 1½ cups.

ELLEN'S BROCCOLI SALAD

As written, this salad is crunchy and very green. It may be varied or enlarged by adding or substituting cauliflower, red bell pepper and/or grated carrot.

1   bunch broccoli, broken into florets
1   Vidalia onion, sliced
2   large celery stalks, sliced
1   green pepper, sliced in strips
1   15-ounce can peas
1   tablespoon red wine vinegar
2   tablespoons lemon juice
3   tablespoons mayonnaise
2   tablespoons chopped parsley
2   tablespoons chopped fresh dill or 1 teaspoon dried dill
1   tablespoon sweet pickle relish
1   teaspoon minced garlic
½   teaspoon seasoning salt
•   freshly ground pepper

Prepare fresh vegetables and set aside. Drain canned peas. In a large salad bowl mix vinegar, lemon juice, mayonnaise, parsley, dill, pickle relish, garlic, seasoning salt and pepper. Stir in fresh vegetables and mix well.

Gently fold in peas. Chill several hours or overnight. Gently stir again before serving. Serves 8-10.

REBECCA CLAYTON
RALEIGH, NC

Nearly every native-born Southerner has a gardening gene, passed down through the generations from ancestors who made their livelihood on a farm. Wherever there is a little plot of ground with sufficient sun, there are onions, cabbages, tomatoes, squash, broccoli, cucumbers and green beans to provide a daily harvest for warm-weather salads. Often the harvest comes from fruit-bearing trees planted long ago — apple, pecan, fig and more.

Apples and jícama sweeten this Winesap Slaw.

WINESAP SLAW

Apples slice into an autumn slaw loaded with Roquefort, pecans and crunchy red cabbage. Jícama is a Mexican root vegetable available in Mexican markets and large grocery stores. Its sweet, nutty flavor adds depth to this colorful combination.

3   cups shredded red cabbage, about 1 medium head

1   cup shredded bok choy, about 1 small bunch

1   cup shredded jícama, about ½ large jícama, peeled

2   medium carrots, peeled and shredded

4   tablespoons raspberry or other fruit vinegar, divided

2   tart apples, such as Winesap or Terry Winter, shredded

¼   cup sesame oil

¼   cup canola oil

•   salt and freshly ground pepper

½   cup chopped pecans

4   ounces Roquefort cheese, crumbled

Begin with red cabbage and bok choy, shredding as finely as possible, using a cutting board and knife. Place in a large serving bowl. Shred jícama and carrots in food processor. Place raspberry vinegar in a small bowl.

Prepare apples for the processor by quartering, peeling and coring them. Submerge apple quarters in raspberry vinegar to prevent darkening; reserve vinegar. Shred apples in food processor. Stir 1 tablespoon of the reserved vinegar into shredded apples just before combining with the other slaw vegetables in the serving bowl.

To prepare dressing: Whisk sesame and canola oils with reserved raspberry vinegar. Add salt and pepper to taste. Pour dressing over slaw and toss well. Add chopped pecans and Roquefort. Serve immediately. Serves 8.

SEVERIN ROESEN (American), *STILL LIFE WITH FRUIT*, c. 1855-60

Severin Roesen, who emigrated to the United States from Germany in 1848, had an artistic career confined to painting fruit and floral still lifes. Although little is known of him, and he achieved only modest success in his lifetime, his work has come to represent Victorian American painting at its most exuberant.

STRAWBERRY-ASPARAGUS SALAD

A light and delicate dressing brings out the spring flavors in asparagus and strawberries. The attractive presentation makes it a nice salad for a buffet.

2　bunches tender asparagus

1　quart strawberries

¾　cup crumbled blue cheese

....

POPPY SESAME DRESSING:

½　cup vegetable oil

¼　cup cider vinegar

1　tablespoon Worcestershire sauce

1　tablespoon grated red onion

1　tablespoon sesame seeds

2　tablespoons poppy seeds

Remove stems from asparagus, steam and cool. Wash strawberries, remove hulls and slice. Make Poppy Sesame Dressing.

Place asparagus on a large platter. Arrange strawberries on top. Shake dressing vigorously and pour over all. Scatter blue cheese on top. Serves 6-8.

POPPY SESAME DRESSING: Whisk ingredients together until well-combined.

SALLY LAZAR
RALEIGH, NC

CHERRY PECAN SALAD

A festive gelatin salad that is perfect for a special occasion when made in decorative or individual molds.

1½　cups canned bing cherries

1　cup cherry juice (juice from cherries with enough water to make 1 cup)

1　package cherry gelatin

1　cup port

1　cup chopped pecans or almonds

Drain cherries into bowl; reserve juice.

In a saucepan, heat juice (and water if needed) to almost boiling; stir in gelatin to dissolve. Set aside to cool. Add port and refrigerate until partially set. Add nuts and cherries. Pour into an oiled 1-quart mold and chill until congealed. Serve with mayonnaise. Serves 8.

ELIZABETH WHITE PERRY
RALEIGH, NC

FROZEN CRANBERRY SALAD

A cool salad that could be used as a light dessert on a hot summer day.

1　16-ounce can whole berry cranberry sauce

1　8-ounce can crushed pineapple, drained

1　8-ounce container plain yogurt

2　teaspoons lemon juice

⅓　cup confectioners' sugar

Mix cranberry sauce, pineapple, yogurt, lemon juice and sugar in a plastic rectangular container. Freeze until set. Cut into squares as you would a sheet cake and serve. As an alternative, pour into a standard muffin pan lined with muffin papers and freeze. Serves 8.

LOUISE WOOTEN TALLEY
RALEIGH, NC

WILD RICE SALAD WITH LEMON JUICE & HONEY MUSTARD DRESSING

Wild rice provides the base for a great salad. A good quality honey mustard will work well with this recipe. If asparagus are not available, substitute sugar snap peas. This salad is even better the next day.

½ cup wild rice

½ cup long grain rice

1 pound zucchini, about 3 small or 2 medium

½ teaspoon salt

1 pound asparagus

1 red or green bell pepper, chopped

½ cup chopped scallions

1 cup sliced green olives

3-4 Roma tomatoes

HONEY MUSTARD DRESSING:

½ cup fresh lemon juice

⅓ cup honey mustard

½ teaspoon salt

½ cup extra virgin olive oil

Prepare wild rice and long grain rice separately according to packages; cool.

While rice is cooking, shred zucchini. (A food processor works well.) Toss with ½ teaspoon salt and set aside. Remove and discard tough ends of asparagus; cut into 1½-inch pieces, keeping tender heads separate. Bring a large pot of salted water to a boil. Add stem pieces, and boil 2 minutes; add heads and boil 2 minutes more. Drain and refresh under cold water.

In large bowl toss together cooled rice, grated zucchini, bell pepper, scallions and olives. Stir in Honey Mustard Dressing. Carefully toss in asparagus. Slice Roma tomatoes into thin wedges and place on top of salad. Serve at room temperature. Serves 10.

HONEY MUSTARD DRESSING: Whisk together lemon juice, mustard and salt. Gradually whisk in olive oil; set aside.

MARINATED CAULIFLOWER SALAD WITH GRAPE TOMATOES

Light but filling, this may be made with bottled or homemade Basil Thyme Vinaigrette.

1 head cauliflower

1 pint grape tomatoes

6 ounces Monterey Jack cheese

½ cup Basil Thyme Vinaigrette

BASIL THYME VINAIGRETTE:

⅓ cup olive oil

⅓ cup vegetable oil

2½ tablespoons red wine vinegar

1 teaspoon Dijon mustard

1 tablespoon water

½ teaspoon basil

¼ teaspoon thyme

½ teaspoon salt

¼ teaspoon pepper

Cut cauliflower into florets and grape tomatoes in half. Dice cheese into ¼-inch cubes. Combine all together in a bowl and toss with dressing. Refrigerate 24 hours before serving. Stir occasionally. Add more dressing if necessary. Serves 8.

BASIL THYME VINAIGRETTE: Whisk ingredients together in a small bowl until well-combined.

NANCY WAY
RALEIGH, NC

ITALIAN BREAD SALAD

Pazanella is the Italian name for this poor man's salad in Italy's culinary history. Bread was added to fill out more expensive ingredients — the bigger the appetite, the more bread was added. Old bread was first soaked in water and then squeezed before adding to the salad. Modern versions toast the bread rather than soak it to make it more palatable. A great accompaniment to almost any dinner.

2½   cups Italian bread cubes, diced ¾-inch

2   tablespoons olive oil

1   large ripe tomato

1   small Kirby cucumber (unwaxed)

½   green pepper

½   cup fresh basil leaves

2   tablespoons capers

2   tablespoons balsamic vinegar

1   clove garlic, minced

•   salt and ground pepper

½   cup extra virgin olive oil

Preheat oven to 375°. Toss bread cubes with 2 tablespoons olive oil. Place on baking sheet and toast for 20 minutes, stirring occasionally, until crisp and brown; cool.

Cut tomato into wedges and remove seeds. Cut wedges into chunks. Cut cucumber into quarters lengthwise, then into chunks. Seed pepper and cut into ½-inch pieces.

In a large bowl, combine toasted bread cubes, tomato wedges, cucumber, green pepper, basil and capers. In separate small bowl, combine vinegar, garlic, salt and pepper. Whisk in olive oil until creamy. Pour over salad ingredients and toss well. Let marinate at least ½ hour before serving to allow vinaigrette to soak into toasted bread. Serves 2-4.

OVERNIGHT LAYERED SPINACH SALAD

This versatile salad was a popular recipe in the first NCMA cookbook shared by the late Mrs. James Ralph Scales. Take to potluck supper or serve on a buffet.

½   pound fresh spinach leaves, chopped

1   10-ounce package tiny frozen peas, blanched

6   strips bacon, cooked and crumbled

2   eggs, hardboiled and chopped

16   cherry tomatoes, halved

½   cup chopped green onions

•   iceberg lettuce

½   teaspoon basil

½   teaspoon oregano

½   cup mayonnaise

½   cup sour cream or plain yogurt

¼-½ cup Parmesan cheese

In a very large straight sided glass bowl (so salad layers can be seen through sides) layer spinach, peas, bacon, eggs, tomatoes, onion and lettuce. Sprinkle basil and oregano over top.

In a small bowl, combine mayonnaise and sour cream. Spread over top of salad. Sprinkle generously with Parmesan cheese. Cover and refrigerate overnight. Do not toss. Serves 6-8.

MRS. JAMES RALPH SCALES 📖
WINSTON-SALEM, NC

TANGY GREEN BEAN SALAD

Cheese, egg and olives give new dimension to a refreshing green bean salad. The base may be made earlier in the day and dressed right before serving

1 pound young green beans

1 clove garlic, minced

½ cup shredded mozzarella cheese

½ cup shredded romaine lettuce

½ red bell pepper, julienned

1 egg, hard boiled and chopped

¼ cup chopped green olives

• salt and pepper

TANGY DRESSING:

⅔ cup olive oil

2 cloves garlic, minced

1 teaspoon Dijon mustard

¼ cup white wine vinegar

1½ teaspoons dried basil

2 teaspoons Worcestershire sauce

Snap ends off beans and drop into boiling water for 7 minutes or until tender, not soggy. Drain, refresh in an ice water bath, drain again and cool.

Combine beans in a medium bowl with garlic, cheese, lettuce, pepper, egg and olives. Cover and refrigerate.

Make Tangy Dressing just before serving. Toss with enough dressing to coat ingredients. Season to taste with salt and pepper. Serves 6-8.

TANGY DRESSING: Whisk ingredients together until well-blended.

JUDITH DICKEY
RALEIGH, NC

TABBOULEH

A most refreshing salad with the crisp flavors of mint and garden vegetables spiked with fresh lemon juice.

¾ cup bulghur

• warm water

2 large tomatoes

2 cucumbers

2 cups chopped parsley

½ cup chopped fresh mint

2 cups chopped green onions

½ cup olive oil

⅓ cup lemon juice

2 teaspoons salt

½ teaspoon black pepper

Rinse bulghur in warm water, drain partially and let soak for 45 minutes. Drain again if necessary and fluff wheat with fork. Chop tomatoes and cucumbers finely and combine with bulghur, parsley, mint and onions. Stir in lemon juice, oil, salt and pepper; mix until blended. Keep chilled. Serves 10.

YVETTE BAINI (MRS. MOUSSA DOMIT)
OCALA, FL

Basil and Tomato Salad with Black Pepper Goat Cheese

BASIL AND TOMATO SALAD WITH BLACK PEPPER GOAT CHEESE

A Caper Vinaigrette dresses up this basil and tomato salad featuring goat cheese rolled in black pepper and herbs.

3	large vine-ripened tomatoes
6	tops of fresh basil
1	head of living Bibb lettuce
2	tablespoons fresh parsley, chopped
2	tablespoons cracked black peppercorns
6	ounces goat cheese
12	Calamata olives

CAPER VINAIGRETTE:

1	teaspoon fresh oregano
1	teaspoon fresh tarragon
1	teaspoon fresh chives
¼	cup balsamic vinegar
1½	tablespoons small capers
1	teaspoon minced garlic
•	pinch red pepper flakes
¼	teaspoon ground black pepper
¼	teaspoon salt
¼	teaspoon sugar
⅔	cup olive oil

Wash tomatoes, basil and Bibb lettuce. Drain thoroughly and pat dry.

Mix chopped parsley and pepper and spread evenly on cutting board or wax paper. Halve goat cheese lengthwise, and roll both pieces in mixture until coated on all sides. Wrap in wax paper and freeze halfway to make cheese easy to slice. When frozen, slice into ½-inch thick slices.

Divide lettuce 6 ways and place onto dinner plates. Slice tomatoes fairly thickly and place 3 slices laying like dominos on each plate at the edge of the lettuce. Add 2 goat cheese slices to each plate, place Calamata olives in the center, and garnish with basil tops. Serve Caper Vinaigrette on the side. Serves 6.

CAPER VINAIGRETTE: Chop oregano, tarragon and chives. In a small bowl, combine herbs with vinegar, capers, garlic, red pepper, black pepper, salt and sugar. Gradually whisk in olive oil, mixing thoroughly. Makes 1 cup.

PICNIC
FARE

More than a place

*M*ore **than a place** to view some of the world's greatest art by the most famous artists of all time, the North Carolina Museum of Art is alive with activity and charged with energy. The Museum experience extends beyond its physical walls onto the manicured, yet natural grounds where you can walk or jog, and later enjoy an outdoor concert, movie or live theatre. It can be a place to meet friends for an afternoon picnic under Thomas Sayre's massive outdoor sculpture, a beautiful backdrop for dining *al fresco.* These easy, portable recipes were selected for their universal palate appeal.

FRANCES' FRESH GARDEN SPREAD

Spread on hearty whole wheat bread for a lunch or picnic, or serve as an hors d'oeuvre on party rye or sourdough slices.

1	cucumber, grated, see note
1	large carrot, peeled and grated
½	cup finely chopped celery
½	cup grated onion
1	teaspoon lemon juice
½	teaspoon salt
1	teaspoon gelatin (½ package)
2	tablespoons hot water
1	cup mayonnaise
¼	cup chopped fresh chives

Combine cucumber, carrot, celery, onion, lemon juice and salt in a medium bowl. Dissolve gelatin in hot water; blend with mayonnaise and vegetable mixture. Refrigerate until chilled and set. Garnish with fresh chives if spread over crackers, or sprinkle over sandwiches. Makes 2½ cups.

NOTE: If the cucumber is store-bought and waxed, peel first. With Kirby cucumbers or fresh from a garden, peeling is not necessary.

FRANCES M. EMORY
RALEIGH NC

WALDORF SANDWICH WITH A LIGHT TOUCH

A traditional Waldorf salad moves into a sandwich in this delicious creation spread over raisin bread, perfect for any picnic basket.

6	ounces cooked turkey breast, cubed
½	cup diced celery
1	small Red Delicious apple, cored and diced
2	tablespoons chopped walnuts
1	tablespoon mayonnaise
1	tablespoon yogurt
⅛	teaspoon nutmeg
⅛	teaspoon cinnamon
4	lettuce leaves
8	slices raisin bread

In a medium-size bowl, combine turkey, celery, apple, walnuts, mayonnaise, yogurt, nutmeg and cinnamon. Cover and refrigerate at least 1 hour or overnight to allow flavors to blend.

To serve: Arrange a lettuce leaf on a bread slice. Spoon ¼ of the turkey mixture over lettuce leaf and top with another bread slice. Repeat with remaining ingredients. Turkey mixture will keep up to 4 days in refrigerator. Serves 4.

GRILLED SALMON AND HUSKY RED

Thin slices of dark pumpernickel sandwich grilled salmon, horseradish cream, tomato chunks and baby spinach leaves.

½ pound salmon fillet

• salt and pepper

• olive oil

½ cup sour cream

1 tablespoon horseradish

1 tablespoon minced shallots

1 teaspoon balsamic vinegar

1 cup fresh baby spinach leaves, washed

2 ripe tomatoes, medium diced

1 tablespoon olive oil

1 teaspoon red wine vinegar

8 slices pumpernickel rye bread

Butterfly salmon fillets or slice lengthwise on the horizontal to yield ¼-inch thick pieces. Sprinkle with salt and pepper and brush with olive oil. Set aside.

In a small bowl combine sour cream, horseradish, shallots and balsamic vinegar. In another bowl toss clean spinach leaves with diced tomatoes, olive oil and red wine vinegar. In a grill pan over medium-high heat cook salmon pieces 1-2 minutes per side until just pink. Do not over cook as fish will dry out.

To serve: Spread horseradish mixture on each of 4 slices of bread; next add salmon fillets, then top with tossed spinach and tomatoes. Top each with second slice of bread. Serves 4.

THE ITALIAN BEEFSTEAK

A meaty slice of tomato adorned with an herbed mascarpone cheese is served on a tomato basil bread. Bravo! Bravo!

2 teaspoons fresh parsley

2 teaspoons fresh basil

2 teaspoons fresh chives

4 ounces mascarpone cheese

• freshly ground pepper

2 beefsteak tomatoes

8 slices tomato basil bread

Chop parsley, basil and chives. Combine with cheese and pepper.

Slice tomatoes ¼-inch thick. Generously spread mascarpone on each bread slice and layer with luscious tomato. Top each with second bread slice. Serves 4.

PIMIENTO BLUE SPROUTWICH

There's nothing quite like the taste of sweet ripe tomatoes combined with any kind of blue cheese. In this winning sandwich, the English Stilton goes southern, courting summer tomatoes, pimientos and fresh sprouts. A vegetable herb wheat bread makes the perfect base for this tantalizing affair.

4 ounces Stilton cheese, crumbled

¼ cup mayonnaise

2 teaspoons minced garlic

2 tablespoons pimiento

½ teaspoon salt

• freshly ground pepper

2 large tomatoes

8 slices vegetable herb bread

2 cups sprouts

Combine Stilton with mayonnaise, garlic, pimiento, salt and pepper.

Slice tomatoes ¼-inch thick. Spread pimiento blue cheese on one slice of herb bread and add a layer of tomato. Pile high with mound of sprouts, cover with second slice of bread. Continue with remaining ingredients. Makes 4 sandwiches.

Goat Lady's Tomato Sandwich with Vidalia Relish

A fresh Vidalia Relish is a perfect topping for this sandwich starring a goat cheese spread and vine-ripened tomatoes. Make the sandwiches a few hours ahead, wrap tightly and refrigerate. You will find the juices from the sweet onion relish will deliciously soak into the bread.

1 loaf crusty French baguette or sourdough bread

4 vine-ripened tomatoes

1 cup arugula, washed and gently patted dry

1 cup Vidalia Relish

THE GOAT LADY'S SPREAD:

3 ounces goat cheese, softened

2 tablespoons heavy cream or half & half

1 tablespoon fresh thyme leaves

VIDALIA RELISH:

4 Vidalia onions

1 small red bell pepper

1 small green bell pepper

3 tablespoons olive oil

2 tablespoons fresh thyme leaves

3½ ounces cider vinegar

1½ ounces water

⅓ cup sugar

½ teaspoon salt

¼ teaspoon pepper

Make Goat Lady's Spread and Vidalia Relish.

Cut baguette in half lengthwise. Spread a thin layer of The Goat Lady's Spread over 1 baguette half. Layer arugula, tomato slices, and Vidalia Relish, then close the sandwich with remaining baguette. Slice into 4 equal pieces on the diagonal. Wrap tightly in plastic and refrigerate until ready to serve. The juices from the sweet onion relish will soak deliciously into bread. Serves 4.

THE GOAT LADY'S SPREAD: Blend all ingredients in a mixing bowl. Refrigerate until ready to use.

VIDALIA RELISH: Slice onions into ¼-inch thick rings. Cut peppers into a ¼-inch dice. Heat oil in a dutch oven over medium-high heat. Sauté onions until they begin to caramelize, about 10 minutes, stirring occasionally. Add peppers and sauté 2 more minutes. Combine thyme, vinegar, water, sugar, salt and pepper and add to onions. Reduce heat, cover and simmer for 30 minutes. Relish will hold up to 2 weeks in the refrigerator. Yields 4 cups.

A tomato sandwich made with goat cheese and a Vidalia relish beautifully survives the morning wait in a lunchbox on a hike in the mountains.

A wicker hamper finds a perch before John Beerman's *Three Trees, Two Clouds.* Fill with Spinach Salad Sandwiches stuffed with Radishes and Arugula, wrapped in colorful, bib-sized napkins. Add the Apple Harvest Pecan Tart (page 194), a favorite wine and trek to a quiet meadow for a luncheon on the grass. Breathe deeply, eat heartily and take in the beautiful skyline.

Spinach Salad Sandwiches with Radishes & Arugula

This stuffed sandwich is great for a picnic. It could also be sliced more thinly and served as an hors d'oeuvre.

2   cups spinach leaves, stems removed

1   cup arugula, plus more for serving

6   medium red radishes

2   flat anchovies

8   ounces cream cheese

4   ounces soft goat cheesee

¼   cup snipped fresh chives

¼   cup chopped parsley

½   teaspoon freshly ground pepper

¼   teaspoon salt

1   plump baguette

Put spinach, 1 cup arugula, radishes and anchovies into bowl of food processor; process until chopped. Add cream cheese and goat cheese and process until well combined, but still chunky. Remove to a bowl and stir in chives, parsley, pepper and salt.

Cut baguette in half lengthwise. Remove top and hollow out top and bottom by removing bread to make a shell of each piece. Spoon cheese mixture generously into the shells letting it run over a bit. Put back together and wrap in foil; refrigerate several hours or overnight. Shortly before serving, carefully separate the 2 halves and add arugula leaves (or lettuce). Put together again and cut into 6 pieces. Serves 6.

Marinated Flank Steak Sandwich

Of course, you can serve this anytime, but it is always a big hit for a tailgate picnic.

1   large flank steak

⅓   cup soy sauce

⅓   cup vegetable oil

⅓   cup sherry cooking wine

1   large garlic clove, crushed

½   teaspoon Tabasco sauce

•   freshly ground pepper

1   large loaf French bread

•   softened butter (do not substitute)

Score flank steak in a diamond pattern on both sides, and place in a glass dish. Mix together soy sauce, vegetable oil, sherry wine, garlic, Tabasco and pepper. Pour over steak, refrigerate overnight.

Grill steak over a hot fire, turning once, until it reaches desired doneness — rare is best for this particular dish because the sandwich should be moist.

Slice bread lengthwise and spread each half with softened butter. Press the loaves together again and wrap in aluminum foil, making an extra piece of doubled foil directly under bread. Warm slightly (do not bake!) in oven about 5 minutes while you slice the meat.

Slice steak crosswise very thinly, keeping your knife at an angle to the grain. Allow it to re-absorb the juices as much as possible. Remove bread from warm oven and separate the two halves. Lay strips of steak on the bottom half until steak is all used up. Pour any remaining juices onto the steak. Cover with the top half of the bread. Place sandwich on doubled thickness of foil. To serve: slice sandwich into 1-2-inch slices, being careful not to cut through foil. Rewrap securely in additional aluminum foil. Keep warm until serving time, but do not re-heat or the meat will turn gray. Serves 4-6.

Carolyn R. Booth
Cary, NC

FESTIVE OPEN FACE SANDWICHES

A variety of cocktail open-face sandwiches makes a pleasing presentation for a festive picnic. Small party rye bread is the easiest to use. Leave in squares or cut some into circles. Featured are just a few suggestions for toppings; use your imagination to create more combinations.

1   loaf cocktail pumpernickel bread (2½-inch square pieces) or thinly sliced white or sourdough bread

•   butter, room temperature

For all combinations, spread bread slices with butter. Add the assorted toppings below, garnish and serve. Allow 3-4 per person.

MUSHROOMS IN SOUR CREAM

½   pound mushrooms, cleaned and sliced

2   tablespoons lemon juice

⅓   cup sour cream

1   tablespoon chopped chives

•   salt and pepper

•   chives for garnish

Toss sliced mushrooms with lemon juice. Add sour cream, chives, salt and pepper. Put 3 or 4 mushroom slices on a buttered piece of bread. Top with chive garnish.

MARINATED CUCUMBERS

3   Kirby cucumbers, washed

½   cup white wine vinegar

¼   cup water

¼   cup sugar

½   teaspoon salt

2   tablespoons fresh chopped dill

•   dill garnish

Thinly slice cucumbers. In bowl mix together vinegar, water, sugar, salt and chopped dill. Pour over cucumbers. Marinate in refrigerator several hours or overnight. Drain well and put 3-4 cucumber slices on brown bread squares. Garnish with dill.

DANISH BLUE AND PEAR

•   Danish blue cheese, carefully sliced with a cheese wire or cheese plane

•   thinly sliced pears

Spread buttered bread with a slice of blue cheese and several pears.

SMOKED SALMON WITH DILL

•   Boston lettuce or leaf lettuce

•   smoked salmon

•   lemon wedges, cut them so the juice can be squeezed on the salmon

•   cucumber twists made from thin bias-cut slices

•   dill, one sprig per sandwich, plus a sprinkling of chopped dill

Place a small piece of lettuce on buttered bread. Top with a generous amount of thinly sliced smoked salmon. Top with a lemon wedge, a cucumber twist and a sprig of dill. Sprinkle chopped dill on top.

JOHN BEERMAN (American), *THREE TREES, TWO CLOUDS*, 1990 © John Beerman

John Beerman's paintings are poetic meditations on the enduring power of nature. *Three Trees, Two Clouds* was inspired by the Haw River country of Alamance County, North Carolina. But the artist has transformed the actual landscape to conjure a radiant, dreamlike vision of nature in which twin spectral clouds hover improbably between the trees. Earth and sky are thus united by uncanny symmetry. In such images the artist finds a mystical order and harmony within nature.

FRANK LONDON (American), *SONG SILENCED*, 1938

This somber, poetic painting by Frank London was executed during the last ten years of the artist's life, yet it is closely linked in spirit to the ecclesiastical art and stained glass that London was designing a decade and a half earlier. Born in Pittsboro, North Carolina, London spent most of his career painting in Europe and learned much from early Dutch still-life painting. *Song Silenced* reflects this inspiration in the peeled lemon, overripe fruit and insects—symbols of the transience of life.

CALIFORNIA KIDS SANDWICH

Peanut butter is the staple in this sandwich. Spread with the honey, carrots and raisins, it's a winner!

12	slices of thin-sliced white bread
1½	cups peanut butter
¼	cup honey
2	cups grated carrots
1½	cups raisins

Have ingredients ready to make sandwiches.

Trim edges of white bread. On 1 slice of bread, spread peanut butter. Next, spread honey over peanut butter. Sprinkle sandwich half with a generous amount of grated carrots and raisins. Cover with 1 plain piece of bread. Repeat the process 5 times for 6 whole sandwiches.

HAM ROLLS WITH HERBED GOAT CHEESE

These ham rolls are a delicious alternative to the traditional picnic sandwich. Use a good quality sliced deli ham.

8	ounces goat cheese, softened
1	teaspoon oregano
1	teaspoon basil
¼	teaspoon thyme
36	slices party ham

In medium bowl, mix goat cheese with oregano, basil and thyme. Spread about 1½ teaspoons on each ham slice covering about ¾ of surface. Roll up starting from the cheese end; chill. About ½ hour before serving, remove from refrigerator and serve at room temperature. Allow 4 to 6 per person. Serves 4-5.

SALAD IN A SANDWICH

Bright and crunchy, these sandwiches gain extra zest from the seasoned mayonnaise. For a picnic: wrap the whole loaf in foil or butcher paper and slice just before serving. Salad greens may be substituted for watercress.

2	bunches watercress, coarsely chopped, large stems removed
1	Vidalia onion, thinly sliced
3	fennel bulbs, thinly sliced
3	tablespoons chopped fennel leaves
⅓	cup toasted chopped walnuts
2	cups torn green leaf lettuce
1	loaf crusty French bread

....

TARRAGON DRESSING:

¼	cup balsamic vinegar
½	cup extra virgin olive oil
2	tablespoons chopped fresh tarragon
2	tablespoons chopped fresh parsley
•	salt and pepper

....

GREEN PEPPERCORN MAYONNAISE:

¼	cup mayonnaise
1	teaspoon Dijon mustard
½	teaspoon crushed green peppercorns

Prepare Tarragon Dressing and place in large salad bowl. Set aside.

Prepare Green Peppercorn Mayonnaise.

Combine watercress, onion, sliced fennel, fennel leaves and walnuts with Tarragon Dressing. Split loaf of bread lengthwise. Spread Green Peppercorn Mayonnaise evenly over each half. Arrange lettuce leaves on bottom half. Top with tossed salad. Cover with top half of loaf. Serves 8.

TARRAGON DRESSING: Place vinegar and herbs in bottom of large salad bowl. Whisk in olive oil. Add salt and pepper to taste.

GREEN PEPPERCORN MAYONNAISE: Combine all ingredients in a small bowl.

The Vidalia, a sweet onion grown only in Vidalia County in Georgia, is harvested in the late spring. This luscious sandwich — combining Vidalias with fennel, watercress and a fresh tarragon dressing — is a feast!

PORK TENDERLOIN SANDWICHES WITH CONFETTI CORN RELISH

If you need to pack a hearty meal for a day of hiking, this is it. The confetti relish is more like a slather of fresh vegetables with dressing. Earmark this for fall tailgates too.

1-1¼	pounds pork tenderloin
3	tablespoons Dijon mustard
1	tablespoon red wine vinegar
1	tablespoon soy sauce
1	tablespoon olive oil
1	clove garlic, minced
½	teaspoon rosemary
½	teaspoon pepper
4-6	soft rolls

CONFETTI CORN RELISH:

1	cup white corn
2	teaspoons vegetable oil
½	cup chopped red pepper
¼	cup chopped red onion
1	cup fresh spinach leaves, chopped
2	tablespoons Dijon mustard
½	teaspoon salt
1	teaspoon pepper
3	tablespoons chopped parsley

Place tenderloin in a reclosable plastic bag. In a small bowl, combine mustard, red wine vinegar, soy sauce, olive oil, garlic, rosemary and pepper. Pour over pork, coating tenderloin well. Cover and refrigerate for at least 2 hours.

Heat gas grill to medium. Grill pork for about 25 minutes (145°-150° on a meat thermometer), turning every 5 minutes to cook evenly. Let rest 10 minutes before carving. (If making the day before, store in refrigerator.)

Slice pork into ¼-inch slices. Put 2-3 pieces on each roll. Wrap tightly for transporting to picnic. When ready to eat, spoon on some of Confetti Relish. Serves 4-6.

CONFETTI CORN RELISH: Cook corn; strain off water. Transfer to a medium bowl. Heat oil in a skillet over medium heat. Cook pepper and onion for about 4 minutes. Add to corn. Return skillet to heat. Add spinach and wilt, stirring for about 2-3 minutes. Transfer spinach to fine mesh sieve. Press excess water from it, then add to corn mixture. Stir in mustard, salt, pepper and parsley. Refrigerate until ready to serve.

TURKEY SALAD

Turkey salad takes on new dimensions with Asian accents, fruit and nuts.

2	pounds cooked turkey breast, diced ½-inch
1	9-ounce can water chestnuts, drained and chopped coarsely
3	cups small diced celery
1	cup slivered almonds
1	large can pineapple chunks, drained
1	tablespoon soy sauce
3	cups mayonnaise
2	tablespoons curry powder
•	pita pockets, optional

In a large bowl put turkey, water chestnuts, celery, almonds and pineapple chunks. In a small bowl mix soy sauce, mayonnaise and curry to make dressing. Mix turkey salad with just enough dressing to moisten.

Serve on lettuce beds with grapes on the side or in pita pockets with shredded lettuce. Serves 12.

BETTY A. NIZICH
CARY, NC

Patty Sue's Rice Salad with Shrimp

Full of crunch and color, this rice salad featuring shrimp is a meal.

3	cups cooked rice
1	15-ounce can mixed vegetables, drained
1	12-ounce can Mexi-corn, drained
2	tablespoons chopped green pepper
2	tablespoons chopped onion
½	cup chopped celery
2	hard-boiled eggs, chopped
2	tomatoes, chopped
1	pound cooked shrimp, peeled
1	cup mayonnaise
¼	cup wine vinegar
¼	cup vegetable oil
•	salt and pepper

In a large bowl combine rice, mixed vegetables, corn, green pepper, onion, celery, eggs, tomatoes and shrimp.

In a separate bowl mix together mayonnaise, vinegar and oil. Add to rice mixture and toss gently. Season to taste with salt and pepper. Chill. Serves 8-10 .

NANCY GREGG
RALEIGH, NC

Asparagus Chicken Penne Pasta Salad

Fresh basil and chives add the zest to this delicious pasta salad. An easy, refreshing summertime meal.

4	boneless chicken breast halves
2	tablespoons olive oil
2	cups dry penne pasta
1	cup asparagus or broccoflower, cut into pieces
1	large ripe tomato, cut into chunks
¼	cup chives, snipped into ¼-inch pieces

BASIL VINAIGRETTE:

⅓	cup white wine vinegar
⅓	cup olive oil
2-3	tablespoons fresh basil, chopped
½	teaspoon sugar
½	teaspoon salt
1	tablespoon capers
•	freshly ground pepper
1	clove garlic, crushed

Make Basil Vinaigrette. Rinse and dry chicken breasts and rub with 2 tablespoons olive oil. Sprinkle with salt and pepper. Grill on range-top grill, browning well on both sides. Grill for 3-5 minutes per side. Check for doneness, being careful not to overcook. Cool and cut chicken into ¾-inch chunks.

While chicken is grilling, cook pasta al dente in salted boiling water. Drain and place in large bowl. Pour vinaigrette over pasta. Add chicken and stir well.

Steam or parboil asparagus or broccoflower in salted water until al dente. Add to pasta; along with tomato. Stir well. Sprinkle chives over salad, toss lightly and adjust seasoning. Serve at room temperature. Serves 4-5.

BASIL VINAIGRETTE: Whisk together all ingredients. Set aside.

Fresh
Catch

CAROLINA SHRIMP IN WINE SAUCE AND PUFF PASTRY BOATS

An excellent dinner entrée made elegant by serving in puff pastry. If you have a large fish-shaped cookie cutter, use it or cut out fish or boat shapes by hand.

2-3   sheets puff pastry
1½   pounds shrimp
¾   cup chopped onion
¼   pound mushrooms, sliced
4   tablespoons butter
3   tablespoons flour
1   cup chicken stock
½   cup sour cream
¼   cup dry white wine
•   salt and white pepper

Thaw puff pastry at room temperature for 20 minutes. Preheat oven to 400°. Gently unfold pastry sheets and cut out six fish or boat-shaped pieces about 4-5-inches in length. Place 2 inches apart on baking sheet. Bake 15 minutes or until golden brown. Remove from oven and when slightly cool, cut out the middle of each pastry to make a shell shape, saving the top piece. Set aside and keep warm.

Peel and devein shrimp. In a large sauté pan cook onion and mushrooms in butter over medium-high heat. Blend in flour and then add chicken stock gradually and simmer until thick, stirring constantly. Add sour cream, wine and shrimp. Continue to simmer until shrimp turn pink. Do not overcook. Season to taste with salt and pepper.

Spoon into pastry shells, garnish with chopped dill or parsley and top with puff pastry crust top. Serves 6.

KAY SHIPMAN SCHOELLHORN
RALEIGH, NC

LIBBA'S SHRIMP AND CHEDDAR GRITS

A hearty version of this savory Southern dish features both country ham and bacon sautéed with fresh shrimp over creamy Cheddar Grits.

¼   pound bacon
¼   pound country ham, cut into strips
½   cup chopped onion
½   pound mushrooms, sliced
1   teaspoon minced garlic
2   tablespoons vegetable oil
1   pound shrimp, peeled and deveined
2   tablespoons lemon juice
½   teaspoon Old Bay Seasoning
3   dashes Tabasco sauce
½   teaspoon salt

CHEDDAR GRITS:

1   cup yellow grits
1   cup grated cheddar cheese, divided
2   eggs, beaten
½   cup milk

Make Cheddar Grits.

In a large skillet fry bacon until crispy. Remove and set aside. Sauté country ham in bacon drippings. Add onion, mushrooms and garlic. Sauté until onions are translucent. Crumble bacon and add to mixture.

In a separate sauté pan, heat oil over medium high. Toss shrimp quickly and cook until pink. Stir in lemon juice, Old Bay, Tabasco and salt. Stir bacon and mushroom mixture into shrimp, and serve over grits. Serves 4.

CHEDDAR GRITS: Preheat oven to 300°. Make grits according to recipe on package. When cooked, cool slightly, then mix in ¾ cup cheese, eggs and milk. Pour into a shallow casserole. Top with remaining cheese. Bake until cheese is melted and eggs set.

LIBBA EVANS
WINSTON-SALEM, NC

GERRIT ADRIAENSZ. BERCKHEYDE (Dutch), *THE FISH MARKET AND THE GROTE KERK AT HAARLEM* (detail), c. 1675-80

SAUTÉED RED SNAPPER WITH SAFFRON CREAM SAUCE

A saffron cream reduction breathes life into fresh snapper. Snow peas and red pepper sautéed in sesame oil complete this beautiful dish.

8	ounces clarified butter, divided, see note
1	cup dry vermouth
1	bay leaf
2	shallots, thinly sliced
2	small celery heart stalks with leaves
1	carrot, roughly chopped
3	peppercorns
2	teaspoons saffron
1	cup clam juice or chicken stock
2	cups heavy cream
•	kosher salt and pepper
¼	cup sesame oil, divided
6	red snapper fillets, skin on
1	tablespoon minced garlic
½	pound snow peas
½	red pepper, julienned
3	tablespoons black sesame seeds
•	parsley or chervil for garnish

Clarify butter and set aside.

In a heavy saucepan bring vermouth, bay leaf, shallots, celery, carrot and peppercorns to a gentle simmer and reduce by half. Add saffron and clam juice and reduce by half. Add cream and simmer for 30 minutes until it is the consistency of cream. Strain and season to taste with salt and pepper.

Heat a large sauté pan with 2 tablespoons clarified butter and 2 tablespoons sesame oil. Pat snapper fillets dry and sauté fish 3 minutes per side. Remove and keep warm adding more butter and oil as needed to cook fish in batches. Sprinkle each fillet with a little salt just before removing from pan.

Begin sauce in another pan by heating ¼ cup clarified butter and 2 tablespoons sesame oil. Add minced garlic, snow peas, and red pepper and toss quickly. Cook stirring over high heat for 2 minutes. Remove pan from heat; vegetables will continue to cook until just tender.

Spoon saffron sauce onto plate. Place snapper on top skin side up. Arrange snow peas and red pepper above fish and sprinkle with black sesame seeds. Serves 6.

CLARIFIED BUTTER: Place butter in a heavy saucepan and melt slowly. Skim foam from surface. Slowly pour off the clear liquid, now clarified butter, leaving milky residue in bottom of pan.

BILL BLAAUW
SWEPSONVILLE, NC

EVIE'S POACHED FISH

A delightfully easy fish dish that may be prepared early in the day and then, amazingly, cooked in the microwave at dinnertime. Use flaky white fish such as sea bass, orange roughy or grouper. The recipe may be multiplied to serve larger parties.

¾	pound fish
1	teaspoon garlic powder
1	teaspoon horseradish
1	teaspoon Dijon mustard
1	teaspoon mayonnaise
1	teaspoon dried minced onions
1	teaspoon shredded Parmesan cheese
1	teaspoon Italian-style bread crumbs
¼	teaspoon paprika
¼	teaspoon dill weed
⅓	cup white wine

Place fish in a dish suitable for the microwave. Distribute seasonings and crumbs over fish in the order listed. Pour wine around fish and cover dish with plastic wrap. Microwave on high for 7 minutes. Adjust time if preparing larger or more fish. Serves 2.

EVELYN (EVIE) DURBIN
CARY, NC

CAPERED SEA BASS IN BLACK BUTTER

The original recipe from Panama, a country abundant with fish, calls for corvina (sea bass), although grouper, flounder or sole would make wonderful substitutes.

4   sea bass fillets (1-inch thickness)
½   cup flour
•   freshly ground pepper
6   tablespoons butter, divided
½   cup capers, drained
•   lime wedges
¼   cup chopped fresh parsley

Rinse fish and pat dry. Season flour with pepper and dredge fillets.

In a sauté pan melt 4 tablespoons butter. Pan fry fish on medium-high heat. Cook 4 minutes each side. Transfer to a warm platter.

Squeeze out as much liquid as possible from capers and add to pan with remaining 2 tablespoons butter. Fry capers at a high heat, stirring quickly until golden brown and crispy. Stir in chopped parsley and spoon over fish. Serve with lime wedges, grilled polenta cakes or mashed potatoes. Serves 4.

MARTA BREWER
RALEIGH, NC

Quick, easy and delicious — Capered Sea Bass in Black Butter.

PAN-ROASTED TUNA WITH POACHED RAISINS AND PIGNOLIA

Salt-encrusted tuna steaks rest in a full-flavored sauce studded with Marsala-soaked raisins and toasted pine nuts.

4 tablespoons coarse sea salt
  or kosher salt

2 teaspoons peppercorns

2 teaspoons fennel seed

4 6-8 ounce tuna steaks,
  ¾-1-inch thick

4-6 tablespoons olive oil,
  divided

• lemon zest curls for
  garnish, optional

....

**MARSALA RAISIN AND
PINE NUT SAUCE:**

¼ cup pine nuts

1 cup Marsala wine

1 cup olive oil

10 cloves whole garlic, peeled

10 dry cured black olives,
  pitted

½ cup minced red onion

• zest of 1 lemon

¼ cup golden raisins

Using a mortar and pestle grind salt, peppercorns and fennel seed. Rub into tuna steaks on both sides (no more than 2 hours before cooking). Cover and refrigerate.

To pan-roast tuna, heat a large heavy bottomed sauté pan on high. Add 2 tablespoons olive oil. Cooking 2 pieces of tuna at a time, sear each side for about 4 minutes. Keep tuna warm in a 200° oven as you cook additional fillets. Ladle sauce onto serving plates (we recommend a salad plate) and position tuna in the center. Garnish with lemon zest curls, if desired. Serves 4.

MARSALA RAISIN AND PINE NUT SAUCE: Toast pine nuts at 350° for 10 minutes. In a small saucepan, heat wine, olive oil, garlic, olives, red onion, lemon and raisins. Bring sauce to a boil for 2-3 minutes. Stir in pine nuts The sauce will be thin with delectable cooked raisins, olives and pine nuts.

GRILLED RUM YELLOW FIN TUNA

Rum, cilantro and a trace of cinnamon sear into fresh tuna steaks.

4 6-ounce tuna steaks, about
  1-inch thick

....

RUM MARINADE:

1 cup Amber rum

2 tablespoons canola oil

1 teaspoon grated lemon peel

2 tablespoons chopped
  cilantro

1 teaspoon vanilla extract

¼ cup lime juice

2 teaspoons honey

½ teaspoon cinnamon

• dash ground allspice

Make Rum Marinade. Place marinade and tuna in a resealable plastic bag; refrigerate 30 minutes.

Remove tuna from plastic bag; discard marinade. Grill tuna over hot coals, 2-3 minutes per side for medium rare. Serves 4.

RUM MARINADE: Blend all ingredients in food processor for 30 seconds.

PEPPERY SCALLOPS

A simple recipe with elegant results. If you often need to produce a company dinner during a busy week, this is a dish to earmark.

1¼ pounds large sea scallops
2 tablespoons melted butter
¼ cup bread crumbs
1 teaspoon basil
½ teaspoon pepper
¼ teaspoon salt
¼ teaspoon garlic powder

Rinse scallops in cold water and pat dry. Toss with melted butter to coat thoroughly.

Mix bread crumbs with basil, pepper, salt and garlic powder. Dip one side of each scallop into crumbs and place breaded-side-up on a baking sheet. Broil 3-5 minutes without turning, depending on size of scallops. Do not overcook. Serves 4.

CONNIE C. SHERTZ
RALEIGH, NC

Peppery Scallops will tilt your world!

PECAN-CRUSTED CATFISH WITH CORN BUTTER SAUCE

A spicy pecan coating mingles wonderfully with mild catfish, while a butter sauce provides the finishing touch.

6   8-ounce catfish fillets

2   cups pecans, coarsely ground

1   teaspoon cumin

1   teaspoon chili powder

1   teaspoon Old Bay seasoning

½   cup chopped fresh parsley

1   teaspoon salt

•   freshly ground pepper

2   eggs

2   tablespoons water

•   cooking spray

....

CORN BUTTER SAUCE:

1½   cups corn kernels

2   tablespoons chopped shallots

½   cup dry white wine

12   tablespoons chilled butter

Preheat oven to 375°. Spray a sheet pan with cooking spray.

Rinse catfish under cold water and pat dry. In a large shallow dish combine ground pecans with cumin, chili powder, Old Bay, parsley and salt. Mix well. Mix eggs with water in another shallow dish. Season fillets with pepper on both sides.

To assemble catfish, dip each fillet into egg wash, then immediately into pecan mixture, taking care to completely coat each fillet with pecans. Place prepared fillets on sheet pan. The fillets can be coated and refrigerated up to 4 hours before serving.

Bake for 12 minutes, checking fillets every 4 minutes to ensure pecans are not burning. If browning too quickly, reduce heat to 350°. To serve, place catfish on a warm salad plate and spoon corn butter sauce around edges. Serves 6.

CORN BUTTER SAUCE: Blanch corn in boiling water briefly; remove from heat and drain. Combine shallots and wine in a heavy-bottomed saucepan and bring to a boil. Continue boiling until almost dry, about 5 minutes. Reduce heat to low. Add butter 1 tablespoon at a time while whisking vigorously. Stir in corn. The sauce will hold for 30-40 minutes. To hold, pour into a double boiler over low steam.

BAKED FISH CURRY

A light yet flavorful meal. Serve with rice and pair with a Zinfandel or Sauvignon Blanc.

2   cups plain yogurt (do not use low-fat)

2   tablespoons lemon juice

1   teaspoon ground turmeric

1   teaspoon ground coriander

1   teaspoon grated ginger

1   clove garlic, minced

½   teaspoon hot curry powder

1   teaspoon dried oregano

½   cup chopped onion

8   white fish fillets such as catfish, sole or cod

1   teaspoon salt

1   teaspoon pepper

3   tablespoons olive oil

½   teaspoon cumin seeds

2   tablespoons honey or chutney

Preheat oven to 350°.

Combine yogurt, lemon juice, turmeric, coriander, ginger, garlic, curry powder, oregano and onion in bowl of food processor. Blend until smooth.

Place fillets in a single layer in a shallow baking dish. Season with salt and pepper. Set aside.

Heat oil in a skillet over medium heat. Add cumin seeds; stir until browned. Add the blended ingredients, stirring constantly. Add honey or chutney to mixture. Pour over fish fillets and bake for 30 minutes.

Serve with curry sauce spooned around fish. Serves 4.

$\mathcal{G}$*ifts* from the sea frequently grace Southern tables in a variety of preparations — marinated, sautéed, baked, fried, poached, smoked, grilled or roasted. Southern cooks add a regional flair to tasty seafood dishes by serving them with grits, breading them with cornmeal and even with another traditional delicacy, pecans, as in the Pecan-Crusted Catfish (page 83).

BAKED SALMON MEDITERRANEAN

A baked entrée means easy preparation for the cook who wants to visit with guests before dinner.

4 salmon fillets, about ½-pound each

1 cup fresh bread crumbs

4 tablespoons capers, rinsed and drained

4 tablespoons green olives, chopped

• salt and pepper

4 tablespoons mayonnaise

Preheat oven to 400°. Spray a flat baking dish with cooking spray.

Carefully skin salmon, or have butcher do it for you. Feel for bones in the thickest part and pull out any you find. Rinse and pat dry.

In small bowl combine bread crumbs, capers, olives, salt and pepper. Lay salmon in dish. Spread each piece with about 1 tablespoon of mayonnaise. Divide crumb mixture among 4 pieces of salmon and press to adhere to mayonnaise. Bake for 15-20 minutes until crumbs are browned and fish flakes easily with fork. Serves 4.

SOFT SHELL CRABS MEUNIÈRE

Scrumptious. A zesty lemon butter sauce features cayenne and white peppers and toasted almonds.

8 soft shell crabs

1-2 cups milk

2 cups flour

1 teaspoon salt

½ teaspoon pepper

¼ teaspoon cayenne

¾ cup butter

1 cup slivered almonds

1 tablespoon lemon juice

½ teaspoon white pepper

• vegetable oil

Have fishmonger clean soft shell crabs, or do it yourself by cutting off eyes with a parallel slice to the face. Lift carapace and lungs and peel off triangular shaped plate on belly.

Soak crabs in 1½-inches of cold milk in a glass pan for 10-15 minutes. In a separate bowl combine flour, salt, black and red peppers. Carefully remove crabs from milk and roll gently in seasoned flour to coat thoroughly. Place on a large platter. Do not overlap.

In a medium saucepan, make Meunière Sauce by melting butter slowly. Stir in almonds and cook butter over low heat until it begins to turn brown. Remove pan from heat and add lemon juice and white pepper. Return to low heat and brown 1 minute more until sauce is the color of hazelnuts.

While sauce is cooking heat enough vegetable oil in a skillet to cover bottom of pan with ¼-inch of oil. On medium-high heat fry crabs up to 3 at a time about 6 minutes or until golden brown on both sides. Keep warm in a 200° oven and continue frying until all are ready. Serves 4.

Serve crabs with a generous spoonful of butter sauce poured over each portion.

ROSEMARY WYCHE
RALEIGH, NC

JAN BRUEGHEL THE ELDER (Netherlandish), *HARBOR SCENE WITH ST. PAUL'S DEPARTURE FROM CAESAREA, 1596*

This small painting exhibits the jewel-like tones and remarkable attention to minute detail for which Jan Brueghel was famous. Vividly demonstrating this technique is the obvious care with which each species of the abundant fish catch is rendered. The setting's festive air and bustling crowd are true to historical accounts of the harbor city, as are the towers of the harbor and the crowds promenading along the seawall. Nearly lost in the mass of humanity is St. Paul, identified by his halo in the lower right corner of the painting.

Cedar Island Shrimp captures the essence of fresh coastal flavors.

CEDAR ISLAND SHRIMP

Fresh herbs abound and highlight the shrimp in this delightfully simple pasta dish.

1-1½	pounds shrimp
3	tablespoons olive oil
4	tablespoons butter
4	shallots, sliced
2	cloves garlic, minced
2	tablespoons fresh parsley
1½	tablespoons fresh oregano
2	tablespoons fresh basil
½	tablespoon fresh thyme
½	tablespoon fresh marjoram
•	red and black pepper
•	salt
1	pound linguini

Clean, devein shrimp. Keep cool.

Heat oil and butter in a large pan over medium heat. Sauté shallots and garlic; do not brown.

Quickly chop parsley, oregano, basil, thyme and marjoram and add with shrimp to pan. Season with red and black pepper and salt. Cook over low flame until shrimp are done (2-5 minutes). Serve over cooked pasta. Serves 4-6.

GEORGANNE C. BINGHAM
RALEIGH, NC

LINGUINI WITH CLAMS AND MUSSELS

Steam the larger littlenecks and make the sauce ahead using the clam broth. Simply reheat on low before cooking the pasta and shellfish. Since clams and mussels and linguini all require large pots, steam the seafood on a hot outdoor grill to free up your stovetop. The aromas will lend authentic clambake appeal to your backyard or patio. Please note that Parmesan cheese is not necessary with seafood.

- 2 dozen large littleneck clams
- 3 cups water
- 1½ cups white wine, divided
- 6 tablespoons butter
- 2 tablespoons minced garlic
- 3 tablespoons minced shallots
- 3 tablespoons flour
- 3 cups reserved clam broth or bottled clam juice
- ⅓ cup chopped parsley
- 2 dozen smaller littleneck clams
- 3 dozen mussels
- 1½ pounds fresh linguini

HERB BUTTER:

- 4 tablespoons butter, softened
- 1 teaspoon chopped parsley
- 1 teaspoon chopped fresh basil
- ¼ teaspoon thyme
- • pinch of pepper

Wash the 2 dozen large clams (shells about 2"-2½" diameter) and steam in a large covered pot with 2 cups water and 1 cup white wine. Once opened (8-10 minutes), remove clams, discard shells, chop clams and set aside. Reserve broth for sauce.

In a large sauté pan, melt butter and sauté garlic and shallots over medium heat 2-3 minutes. Stir in flour and cook gently to make a roux. Whisk in clam broth until a thin sauce is achieved. Add chopped clams and parsley and simmer 2 minutes. The entree may be made ahead to this point and refrigerated. Reheat before stirring into cooked pasta.

Just before dinner, prepare small littlenecks (shells about 1½" in diameter) and mussels for steaming. For clams add 2-inches water and ¼ cup white wine to either a steamer basket or large soup size pot. For the mussels, add ¼ cup wine to 1-inch water in another similar pot. Over high heat, the clams will cook 5-8 minutes until open; the mussels 3-5. Check every few minutes. Reserve the mussel broth. Cooking the clams and mussels this way is done easily on a gas grill.

In another large pot, bring 3 quarts salted water to boil. Add fresh pasta, bring back to boil and cook 3-5 minutes. Drain pasta and place in large serving bowl; stir in the reserved clam sauce. Divide pasta among 6 plates. Lay 4 steamed clams and 5 steamed mussels in the shell on each serving. To dress each dish, add 2 tablespoons Herb Butter to mussel broth. Stir gently and spoon this herbal juice onto open shellfish. Serves 6.

HERB BUTTER: Blend ingredients together in a small bowl. Refrigerate until ready to use.

SPAGHETTINI WITH SMOKED SALMON AND ARTICHOKE HEARTS

Smoked salmon and artichoke hearts spiff up this easy to assemble pasta. Alice Welsh suggests serving it with a Chianti or Barola wine.

- 1 tablespoon minced shallots
- 1 teaspoon minced garlic
- 4 tablespoons butter
- 1 cup heavy cream
- 2 tablespoons white wine
- ½ pound smoked salmon, divided
- 1 14-ounce can artichoke hearts, cut in quarters, optional
- ½ teaspoon salt
- • fresh ground pepper
- 1 pound spaghettini
- • lemon wedges
- 2 tablespoons chopped parsley

In a large saucepan sauté shallots and garlic in butter for 3-5 minutes. Add cream and wine and bring to boil. Cook until cream thickens.

Cut salmon into small pieces and save out some for garnish. Add remaining salmon to sauce with drained, quartered artichoke hearts. Heat through; season with salt and pepper.

Cook pasta al dente in a large pot of boiling water. Drain; toss with sauce. Garnish each plate with reserved smoked salmon, lemon wedges and chopped parsley. Serves 3-4.

ALICE M. WELSH
CHAPEL HILL, NC

STRICTLY VEGETARIAN

FARMER'S MARKET BOWTIES

Simplicity reigns in this delightful vegetarian pasta.

2   cloves garlic, minced

1   small onion, sliced thin

½   pound green beans

1   small Chinese eggplant,
    see note

2   tablespoons olive oil

1   14.5-ounce can diced
    tomatoes

1   teaspoon salt

¾   teaspoon ground pepper

¼   teaspoon garlic powder

1   pound bowtie pasta

4   ounces feta cheese

In a large pot, boil 4 quarts water for pasta. While you wait for the water to boil, prepare garlic and onions. Cut green beans in half, and dice Chinese eggplant into 1-inch pieces.

In a large sauté pan, heat olive oil over medium-high heat. Add garlic and onion, and sauté 3 minutes. Stir in beans and eggplant, cook 3 minutes. Add tomatoes, salt, pepper and garlic powder. Reduce heat and simmer 5 minutes.

Cook bowtie pasta about 8 minutes until al dente. Drain and pour into a large serving bowl. Pour vegetable sauce over top. Sprinkle with crumbled feta cheese. Serves 4-6.

NOTE: If Chinese eggplant is difficult to find, a small eggplant will suffice. Quarter lengthwise and then slice into 1-inch thick pieces.

PUTTANESCA

The pungent ripeness of southern Italy breathes life into this simple pasta dish inspired by the Villa Le Balze in Fiesole.

2   cloves garlic

3   anchovy fillets

3   tablespoons olive oil

1   15-ounce can crushed
    tomatoes

½   cup small black pitted
    olives

1   tablespoon capers

•   freshly ground pepper

1-1½ pounds spaghetti

Mince garlic cloves and anchovies. Cook in olive oil in a heavy saucepan over medium heat about 3 minutes. Stir in tomatoes, olives and capers. Season with pepper. Cook covered on low heat 30 minutes, stirring occasionally.

Cook pasta in boiling water; drain and toss with sauce. Serve immediately. Serves 4-6.

SCOTTY STEELE
RALEIGH, NC

THE MAZE'S PENNE PASTA

A popular entrée shared by a restaurant once located in Winston-Salem called The Maze. Broccoli-rabe would be a great alternative when asparagus aren't in season.

8-10 ounces penne pasta

2   tablespoons butter

½   cup sliced onion

½   pound asparagus, cut into
    1½-inch pieces

½   cup sun-dried tomatoes
    (in oil)

2   cloves garlic, minced

1   teaspoon salt

½   cup heavy cream

½   cup crumbled feta cheese

Cook penne pasta. Drain, running cold water through it, and set aside.

Melt butter in a large heavy-bottomed sauté pan. Cook onion for 2-3 minutes before adding asparagus, chopped tomatoes, garlic and salt. Cook 5-7 minutes before adding cooked pasta and cream. Simmer until thickened.

Divide between 2 plates. Top with feta cheese and serve immediately. Serves 2.

MARY M. BLAKE
RALEIGH, NC

NEIL WELLIVER (American), *BREACHED BEAVER DAM* (detail), 1975

Summer Pasta with Brie — a festive yet light entrée.

$\mathcal{M}ild$ **climate means Southerners** may dine *al fresco* most of the year. Whether it's an intimate supper with friends or a neighborhood block party, good food served outdoors with music supplied by chirping katydids or the gentle sounds of the surf is an important part of our Southern heritage.

Summer Pasta with Brie

Fresh, light and colorful — a perfect casual supper for a hot summer's eve.

12	ounces Brie cheese
¾	pound Roma tomatoes
1	cup fresh basil leaves, chopped
2	cloves garlic, minced
1	tablespoon coarsely ground pepper
¾	cup olive oil plus 1 tablespoon, divided
1	cup Calamata olives, pitted
1	pound linguini or penne

Wrap Brie securely in plastic wrap and freeze for 1 hour. Unwrap, cut off rind and coarsely shred cheese into a large bowl.

Cut tomatoes lengthwise into sixths. Combine with cheese, basil, garlic, pepper, ¾ cup olive oil and olives. Toss lightly, cover and let sit at room temperature for 4 hours.

Cook pasta in a large pot of boiling water with 1 tablespoon oil added. Cook until just tender. Drain well. Toss gently with reserved brie mixture and serve immediately. Serves 6.

GAB SMITH
RALEIGH, NC

Roasted Vegetable Paella

In Spain and Portugal, seasonal vegetables are chosen from the array available at the market. For robust flavor, roast tomatoes and onions before adding to the dish.

4	Roma tomatoes
2	red onions
•	olive oil
•	salt and pepper
2	cups sugar snap peas
1	8-ounce package frozen artichoke hearts
1	bunch asparagus
2	carrots, julienned
6	cups vegetable broth
½	teaspoon saffron threads
1	large Spanish onion, chopped
1	green pepper, chopped
1	red pepper, chopped
4	cloves garlic, minced
½	teaspoon paprika
1	bay leaf
½	teaspoon salt
1	cup dry white wine
2	cups Arborio rice, see note

Preheat oven to 425°. Trim Roma tomatoes and cut into quarters. Peel and trim red onion, cut in wedges. Brush a baking sheet with olive oil. Place tomatoes and onions on pan for roasting. Brush vegetables with olive oil. Season with salt and pepper. Roast in oven for 10-20 minutes, until vegetables are softened and beginning to brown.

To prepare remaining vegetables, bring a large pot of water to a rolling boil. Place snap peas, artichokes, asparagus and carrots in water for 2-4 minutes. Drain and refresh with cold water to stop further cooking. Set aside.

Heat vegetable broth and saffron in saucepan over low heat for 10-15 minutes.

In a 4-quart heavy skillet, Dutch oven or electric wok, heat 3 tablespoons of olive oil. Sauté onion and peppers for 6-7 minutes. Add garlic, paprika and bay leaf and sauté for 1-2 minutes. Add rice and salt, and cook 3-4 minutes. Add heated broth and wine and stir.

Preheat oven to 350°. At this stage, transfer broth to a ceramic paella dish for baking or preparation may continue in the wok. Add blanched vegetables and push into broth without stirring. Top with roasted tomatoes and onion. Do not stir. Bake, uncovered, in oven or continue cooking in wok for 15-20 minutes until rice is plump and cooked through. Remove and cover loosely with foil. Let sit for 10 minutes before serving. Serves 8.

NOTE: Arborio rice can be replaced with long grain rice. Reduce vegetable broth to 4 cups.

ROASTED RED PEPPER RISOTTO with Goat Cheese

The special variety of Italian rice called Arborio is the key to risotto. The hard, fat grain absorbs quantities of liquid without becoming mushy. Always use a wooden spoon and stir constantly. Wait until liquid is absorbed before adding more. This recipe features easy techniques for roasting peppers and garlic that you will want to earmark for use in other recipes.

5	red bell peppers, roasted, see note
5-6	cloves garlic, roasted, see note
1	tablespoon olive oil
1	medium onion, finely diced
2	cups Arborio rice
½	cup white wine
6	cups vegetable broth, heated to a boil
½	cup unsalted butter
8	ounces goat cheese, softened
•	fresh thyme for garnish

Roast peppers and garlic separately.

In a medium saucepan, heat olive oil over medium heat. Add onion and sauté about 5 minutes. Add rice and sauté for 1 minute. Add white wine, stirring constantly. Add 1 cup boiled broth, stirring constantly until the rice absorbs liquid. Continue to cook adding about ½ cup liquid at a time, making sure that all the liquid is absorbed before adding final ingredients.

Slice roasted red pepper into strips. Puree in a food processor until smooth. This should yield about 1 cup puree. Set aside.

Stir in red pepper puree, roasted garlic, butter and goat cheese. Cook mixture briefly over medium heat, stirring constantly until butter and cheese are blended. Garnish portions with fresh thyme and serve immediately. Serves 6.

To roast peppers: Preheat oven to 450°. Brush each pepper lightly with olive oil and place on a baking pan. Roast for 20 minutes, turning peppers 3-4 times. When done, the skin will be blistered and charred. Remove from oven and place peppers in a paper bag for 5 minutes. Remove peppers and carefully peel skins off. Cut peppers open, remove stems, ribs and seeds.

To roast garlic: Preheat oven to 350°. Toss unpeeled cloves in 1 tablespoon olive oil, place in a covered baking pan and cook for 30 minutes or until soft. Press cloves through a fine sieve and set aside the roasted garlic puree. This should measure 1 tablespoon.

WILD MUSHROOM AND SUGAR SNAP PEA RISOTTO

The essence of wild mushrooms and fresh sugar snap peas infuses this risotto with the wafting breezes of springtime's woodlands.

¼	pound sugar snap peas, about 1 cup
¾	pound mixed wild mushrooms, such as cremini and shiitake
3	tablespoons butter
2	teaspoons minced garlic
2	tablespoons olive oil
2	tablespoons minced shallots
1	cup Arborio rice
½	cup white wine
3½	cups vegetable stock, heated to a boil
¼	teaspoon Parmesan cheese
¼	teaspoon salt
¼	teaspoon pepper

Wash and "string" sugar snap peas. Blanch in large pot of boiling, salted water for 1 minute only. Drain and plunge into ice water to stop cooking process. Drain; cut in half diagonally. Set aside.

Wipe mushrooms clean with mushroom brush or paper towels. Slice, discarding tough stems of shiitake mushrooms. Melt butter in large skillet over medium-high heat; add garlic and mushrooms. Sauté about 4 minutes until lightly browned and slightly limp. Set aside.

In a heavy 3-quart or larger saucepan, heat olive oil over low heat. Add shallots and sauté about 1 minute until golden. Add rice and stir to coat. Increase heat to medium; add wine and cook, stirring, until all liquid is absorbed. Add vegetable stock ½ cup at a time every few minutes as it gets absorbed. Cook and stir until all the liquid is absorbed before adding more.

When rice is tender and all the stock is absorbed, stir in mushrooms, sugar snap peas, and Parmesan cheese. Heat through, season with salt and pepper and serve immediately. Serves 4.

A feast of textures for the palate — Wild Mushroom and Sugar Snap Pea Risotto.

$\mathcal{W}\!hen$ **asked for the** secret to good meals, every top chef will answer that he uses "the freshest ingredients." Perhaps the reason why the South has such a fine reputation for good food lies in its history as an agricultural community. With an abundance of fresh vegetables just a few steps from the kitchen door, every meal can be a culinary delight. And the meat can be optional.

SPINACH QUINOA BURGERS WITH ROASTED RED PEPPER MAYO

Great vegetarian flavor for weekend entertaining. Quinoa, sometimes called the "Mother Grain" by the Aztecs, must be rinsed in water before cooking to remove a little substance called saponin. Spread with Roasted Red Pepper Mayo on page 110.

⅓ cup raw quinoa

2 cups fresh spinach, finely chopped

¼ cup finely chopped red pepper

¼ cup finely chopped yellow pepper

½ cup grated zucchini

½ cup grated carrot

½ cup chopped red onion

½ cup chopped parsley or cilantro

1 clove garlic, minced

½ cup toasted pecans, finely chopped

½ cup dry bread crumbs

1-2 eggs, beaten

Rinse quinoa in cold water; drain through a fine strainer. Cook, covered, in ⅔ cup boiling water until liquid is absorbed, about 10 minutes.

In a medium bowl, combine spinach, red and yellow peppers, zucchini, carrot, onion, parsley, garlic, pecans and bread crumbs. Mix well. Stir in quinoa and beaten eggs. Add more bread crumbs to make a consistency that holds together. Form into patties.

Sauté in a skillet over medium heat about 4-5 minutes per side. Keep warm in a 200° oven. Serve with Roasted Red Pepper Mayo. Serves 4.

RED BEANS & QUINOA

A play on one of Louisiana's best known contributions to American regional cuisine — red beans and rice. Seasoned red beans are served over quinoa, a common grain in South American cuisine that has a texture similar to couscous.

1 pound dry red beans

3 tablespoons olive oil

1½ cups diced onion

1 shallot, minced

1 green bell pepper, ¼-inch dice

¼ cup chopped parsley

½ teaspoon cayenne pepper

1 teaspoon thyme

1 tablespoon basil

4 cups vegetable stock

½ teaspoon freshly ground pepper

2 teaspoons salt

QUINOA:

1 cup quinoa

2 cups water

1 teaspoon salt

2 teaspoons pepper

Rinse beans, drain and pour into a large pot. Cover with 6 cups cool water and soak 2 hours. Drain beans into a colander and rinse.

In same pot that beans were soaked, heat olive oil over medium-high heat. Sauté onion and shallot 3 minutes. Add bell pepper and sauté 1 minute longer. Add drained beans, parsley, cayenne, thyme, basil, water or vegetable stock and pepper. Bring to a boil and reduce heat to low. Simmer gently 1½ hours, stirring occasionally to prevent beans from sticking. Add salt and simmer 1 hour longer, until beans are cooked through. Add ½-1 cup water or stock if needed toward end of cooking. Serve over hot quinoa. Serves 4-6.

QUINOA: Rinse quinoa well before cooking by placing in a fine sieve and immersing in cool water. Drain until water runs clear. Put quinoa, water, salt and pepper in a small saucepan with a tight fitting lid. Bring to a boil, reduce heat to low and simmer for 15 minutes, covered, or until water is absorbed. Fluff with a fork before serving. Makes 3 cups.

Gilbert and George have been artistic collaborators since 1967 and developed a format — exemplified by *Cabbage Worship* — for their billboard-sized "photo pieces": rectangular photographs abutted to form a grid and creating one overall image. This piece, from a series of works about current spiritual crises titled *Modern Faith*, offers a commentary on the fanaticism of cult worship. The object of devotion is not a deity but a head of cabbage, lampooning how human beings place their faith in dubious causes.

GILBERT AND GEORGE (British), *CABBAGE WORSHIP*, 1982   © Gilbert and George

An Autumn Vegetable Stew over Bulghur Pilaf

A delicious combination of corn, acorn and butternut squash. Served over bulghur pilaf, this is a fighting team against a cold blustery day.

1	small acorn squash
¾	cup water
1½	cups corn, fresh or frozen
2½	teaspoons salt, divided
2	tablespoons olive oil
1	cup diced onion
2	celery stalks, ½-inch dice
1	white turnip, peeled, ½-inch dice
1	small butternut squash, peeled, seeded, ½-inch dice
1	large russet potato, peeled, ½-inch dice
3	carrots, ½-inch diagonal slice
3	cups vegetable stock
1	green bell pepper, ½-inch dice
1	red bell pepper, ½-inch dice
¾	teaspoon ground nutmeg
¼	cup fresh sage, chopped
1	teaspoon pepper

BULGHUR PILAF:

2	tablespoons olive oil
½	medium onion, chopped
1½	cups bulghur
1	teaspoon salt
½	teaspoon dried sage
3	cups water or vegetable broth

Preheat oven to 350°. Cut acorn squash in half, seed and place cut side down in a baking dish with ¾ cup water. Bake 45 minutes until soft. Cool and scrape squash from shell. Place in a food processor bowl.

Shuck corn and place in a large pot of water with 1 teaspoon salt. Cook 6 minutes, drain and let cool enough to handle. Cut corn off cobs, then scrape the "milk" from each cob using the back of your knife. Place cut corn and corn milk into food processing bowl with acorn squash. Process mixture until slightly smooth, about 1 minute.

In a large Dutch oven, heat olive oil over medium-high heat. Sauté onion and celery 3 minutes. Add turnip and butternut squash, cover and cook 5 minutes. Add potato and carrot, cover and cook 2 more minutes.

Add vegetable stock and corn and acorn puree, bring to a simmer, uncovered. Reduce heat to low and simmer 20 minutes. Add green and red bell pepper, nutmeg, sage, the remaining 1½ teaspoons salt and black pepper to stew, simmer 10 minutes more, remove from heat. Ladle stew in bowls over Bulghur Pilaf. Serves 6.

BULGHUR PILAF: In medium-sized heavy saucepan, heat olive oil over medium-low heat. Add onion and sauté about 5 minutes until soft. Add bulghur, salt and sage; stir to coat bulghur with the oil. Add water or broth and bring to a boil. Reduce heat to low, cover and simmer 15 minutes, or until water is absorbed.

Fall's harvest blends into an Autumn Vegetable Stew served over Bulghur Pilaf.

FRESH HERB VEGGIE BURGERS

You will relish these savory veggie burgers, perfect for a casual cookout with friends.

½ pound mushrooms

1 cup very thinly sliced green cabbage

½ cup finely chopped green bell pepper

1 teaspoon fresh oregano

1 teaspoon fresh basil

4 tablespoons fine, dry bread crumbs

2 tablespoons tomato sauce

⅛ teaspoon pepper

¾ teaspoon salt

1 egg white

4 hamburger buns, toasted

2 tablespoons ranch dressing

4 curly leaf lettuce leaves

4 slices tomato

4 slices onion

Coat a large non-stick skillet with cooking spray. Thinly slice mushrooms and sauté over medium-high heat. Add cabbage and bell pepper; sauté 3 minutes. Remove from heat; stir in minced oregano and basil. Cool 10 minutes.

Combine bread crumbs, tomato sauce, pepper, salt and egg white in a medium bowl. Add cabbage mixture; stir well. Divide mixture into 4 equal portions, shaping into ½-inch thick patties.

Coat grill rack with cooking spray; place over medium hot coals. Place patties on rack; grill for 5 minutes on each side or until desired doneness. (You may also pan sauté, bake in 450° oven or even broil.)

Toast buns on grill or under broiler.

Spread 1½-teaspoons ranch dressing over top half of each bun. Line bottom halves with lettuce leaves, then top with a patty, tomato slice, onion slice and top half of bun. Serves 4.

KICKIN' THREE BEAN CHILI

This chili kicks of jalapeño while the portobello mushrooms add a heartiness favored by meat lovers and vegetarians alike. Masa harina, a Mexican flour made from sun or fire-dried corn kernels used to make corn tortillas, presents an unexpected corn flavor.

2 tablespoons olive oil

3 cloves garlic, minced

1 cup diced onion

2 small carrots, diced

2-3 jalapeño peppers, seeded and minced

3 large red or yellow bell peppers, diced

1½ pounds portobello mushrooms, ¾-inch dice

1 14-ounce can black beans

1 14-ounce can pinto beans

1 14-ounce can kidney beans

3 tablespoons chili powder

2 tablespoons ground cumin

1-2 tablespoons hot sauce

½ cup masa harina

4 cups vegetable stock or water

2 teaspoons salt

1 teaspoon pepper

• cooked brown rice

Heat olive oil in a large soup pot over medium-high heat. Add garlic and onion and sauté about 5 minutes. Add carrots, jalapeños, bell peppers and mushrooms and cook 8-10 more minutes until tender.

Add beans with juice and bring to a simmer. Add chili powder, cumin and hot sauce. Simmer 5 minutes.

Stir in masa harina and vegetable stock and bring to a boil. Add salt and pepper. Reduce heat and simmer uncovered for 20 minutes, stirring occasionally. Serve over rice. Serves 8.

WEEKEND
ENTERTAINING

$\mathcal{W}$eekends are sacred: a welcome reprieve from the weekday hustle and bustle of juggling work, school and family schedules. The recipe for the perfect weekend lies in striking the right balance between routine chores, relaxation and fun — with the emphasis on fun. This chapter was put together with convenience in mind, featuring a variety of entrées for the grill and other "participation" foods that are suitable for gatherings of all kinds. Try staging an early barbecue, light supper or tailgate party prior to the evening's cultural entertainment — a stroll among the sculptures and gardens in the Museum Park followed by a movie, concert or theatrical performance at the outdoor amphitheatre. Truly nothing could be finer.

BASIL BLUE AND SMOKED SALMON PIZZAS ON THE GRILL

Grilling pizza is another way to vary the flavor of this beloved staple in our diet. Prepared pizza crusts, or Bobolis, are readily available in grocery stores. Spread these with toppings and head to the grill. A slight re-heating to melt cheese and soften ingredients is all that's in order.

BASIL BLUE PIZZA:

- 1 prepared pizza crust, or Boboli
- 1 large tomato
- ¼ cup fresh basil leaves
- • olive oil
- ½ pound Gorgonzola cheese

SMOKED SALMON PIZZA:

- 1 prepared pizza crust or Boboli
- ½ pound Fontina cheese
- ¼ pound smoked salmon slices
- • olive oil
- ¼ cup chopped red onion
- 2 tablespoons capers

BASIL BLUE PIZZA: Finely chop tomato; wash basil leaves and pat dry. Brush crust with olive oil and crumble Gorgonzola over surface. Scatter tomato and arrange basil leaves in an artistic design. Drizzle with 1 tablespoon olive oil, then grill according to instructions below. Serves 3-4.

SMOKED SALMON PIZZA: Slice Fontina thinly. Cut salmon into small pieces. Brush pizza crust with olive oil. Lay cheese on crust. Scatter smoked salmon, onions and capers on top. Drizzle a little more olive oil, then grill. Serves 3-4.

To grill pizzas: Slide crust with toppings toward, but not directly over hot coals or flames. Keep pizza near the corner of the grill so only one quarter of crust is over direct heat. Rotate pizza with tongs to cook evenly. The pizza is done when vegetables are hot and cheese is melted. Cook 5-6 minutes.

To bake in a conventional oven: Preheat oven to 450° and bake 10 minutes or until cheese is golden brown and bubbly.

PREVIOUS PAGES: **CLAUDE HOWELL** (American), *BEACH UMBRELLAS (detail)*, 1954

A grilled feast for a dozen favorite friends — Tangy Tandoori Chicken.

TANGY TANDOORI CHICKEN

This recipe marinates up to 15 pieces of chicken, although we recommend boneless breasts so the meat can be cooked with more marinade. Serve this delightfully spicy dish for your next neighborhood gathering with a Curried Basmati Rice, page 203. The ease of the menu will please the host.

4	cups plain yogurt
2	tablespoons white vinegar
4-5	cloves garlic, chopped
3	medium onions, chopped
2	tablespoons lemon juice
4	tablespoons cumin
2-4	tablespoons crushed red pepper
2	tablespoons salt
3	tablespoons pepper
2	tablespoons white pepper
½	teaspoon cinnamon
2	tablespoons ground coriander
¼	cup chopped fresh cilantro (optional)
•	up to 15 boneless chicken breasts halves

Place yogurt, vinegar, garlic, onions, lemon juice, cumin, red pepper, salt, black pepper, white pepper, cinnamon, coriander and cilantro in blender or food processor for a few minutes.

Remove skin and fat from chicken. Pour marinade over chicken and refrigerate overnight. Grill chicken until done.

JUDITH DICKEY
RALEIGH, NC

GEORGE INNESS (American), *UNDER THE GREENWOOD*, 1881

Geoorge Inness painted what he termed the "civilized landscape": an inhabited nature on a human scale, as opposed to the grandeur and spectacle of the American wilderness depicted by several of his contemporaries. Through his landscapes, Inness sought a profound and emotional correspondence between himself (or the viewer) and the natural world. *Under the Greenwood* invokes a pastoral life of peace and harmony and thus offers a poetic alternative to the starker realities of modern life.

GRILLED CHICKEN HAVARTI SANDWICHES

Please your guests with this twist on an old favorite. Red onions and tomatoes complement the unique buttery marinade.

½ cup butter

1 cup soy sauce

1 cup dry sherry

1 medium yellow onion, thinly sliced

1 tablespoon pepper

6 boneless chicken breast halves

6 buns

½ cup Dijon mustard

6 slices Havarti cheese

....

RED ONION TOMATO RELISH:

2 tablespoons olive oil

1 cup thinly sliced red onion

1 cup diced tomato

2 tablespoons chopped parsley

1 tablespoon Dijon mustard

2 tablespoons white wine vinegar

¼ teaspoon salt

¼ teaspoon pepper

In 1-quart saucepan, melt butter over low heat. Add soy sauce, sherry, onion and pepper. Bring to a boil. Reduce heat to medium; simmer for 5 minutes.

Arrange chicken in a glass or plastic container just large enough to hold the chicken. Cool marinade for 5 minutes. Pour over chicken. Cover and refrigerate at least 2 hours and up to 24 hours — the longer, the better.

Prepare a charcoal or gas grill to medium heat. While grill is heating, wrap buns in foil. Heat in a 200° oven.

Grill chicken for 5 minutes on each side. If breasts are extra thick, grill 1-2 minutes longer per side. Top each breast with a slice of cheese for last minute of cooking. Serve on warm buns with Dijon mustard and Red Onion Tomato Relish. Serves 6.

RED ONION TOMATO RELISH: In a large skillet, heat olive oil over medium heat. Add onion. Cook until soft and wilted. Stir in tomatoes and parsley. Cook for 2 minutes. Set aside. In small bowl whisk mustard, vinegar, salt and pepper together. Add to onion mixture. Refrigerate in a small serving bowl until ready to use. Makes 2 cups.

BOWTIES WITH SAUSAGE, TOMATOES AND CREAM

An easy, pull-together pasta for a weekend of relaxation. Other kinds of sausage such as venison make a good substitute.

2 tablespoons olive oil

1 pound sweet Italian sausage

½ teaspoon crushed red pepper

½ cup diced onion

3 cloves garlic, minced

1 28-ounce can Italian diced tomatoes

1½ cups whipping cream

½ teaspoon salt

¾ pound bowtie pasta

3 tablespoons fresh minced basil

• Parmesan cheese

¼ cup chopped fresh parsley

Heat oil in large heavy skillet over medium heat. Remove casings from sausage, crumble and cook in oil with crushed pepper until sausage is no longer pink, about 7 minutes. Add onion and garlic and cook another 5-7 minutes until tender. Drain tomatoes, chop coarsely and stir into sausage along with cream, salt and basil. Simmer until mixture thickens slightly, about 4 minutes.

In a separate pot of boiling salted water, cook pasta al dente. Drain pasta and add to simmering sauce. Garnish with Parmesan and parsley. Serves 4.

CHERYL MAUPIN
RALEIGH, NC

FLANK STEAK TERIYAKI

No need for dining out at a Japanese steak house with this recipe in your files. It's a winner! A Gingered Cabbage was developed to pair with this easy grilled entrée.

1	2-3 pound flank steak
¾	cup vegetable oil
½	cup soy sauce
1½	teaspoons ground ginger
2	tablespoons lemon juice
1½	tablespoons molasses
½	teaspoon dried minced onions

GINGERED CABBAGE:

2	cups thinly sliced bok choy with leaves
4	cups thinly sliced napa cabbage
3	tablespoons olive oil
2	tablespoons sesame oil
2	tablespoons julienned daikon radish
2	tablespoons minced peeled ginger
⅔	cup beef stock
1	tablespoon rice vinegar

Trim fat and surface tissue from flank steak. Place in a large baking dish and with a fork, punch holes over surface of both sides. Make marinade by combining remaining ingredients and pouring over steak. Let stand 6-8 hours or overnight in refrigerator.

Before cooking, remove steak from marinade and discard marinade.

Grill over hot fire 5 minutes per side or until center is pink. Slice thinly across grain on the bias. Serves 4-8.

GINGERED CABBAGE: As you slice bok choy, separate sliced stalks from leaves and combine leaves with napa cabbage. In a high-sided skillet heat oils over medium-high and lightly brown bok choy stalks. Cook for 5 minutes, then add bok choy leaves and napa cabbage, radish and ginger. Continue to cook until lightly browned. Add beef stock, reduce heat to medium, cover and braise until liquid is absorbed and cabbages are tender, about 10 minutes. Stir in rice vinegar, simmer 1 minute; keep warm.

EMILY S. BOWEN
PINEHURST, NC

BOURBON MUSTARD SPARERIBS

Simplicity at its best; just the smell of these ribs baking makes your mouth water. They marinate overnight so this is an easy entertaining dish.

10-12	pounds country style pork spareribs
¼	cup orange juice
½	cup soy sauce
1	cup brown sugar
2	tablespoons Worcestershire sauce
1	cup Dijon mustard
¼	cup finely chopped red onion
½	cup bourbon

Separate ribs by slicing vertically between the bones. Arrange in a large non-aluminum baking pan or glass dish.

Make marinade in a medium bowl by combining orange juice and soy sauce. Blend in the brown sugar, Worcestershire sauce and mustard. Add red onion and bourbon, stirring well. Measure 3 cups of marinade and pour over ribs. Set aside 1 cup of marinade for basting. Marinate spareribs in the refrigerator overnight.

The next day, bake ribs on a rack in a roasting pan, uncovered, at 350° for 1½-2 hours. Baste with marinade every 20-30 minutes of cooking. Just before serving grill ribs over hot coals 5-10 minutes, basting with marinade. These ribs may also be finished off under the broiler. Serves 8.

Hoisin Ribs turn casual entertaining into a winning occasion.

HOISIN RIBS

Take these mouth-watering ribs, a recipe shared by a friend of Karel Shultz, to your next tailgate. Marinate overnight and bake the next morning — the crowd will carry you into the end zone! Fried chicken doesn't have to be the only thing that's finger-lickin' good!!

2	racks baby back ribs
1	cup ketchup
2	tablespoons brown sugar
⅓	cup hoisin sauce
2	tablespoons soy sauce
2	tablespoons dry sherry
1	clove garlic, minced

Cut ribs into sections of 2-3 rib portions.

In a bowl combine remaining ingredients. Arrange ribs in a single layer in a glass baking dish. Pour sauce over, turning ribs to coat all sides. Cover and refrigerate overnight.

Preheat oven to 375°. Turn ribs over in marinade again before baking for 1½ hours. Baste occasionally and add a little water as needed so sauce doesn't over-thicken. Serves 6.

KAREL SHULTZ
RALEIGH, NC

LAMB SHISH KEBABS

A hungry group of friends will devour these succulent shish kebabs, a recipe from Scotty Steele's mother. Serve with seasoned rice or couscous.

- 2 pounds boneless lamb
- 1 green pepper, cut in 1½-inch pieces
- 12-16 cherry tomatoes
- 8 mushrooms caps
- • small onions, quartered
- 2 teaspoons A-1 Sauce
- 2 tablespoons prepared barbecue sauce
- 1 tablespoon brown sugar
- 3 tablespoons red wine

··

LAMB MARINADE:

- ½ cup vegetable oil
- ¼ cup lemon juice
- 1 tablespoon tarragon or wine vinegar
- 1 clove garlic, minced
- ¼ teaspoon thyme
- ½ cup finely chopped onion
- ¼ cup red wine

Cut lamb into 1½-inch pieces. Prepare marinade. Pour over lamb and refrigerate 6 hours or more.

At cooking time, drain meat reserving marinade for sauce. Alternate lamb cubes on skewers with green peppers, tomatoes, mushroom caps and onions. Grill, turning to brown on all sides.

In a saucepan combine reserved marinade, A-1 sauce, barbecue sauce, brown sugar and wine. Bring to a boil and simmer 5 minutes until smooth and hot. Serve over kebabs. Serves 4.

LAMB MARINADE: Whisk together all ingredients in a medium bowl.

SCOTTY STEELE
RALEIGH, NC

SKEWERED SHRIMP IN BEER

If these shrimp don't get soused from soaking in beer overnight, their brief visit to a hot grill and a dose of lemon butter will put them over the edge.

- 2 pounds raw, medium shrimp
- 1½ cups beer
- 1 tablespoon fresh chopped chives
- 2 teaspoons Dijon mustard
- 1 clove garlic, minced
- 1 teaspoon salt
- • generous grind of fresh pepper
- • wooden skewers soaked in water at least 1 hour
- 3 tablespoons butter, melted
- 1 tablespoon lemon juice

Peel raw shrimp; devein if necessary. Combine beer, chives, mustard, garlic, salt and pepper and pour over prepared shrimp. Marinate for 8 hours or overnight, stirring from time to time.

Thread shrimp on soaked skewers leaving a small space between each one. Combine melted butter and lemon juice. Place skewers over hot coals and grill about 2 minutes on each side, brushing frequently with the lemon butter. The shrimp are done when they turn pink; do not overcook. Serves 6.

Claude Howell's Boiled Shrimp: "Did you know that if you

press the tail of the shrimp and pump it, the entire shell slips off in one movement?
I should know, I once was the champion shucker in New Hanover County. When the
shrimp are right, and so often they are, we do this: Boil them briefly, no more than 3
minutes, just until they turn pink. Add salt, bay leaves, allspice and Szechuan pepper if
you can find it. Cover the table with paper. Give everyone a bowl with a sauce made of
homemade mayonnaise, chili sauce, tomato ketchup, dash of Tabasco, tablespoon
Worcestershire, pinch of dill and oregano. Everyone shucks his own shrimp."

— Artist Claude Howell, (1915-1997)

SPICY SHRIMP

*During the summer months at their home on Bogue Banks, this dish is a Fitzpatrick family favorite. Originally shared by a friend
from Shugaloc, Mississippi, the recipe has been fine tuned by the Fitzpatricks with touches of their own. Serve with hot French bread.*

1-1½ pounds unpeeled shrimp, headed
1 cup butter
1 8-ounce can tomato sauce
½ cup fresh lemon juice
1 cup olive oil
1 teaspoon salt
1 teaspoon pepper
1 teaspoon red pepper flakes
4 teaspoons Zatarain's liquid crab boil
2 teaspoons fresh rosemary

Wash shrimp thoroughly and set aside.

In a saucepan melt butter. Whisk in tomato sauce, lemon juice and olive oil.
Add salt, pepper, red pepper flakes, crab boil and rosemary. Stir in unpeeled
shrimp. Cover and cook on medium heat stirring often for 3-4 minutes.

To serve: Pour shrimp with sauce into a large bowl and serve family style with
lots of napkins. Serves 2-3.

JOYCE FITZPATRICK
RALEIGH, NC

BACKFIN CRAB ON CORNMEAL CRUSTED TOMATOES

Crabmeat salad rests atop slices of ripe summer beefsteak tomatoes in this knockout main course.

1   pound backfin crabmeat

1   lemon, juiced

1   cup finely minced celery
     (use tender center stalks)

2-3   ripe beefsteak tomatoes

•   salt and pepper

3   eggs

1   cup cornmeal

⅓-½   cup olive oil

½   cup fresh basil leaves,
     divided

SHALLOT VINAIGRETTE:

⅓   cup white wine vinegar

1½   tablespoons minced
     shallots

½   teaspoon Dijon mustard

½   teaspoon salt

•   freshly ground pepper

1   cup olive oil

Pick through crabmeat, feeling with your fingertips to remove any tiny pieces of shell. Season with lemon juice. Combine crabmeat with celery in a medium-sized glass bowl and slowly add up to 1¼ cups Shallot Vinaigrette, reserving ¼ cup. Cover and refrigerate for an hour or two.

At serving time, remove stem and white core from tomatoes. Cut into eight 1-inch thick slices. Sprinkle tomatoes with salt and pepper.

Lightly beat eggs in a small bowl. Measure cornmeal into a pie plate.

Heat a large skillet over medium high heat. Add oil 3 tablespoons at a time. Dip tomato slices first in egg, then in cornmeal to coat. Cook 4 minutes per side. Drain cooked tomatoes on paper towels or rack. Dip and cook remaining tomatoes, adding more oil when necessary.

Remove a few whole basil leaves for garnish, then lightly chop remaining basil. Sprinkle chopped basil over each tomato. Mound ½ cup crab salad on each slice, allowing 2 per person. Drizzle a little of the remaining dressing over the top and garnish with a whole basil leaf. Serves 4.

SHALLOT VINAIGRETTE: Place vinegar, shallots, mustard, salt and pepper in food processor. Process until smooth and shallots are minced. While the machine is running, slowly pour olive oil through spout and process until creamy. Yields 1½ cups.

SPICY CATFISH SANDWICHES

Capers and seafood seasoning add pizzazz to a simple sandwich. For spicy seasoning use Paul Prudhomme's Seafood Magic or the Cajun or blackening blends found in the spice section of grocery stores. Dee Cook adapted this from The Art of Cooking for the Diabetic *by Mary Abbott Hess.*

1½   tablespoons mayonnaise

1   teaspoon lemon juice

½   teaspoon capers, drained

½-1   tablespoon spicy seasoning

4   catfish fillets

2   tablespoons butter, divided

4   sandwich buns

•   lettuce leaves

•   tomato slices

In a small bowl mix mayonnaise, lemon juice and capers; set aside.

Rub spicy seasoning on both sides of catfish. Melt 1 tablespoon butter in a large skillet on medium high. Add catfish and cook 3-4 minutes on each side, depending on size of fillets. Transfer fish to paper towels to drain.

Brush 1 side of buns with remaining 1 tablespoon butter. Place in skillet and brown lightly. Spread buns with mayonnaise mixture, add catfish, lettuce and tomato. Serve immediately. Serves 4.

DELORES (DEE) COOK
APEX, NC

A southern delicacy —
Backfin Crab on Cornmeal
Crusted Tomatoes, inspired by
the coastal waters
painted by Ben Berns.

BEN BERNS (Dutch), *SWAMP MALLOWS*, 1995

BASIL SUN-DRIED TOMATO SALMON BURGERS

Pungent fresh basil and sun-dried tomatoes add elegant flavor to the salmon.

1¼   pounds salmon fillets, skin removed

¼   cup dry bread crumbs

½   cup sour cream

¼   cup finely chopped onion

1   clove garlic, minced

1   tablespoon chopped fresh basil

¼   cup sun-dried tomatoes in oil, chopped

•   salt and pepper

4   large Kaiser rolls, sliced

....

ROASTED RED PEPPER MAYO:

⅓   cup roasted red bell pepper, chopped

¼   cup mayonnaise

1   clove garlic, minced

¼   teaspoon red pepper flakes

Cut salmon into 2-inch pieces. Place in food processor and pulse quickly off and on 4-5 times until coarsely chopped. Do not over process. Place in medium mixing bowl and carefully fold in bread crumbs, sour cream, onion, garlic, basil and sun-dried tomatoes. Add salt and pepper to taste.

Pat into 4 burgers. Grill 4-5 minutes per side. Place on toasted rolls and top with Roasted Red Pepper Mayo. Serves 4.

ROASTED RED PEPPER MAYO: Roast red bell peppers according to instructions on page 92. Chop peppers and combine with mayonnaise, garlic and red pepper flakes.

ROASTED ASPARAGUS FONTINA PITA MELTS

Warm vegetables, prosciutto and melted cheese tucked into pita shells are a hit. A sweet variety of onion such as Vidalia or Maui complements the full flavor of roasted vegetables. Tender young green beans may be substituted for asparagus.

1   pound asparagus spears, thinly sliced on bias

1   cup sliced red onion or Vidalia onion

2   ounces chopped prosciutto

1   tablespoon virgin olive oil

1   tablespoon freshly chopped dill

•   kosher salt and freshly ground pepper

4   Greek-style pita breads

6   ounces Fontina cheese, thinly sliced

Preheat oven to 375°.

Cut asparagus about 1½- to 2-inches long on the bias. Combine with onion, prosciutto, oil and dill in medium roasting pan or oven-proof skillet. Mix to coat ingredients with oil. Season with kosher salt and pepper. Roast for 25-30 minutes, stirring after 15 minutes to roast evenly. Remove from oven.

Evenly distribute vegetables on top of whole pita breads. Lay cheese slices on top; fold over and eat. Serves 4.

SALADE NIÇOISE WITH FRESH TUNA

A delightful medley of Mediterranean flavors. Serve with a French baguette for a hearty one-dish meal. Do all your cooking and slicing ahead. Marinate, then assemble at mealtime.

1   pound fresh tuna

¾   pound green beans

½   pound new potatoes

½   red onion, divided

2   tomatoes

2   hard-boiled eggs

1   cup pitted Niçoise or black olives, halved

•   salt and pepper

1   head Boston lettuce

NIÇOISE VINAIGRETTE:

½   cup olive oil

¼   cup vegetable oil

¼   cup red wine vinegar

1   teaspoon Dijon mustard

1   tablespoon water

½   teaspoon basil

½   teaspoon thyme

1   teaspoon minced garlic

1   teaspoon salt

½   teaspoon black pepper

Make vinaigrette and set aside at room temperature. Slice tuna into steaks, 1-inch thick. Marinate tuna in ⅓ cup vinaigrette in refrigerator for 2 hours.

To prepare vegetables: snap ends off green beans and steam 7-8 minutes until just tender. Cool and refrigerate. Cut new potatoes in half and cook in boiling water 20 minutes or until done. Drain and cool. Cut potatoes in 1-inch pieces and refrigerate. Slice red onion into very thin rounds; separate onion layers. Cut tomatoes and eggs into wedges.

Grill fish under broiler for 5 minutes on each side. Let cool and cut into bite-size pieces.

In a medium bowl combine tuna, green beans, olives and potatoes. Add only half the sliced onions and ¾ cup vinaigrette. Season to taste with salt and pepper. Cover and refrigerate for 1 hour to let flavors blend.

Arrange Boston lettuce as a bed on 4 plates; divide Tuna Niçoise. Garnish with tomato, egg wedges and remaining sliced onions. Drizzle a little of remaining vinaigrette over each salad. Serves 4.

NIÇOISE VINAIGRETTE: In a small bowl combine oils and vinegar with mustard, water and seasoning. Yields 1½ cups.

COVERED
DISH

CORN PONE CASSEROLE

Corn pone is an eggless cornbread that is most often shaped into small rounds and fried or baked. Here it becomes a delightful topping to an easy baked chili casserole.

1	pound lean ground beef
1	cup diced onion
4	teaspoons chili powder
1	28-ounce can diced tomatoes
1½	teaspoons sugar
1½	teaspoons salt
¼	teaspoon pepper
1	16-ounce can red kidney beans, drained
1	cup grated cheddar cheese
1	package Jiffy Corn Muffin Mix
⅓	cup milk
1	egg

In a large saucepan over medium-high heat, cook beef and onions until all pan juices evaporate and meat is browned, stirring occasionally. Stir in chili powder, cook one minute. Stir in tomatoes with liquid, sugar, salt and pepper. Bring to a boil over high heat. Lower heat, cover and simmer 30 minutes, stirring often. Stir in beans.

Spoon mixture into a 9-inch x 13-inch casserole dish. Spread cheddar cheese over meat mixture.

Preheat oven to 400°. Prepare corn muffin mix batter according to package instructions. With the back of a spoon, spread batter evenly over meat mixture. Bake uncovered 15-20 minutes until golden and a toothpick inserted into cornbread comes out clean. Serves 6-8.

CONNIE C. SHERTZ
RALEIGH, NC

STUFFED CABBAGE

Adapted from The Jewish Cookbook, *this recipe is a crowd-pleaser. The number served depends on the size of the cabbage as well as the number of hearty appetites.*

1	large head cabbage
1	pound ground beef
¾	cup cooked rice
1	cup chopped onion
½	teaspoon salt
¼	teaspoon pepper
2	cups canned tomatoes
½	cup raisins
2	tablespoons brown sugar
2	cups or more V-8 juice
•	lemon juice

Boil cabbage in a large pot of water for 5 minutes and separate the leaves when cool enough to handle.

In another bowl mix together ground beef, rice, onion, salt and pepper. Select the largest, softest cabbage leaves and lay out on work surface. Put 3 tablespoons meat mixture into each and fold up cabbage leaves over meat like a packet. Continue with remaining meat mixture.

Preheat oven to 325°. Line a large pot or roasting pan with remaining cabbage leaves. Place the stuffed bundles seam side down or tied with butcher's string on cabbage leaf lining. Add canned tomatoes, raisins, brown sugar and a dash of salt to the bundles. Add enough V-8 juice to cover. Cover pan and bake for 2½-3 hours. Add more V-8 as necessary to keep the bundles covered and moist.

Once baked, taste the sauce and adjust the seasoning with lemon juice and/or brown sugar to achieve desired sweet and sour balance. Makes 10-12 bundles.

ELIZABETH K. LEVINE
RALEIGH, NC

PREVIOUS PAGES: **CHRISTIAN MAYR** (American), *KITCHEN BALL AT WHITE SULPHUR SPRINGS, VIRGINIA* (detail), 1838

A GAHNTZE TZIMMES

Yiddish for "A Grand Production", this simple boneless brisket is so-called for the 5½ hours cooking time, a recipe adapted from
Love and Knishes (Vanguard Press, 1956) by Sara Kasden. Here the essence of prunes is baked into the brisket, its delightful
sweetness enhanced by carrots, apricots and sweet potatoes. Serve at your next large family gathering.

3-4	pounds boneless brisket
2	tablespoons olive oil
3	large carrots
½	pound pitted prunes
½	pound dried apricots
1	lemon, thinly sliced
3	large sweet potatoes
•	juice of one orange
5	cups boiling water
1½	tablespoons brown sugar
2	tablespoons flour

Preheat oven to 400°. Trim excess fat from brisket. Heat oil in large skillet or Dutch oven over medium-high heat. Add brisket and brown on all sides. Transfer to a roasting pan. Peel carrots and cut in 1-inch rounds. Place around meat along with prunes, apricots and lemon slices. Peel sweet potatoes and cut into 1-inch thick slices. Place over meat and fruit.

Combine orange juice and boiling water. In a separate bowl mix brown sugar, flour and enough cold water to make a thin paste. Add to orange liquid. Pour over meat and, if necessary, add enough boiling water to bring liquid to top of meat.

Bake at 400° for 1 hour. Reduce heat to 325° and bake another 4 hours. Uncover and bake 30 minutes more. Slice brisket and surround with the cooked vegetables and fruit. Serves 8-10.

ELIZABETH K. LEVINE
RALEIGH, NC

Sweet fruit makes
A Ghantze Tzimmes
a crowd pleaser.

JAN LIEVENS (Dutch), *THE FEAST OF ESTHER*, c. 1625

The masterpiece of Lievens's early career, *The Feast of Esther* was at one time attributed to Rembrandt. The artists were colleagues in Leiden and may have shared a studio. The scene depicts a dramatic moment when the enjoyment of the savory pie is interrupted as Queen Esther exposes a plot against the Jews of Persia to her husband, King Ahasuerus.

KHORESH BADEMJAN

A homespun international dish. Serve with couscous and salad.

1   large eggplant
•   salt
½   cup vegetable or olive oil
1   large onion, chopped
1   pound ground beef or lamb
½   teaspoon pepper
½   teaspoon nutmeg
½   teaspoon cinnamon
1   tablespoon minced garlic
2   large tomatoes, sliced
•   dash paprika
•   1 cup plain yogurt

Cut eggplant in half, lengthwise and then cut again crosswise into ½-inch slices. Wash in colander and sprinkle with salt; let sit 20 minutes. Wash again to remove salt and pat dry with paper towel.

Preheat oven to 350°. Grease a pie pan or an 8-inch x 8-inch baking dish.

Heat oil in a skillet over medium high and sauté eggplant in batches until golden brown. Sauté onions in same skillet and set aside. Brown meat and season well with 1 teaspoon salt, pepper, nutmeg and cinnamon.

Line bottom of pan with half the eggplant slices. Add garlic, browned meat and sliced tomatoes. Top with remaining eggplant. Sprinkle onions over top then a dash of paprika. Bake for 20-30 minutes. Serve topped with a dollop of yogurt. Serves 4-6.

ASSAD MEYMANDI
RALEIGH, NC

MOUSSAKA

Originally from Greece, moussaka is a popular dish throughout most of the Near East. Variations on this dish can include the addition of artichokes and potatoes. The best thing about this dish, a popular inclusion in the first NCMA cookbook, is that you can "make, bake and serve later." It's best when served slightly warm — not hot, not cold.

4   large eggplants
•   salt and pepper
•   flour
•   vegetable shortening

MEAT SAUCE:

2-3 tablespoons olive oil
2   medium-size onions, chopped
3   pounds ground chuck or ground lamb
2   tablespoons salt
1   teaspoon pepper
½   cup chopped fresh parsley
1   clove garlic, chopped
1   8-ounce can tomato sauce
2   fresh tomatoes, chopped
½   cup red wine

EGG SAUCE:

1   quart milk
½   cup butter
6   tablespoons flour
1   teaspoon salt
6   eggs, well-beaten
½   teaspoon grated nutmeg
1   cup Parmesan cheese

Wash eggplants and slice ½-inch to ¾-inch thick. Salt and pepper each slice and flour lightly.

In a large skillet, heat enough shortening to cover bottom of a skillet. Brown eggplant lightly, then remove and drain on paper towels. For every skillet of eggplant slices, wipe out pan with paper towel so no burnt flour will be left in skillet. Add clean shortening and continue process until all eggplant is browned.

To prepare Meat Sauce: In large skillet, sauté onion in oil for 1 minute. Add ground beef, and/or lamb, salt and pepper to taste; brown, stirring constantly until meat has no raw appearance. Add parsley, garlic, tomatoes, tomato sauce and red wine. Cook 10 minutes and set aside.

To prepare Egg Sauce: Pour milk into a large saucepan and heat to scalding. Remove from heat before it scorches. Meanwhile, in another large saucepan, melt butter over low heat, and stir in flour to make a roux. Add salt, well-beaten eggs, and stirring constantly, gradually add scalded milk. Cook on medium heat until thickened and stir in nutmeg.

Preheat oven to 350°. In a 12-inch x 18-inch x 4-inch baking dish, place 1 layer of eggplant. Pour meat sauce over eggplant and place another layer of eggplant over meat sauce. Pour egg sauce over top and sprinkle freely with grated cheese. Bake 1 hour. Remove from oven and allow to cool to room temperature. Cut into 3-inch or 4-inch squares. Serve with a spatula. This keeps well in refrigerator. If frozen, reheat in a warm 300° oven before serving. Serves 12.

MARIAN ARETAKIS
RALEIGH, NC

HEARTY MIDDLE EASTERN TART

A tart that seems to capture both exotic yet homespun flavorings in the same bite. Fresh mushrooms, spinach and turkey are stirred into Middle East staples such as lentils and basmati rice.

1½ cups dried lentils

4 cups chicken broth (or vegetable broth)

2 tablespoons Middle Eastern Spice Mix, divided, recipe below

1½ teaspoons salt, divided

¼ cup plus 2 tablespoons olive oil, divided

3 cups sliced onions (2 large)

¾ cup toasted pine nuts

1 pound mixed mushrooms, sliced

1 pound fresh spinach, roughly chopped (10 cups)

1 cup Basmati rice

1½ cups golden raisins

4 cups cooked turkey (chopped or shredded)

2 sheets puff pastry, thawed (one 17.3-ounce box)

1 egg beaten with 1 tablespoon water (for egg wash)

....

MIDDLE EASTERN SPICE MIX:

1 tablespoon cumin

1 teaspoon cardamom

½ teaspoon allspice

½ teaspoon coriander

½ teaspoon cloves

1 teaspoon freshly ground pepper

1 teaspoon red pepper flakes, crushed

½ teaspoon ginger

1 teaspoon turmeric

1 teaspoon salt

1 tablespoon paprika

1 teaspoon cinnamon

Wash and pick over lentils. Put into a large pot and cover with 8-10 cups water. Bring to a boil. Boil 2 minutes. Remove from heat and let stand, covered, 30 minutes. Drain and rinse discarding water. Return to pot along with the chicken broth, 1 tablespoon Middle Eastern Spice Mix and 1 teaspoon salt. Bring to a boil, partially cover, and cook until almost tender, about 10 minutes.

Meanwhile, heat ¼ cup olive oil in large heavy skillet or Dutch oven. Add onions, 1 tablespoon of the spice mix and ½ teaspoon salt. Cover and cook very slowly until soft, 20-25 minutes, stirring occasionally.

To toast pine nuts, put in heavy skillet over medium heat, stir and shake pan until nuts are golden, 2-3 minutes.

Heat remaining 2 tablespoons olive oil in large pot over medium-high heat. Add sliced mushrooms and sauté, stirring frequently, about 5 minutes. Reduce heat to medium and add spinach. Cover and cook until spinach is wilted, about 5 minutes.

When onions are soft add toasted pine nuts, basmati rice and raisins to pan. Cook 3-4 minutes stirring frequently. Add to lentil mixture along with the cooked mushroom/spinach mixture and turkey. Return to a boil, then reduce heat to low, cover and cook about 10 minutes until liquid is absorbed by rice, add a bit more liquid if it is getting too dry. Taste to correct seasoning adding more salt or spice mix if desired. (Dish may be made ahead to this point. Reheat before putting into pastry crust.)

Preheat oven to 400°.

Unfold 1 pastry sheet on floured board. Roll out into a 15- to 16-inch square big enough to line bottom and sides of a 10-inch x 2½-inch springform pan with a ½-inch overhang. Put in ungreased pan and trim leaving the ½-inch overhang; reserve scraps. Fill with warm lentil mixture. (It is important that the pan be full in order to support the top crust.) Roll out second pastry sheet and cut a circle to fit the top of the pan with about ½-inch overhang (about 11 inches). Brush bottom crust edges with egg wash. Put top crust on top pressing edges to seal. Fold overhang under and crimp edges. Brush top with egg wash.

Cut scraps into design if desired to decorate top of tart. Arrange on top of tart and brush décor with egg wash. Make a couple of slits in top crust to allow steam to escape. Bake on bottom rack of oven for 35-40 minutes until golden brown. Let sit 10-15 minutes for easier slicing. Remove sides of spring form pan, cut into wedges and serve. Makes 8 entrée servings.

NOTE: This tart could be make as a vegetarian entrée if desired, by leaving out the turkey and substituting vegetable broth for the chicken broth. It is important, however, to have the pan full to support the crust, so increase the lentils to 1 pound and add a bit more liquid if needed.

MIDDLE EASTERN SPICE MIX: Combine well and store in jar. Use to season rice, lentils, meats, etc.

Hearty Middle Eastern Tart — created to depict the savory tart in Jan Lievens' painting, The Feast of Esther.

Who **doesn't love a potluck** dinner? Food, fellowship and covered dishes reign supreme at these informal gatherings where everyone contributes by bringing a dish or two. While Museum events are usually catered affairs, docents and staff enjoy getting together for their own potlucks. It's a tasty opportunity to try new foods, swap recipes, trade cooking tips and catch up on all the latest. These make-ahead crowd pleasers are recipes from Museum staff and docents who enjoy the socializing and savory sampling prevalent at these special meals.

Chicken Cacciatore

Good flavor emerges from this simple stovetop preparation. Serve with baked polenta squares, orzo or bowtie pasta.

4	chicken breasts
¼	cup olive oil
1	teaspoon minced garlic
¼	teaspoon oregano
1	14-ounce can chunky Italian style tomatoes
1	cup white wine
•	salt and pepper
¼	cup chopped fresh parsley

Rinse chicken breasts and pat dry. Heat oil in a heavy-bottomed skillet over medium-high heat and brown chicken evenly. Stir in garlic, oregano, tomatoes and white wine. Cover and cook slowly about 40 minutes until sauce is like gravy. Season to taste with salt and pepper. Sprinkle fresh parsley over chicken just before serving. Serves 4.

HERIETA SCHENKEWITZ
RALEIGH, NC

Chicken Curry à la Hazel

A delightful quick cook main course that's easily transportable to a gathering of friends. The Scotch Bonnet pepper called for in this recipe is extremely hot, even with the seeds removed. For a "cooler" version, substitute a jalapeño pepper.

2½	pounds boneless chicken breasts
4	tablespoons butter
1	large onion, choped
2	tablespoon chopped celery
1	teaspoon fresh minced ginger
1	Scotch Bonnet pepper, seeds removed, minced
1½	teaspoons Madras curry powder
½	teaspoon turmeric
¼	teaspoon fenugreek, available in health food stores
1½	teaspoons fresh thyme
½	teaspoon cumin
1	tablespoon fresh chopped parsley
½	cup chicken stock
•	salt and white pepper

Cut chicken breasts into bite-size strips. In a large, hot skillet, melt butter and sauté chicken, onion and celery for 1 minute. Add ginger, pepper, curry powder, tumeric, fenugreek, thyme, cumin, parsley and chicken stock. Blend well and simmer 15 minutes more on medium heat. Season with salt and pepper.

Serve over cooked white rice accompanied by your favorite chutney. Serves 4.

GUATEMALA, MAYAN, *CYLINDER VASE, c. 700-800*

SOUR CREAM CHICKEN ENCHILADAS

A popular Tex-Mex casserole to make ahead for a hungry crowd.

4	boneless chicken breasts
2	cans cream of chicken soup
1	cup low-fat sour cream
1½	teaspoons dried minced onion
2	4-ounce cans chopped green chilies
12	6-inch flour tortillas
1	cup shredded sharp cheddar cheese

Cook chicken and cut into small dice. Set aside.

Preheat oven to 350°.

In a medium saucepan combine soup, sour cream, dried onion and green chilies. Heat and stir until smooth. Spread chicken down the middle of each tortilla. Top with 2 tablespoons soup mixture, roll up and arrange in a greased 9-inch x 13-inch pan.

Pour remaining soup over top of tortillas and sprinkle with cheese. Bake 40- 45 minutes. Serves 6.

SALLY LAZAR
RALEIGH, NC

SMOKED CHICKEN AND WILD MUSHROOM CAZUELA

Use mushrooms such as porcini, chanterelles or shiitake. A wonderful make-ahead casserole dinner. If you have a smoker, rather than grill the chicken, smoke it over hickory.

•	olive oil
3	pounds chicken breasts (on the bone)
1	tablespoon butter
1	small onion, chopped
1	tablespoon minced garlic
2	cups chopped wild mushrooms
¾	cup chicken broth
3	eggs
1½	cups flour
1	teaspoon baking powder
¼	cup fresh cilantro
1	tablespoon crushed red chillies
1	teaspoon oregano
1	teaspoon cumin
1	teaspoon salt
2½	cups grated Monterey Jack cheese, divided
12	red jalapeño tortillas

. . . .

TOMATO TOPPING:

1	teaspoon olive oil
¼	cup chopped onion
2	cups canned tomato sauce
1	tablespoon chili powder
1	teaspoon paprika
½	teaspoon cumin

Brush chicken with olive oil and grill until done.

Melt butter in a medium sauté pan over medium high heat and sauté onion, garlic and mushrooms for 2 minutes. Add chicken broth and cook on high heat for 2 more minutes; let cool.

In a large bowl mix eggs, flour and baking powder. Chop cilantro, and add with red chilies, oregano, cumin and salt.

Debone cooked chicken and chop into ½-inch cubes. Combine chicken with egg mixture; add mushroom mixture and 1 cup Monterey Jack cheese.

Preheat oven to 350°.

In a hot skillet heat enough oil to cover entire bottom of pan. Slightly cook the tortillas on both sides to soften. Line the sides and bottom of a 9-inch x 13-inch pan with the tortillas. Fill pan with chicken mixture; top with remaining cheese. Bake for 35-40 minutes or until a toothpick comes out clean. Serve with Tomato Topping. Serves 6.

TOMATO TOPPING: In a small saucepan cook the oil and onion for 2 minutes. Add tomato sauce and chili powder, paprika and cumin. Simmer 20 minutes more. Yields 2 cups.

ANTHONIE PALAMEDESZ. (Dutch), *MERRY COMPANY*, 1632

Images of well-dressed couples participating in activities of the type illustrated here were known as "merry companies" in seventeenth-century Holland. The interpretation of these activities has contributed significantly to our understanding of Dutch painting. For example, games played by groups of men and women, particularly tric-trac (backgammon), which two of the figures at the table appear to be playing, were often likened to the game of love.

CHICKEN TETRAZZINI

A great one-dish meal for a busy weekday supper to transport to a dinner meeting.

1½	cups broken spaghetti
2	teaspoons butter or margarine
½	cup chopped onion
¼	cup chopped green pepper
1½	cups chopped cooked chicken
½	cup chicken stock
¼	cup pimientos, chopped
1	10-ounce can cream of chicken soup
½	teaspoon salt
½	teaspoon pepper
2	cups shredded sharp cheddar cheese (8 ounces), divided

Preheat oven to 350°. Grease a 2-quart casserole.

Cook spaghetti pieces in boiling water, according to package directions. Drain and place in large bowl.

Melt butter in small skillet over medium heat and sauté onion and green pepper until tender. Combine with pasta, chicken, stock, pimientos, chicken soup, salt, pepper and 1 cup of the cheese.

Spoon into casserole and top with remaining 1 cup cheese. Bake for 45 minutes.

The casserole may be frozen baked or unbaked. Serves 4.

FRANCES M. EMORY
RALEIGH, NC

DEEP-DISH SPAGHETTI PIE

This recipe is a winner. A make-head recipe for a hungry group of friends.

6	ounces uncooked spaghetti
2	tablespoons butter
2	eggs, well beaten
⅓	cup grated Parmesan cheese
1	pound Italian sausage, mild or hot
½	cup chopped onion
¼	cup chopped green pepper
1	8-ounce can chopped or stewed tomatoes
1	6-ounce can tomato paste
1	teaspoon sugar
1	teaspoon oregano
¼	teaspoon garlic salt
1	cup cottage cheese, drained
½	cup shredded mozzarella cheese (2 ounces)

Butter a 10-inch deep-dish pie plate.

Cook spaghetti in boiling salted water. Drain and place in a large bowl. You should have about 2½ cups. Stir in butter, eggs and Parmesan. Press spaghetti mixture into buttered dish to make a crust.

If sausage is in links, remove from casing. In a large saucepan, crumble sausage and cook with onion and pepper until vegetables are tender and meat is brown. Drain off fat. Stir in tomatoes, tomato paste, sugar, oregano and garlic salt. Heat through.

Preheat oven to 350°. Spread cottage cheese over bottom of spaghetti crust. Spoon meat mixture into pie. Bake uncovered for 20 minutes. Sprinkle mozzarella cheese over top and bake 5 minutes more or until cheese is melted. Serves 6.

EVELYN (EVIE) DURBIN
CARY, NC

FROM FAUNA TO FOWL

BEULAH'S VEAL BIRDS

A family favorite created by Beulah Wellborn, longtime cook and the inventor of many delightful original recipes.

8	pieces of veal scaloppine
1	tablespoon butter
2	tablespoons finely chopped onion
2	tablespoons finely chopped celery
3	slices dry bread
1	cup crumbled cornbread
1	egg, lightly beaten
¼	teaspoon salt
¼	teaspoon pepper
½	cup flour plus 1 tablespoon, divided
2	tablespoons vegetable oil
1½-2 cups chicken stock	

Pound veal out to ¼-inch thickness. Set aside.

Melt butter in a small skillet over medium heat, and sauté onion and celery 3 minutes. In a medium bowl, crumble bread with cornbread. Stir in sautéed onion and celery, egg, salt and pepper. Spread each veal scallop evenly with stuffing leaving a ¼-inch margin all around edge. Roll up and secure with a toothpick.

Preheat oven to 350°. Put ½ cup flour in a bowl. Roll each "bird" in flour. Heat oil in sauté pan on medium-high heat and brown veal rolls on all sides. Transfer to a baking dish, reserving pan.

To pan, add 1 tablespoon flour to oil, and cook 1-2 minutes to make a roux. Stir in 1½ cups chicken stock. Bring to boil and simmer until thickened. When thickened, pour sauce over veal. Cover and bake 45 minutes. Add more chicken stock during cooking if needed to provide gravy. Uncover and cook 10 minutes more. Serves 4.

EMILY LAMBETH
THOMASVILLE, NC

SEARED VEAL CHOPS WITH SAUTÉED SHIITAKES

This easy main course is served with a sauce of mushrooms and pan juices, allowing all its flavor to emerge. Request thick chops cut from the center. A nice Burgundy or Cabernet Sauvignon would complement the veal.

2	tablespoons vegetable oil
2	1-inch thick veal chops
•	salt and pepper
1	tablespoon butter
2	tablespoons thinly sliced shallots
1	tablespoon fresh chopped thyme
1	cup sliced shiitake mushrooms or other wild variety such as portobello
⅓	cup Madeira
•	fresh thyme sprigs for garnish

Preheat oven to 400°. Heat oil in ovenproof skillet over medium heat. Season chops with salt and pepper and add to hot pan. Sear for 2 minutes on each side. Place pan in oven and roast for 6-7 minutes for medium-rare. Transfer veal to a warm plate and tent with foil, reserve pan.

Add butter to pan and melt over medium heat. Add shallots and cook for 3 minutes. Add thyme and mushrooms and sauté for 2 more minutes. Add Madeira and reduce mixture for another 2-3 minutes. Add a dash of salt and pepper.

To serve, place chops on warm plates and spoon mushrooms over and around the meat. Garnish with fresh thyme. Serves 2.

PREVIOUS PAGES: **WINSLOW HOMER** (American), *WEANING THE CALF* (detail), 1875

BRAISED PORK WITH APPLES AND ONIONS

This fragrant, homespun dish signifies bistro fare. The pork flavors the sauce while the aromatic vegetables are used to thicken it. Serve with rosemary mashed potatoes and crusty bread to complete your dinner.

- 1 2¼ to 3 pound boneless pork shoulder (Boston Butt), fat on, tied if necessary
- • salt and pepper
- 4 slices thick bacon
- 2 cups diced onion
- 1 cup diced carrots
- 2 Granny Smith apples, cored and diced
- 3 cloves garlic, cut in half
- 4 cups chicken broth
- ¼ cup apple cider
- 1 sprig fresh rosemary
- ¼ cup cider vinegar

Liberally salt and pepper roast. Place roast fat-side down, in a medium-hot frying pan. Over medium-low heat, slowly render (melt) fat from meat, about 15 minutes. Brown roast on all sides. Remove and place in a roasting pan, fat-side up. Reserve frying pan.

Preheat oven to 325°. Cut bacon in ½-inch pieces. Cook in reserved skillet until crisp; set aside. Pour off all but 1 tablespoon of fat from skillet. Add onions, carrots, apples and garlic to pan and sauté over medium heat for 10 minutes. Add chicken broth, cider, rosemary sprig and vinegar. Bring to a boil, immediately pour over roast. Cover with foil.

Roast for 2 hours. Check meat for tenderness by sticking a fork into center. Juices will run clear. Cook for up to 30 minutes more if necessary. Transfer roast to cutting board.

To make a sauce: Bring braising liquid to a simmer over medium heat. Skim fat and remove rosemary sprig. Transfer ¼ onions, carrots and apples with liquid to blender and puree until smooth. Stir puree back into skillet. Add reserved bacon. Check sauce for seasoning, adding a drop of vinegar for tartness if desired.

To serve, slice roast in ¾-inch slices. Arrange meat over mashed potatoes flavored with garlic and rosemary. Spoon sauce over pork and potatoes before serving. Serves 4.

ROLLED ROAST PORK LOIN WITH SPINACH, TOMATO & MUSHROOMS

Pure elegance will grace the table on which this succulent pork roast is served. Make use of the method for rolling out the pork loin — it is really rather simple to do.

- 1 2-pound pork loin trimmed of fat and silverskin
- 1 pound fresh spinach, washed
- 2 large tomatoes, peeled, seeded and diced
- ½ pound mushrooms, sliced
- 3 large cloves garlic, chopped
- 1 tablespoon fresh basil
- 1 teaspoon dried oregano
- • salt and pepper
- • olive oil

You will be cutting the pork loin to form a large sheet. Cut meat about ¼-inch above and level with the cutting board, continuously cutting and rolling the loin until a single even sheet is formed.

Prepare separately the spinach, tomatoes and mushrooms. First, braise spinach in olive oil and set aside. Next, sauté tomatoes with basil and half the garlic in olive oil and set aside. Finally, sauté sliced mushrooms with pepper and remaining garlic and set aside. Chill all ingredients.

Preheat oven to 375°. Layer spinach, mushrooms and tomatoes on the pork loin and re-roll the pork sheet. Rub more olive oil on the outside of the pork roast and season the top with oregano, salt and pepper. Seal loin in oiled aluminum foil and bake 1½ hours. Serves 4-6.

$\mathcal{A}n$ **elegant entrée for** an autumn dinner party, Stuffed Pork

Tenderloin with Juniper Berry Sauce may be cooked the day before, freeing the

host to spend precious time with guests. This could also become the centerpiece

to a holiday meal.

Stuffed Pork Tenderloin with Juniper Berry Sauce

An apple stuffing embellishes a pork tenderloin filled with an unusual juniper berry sauce. Juniper berries are the fruit of the evergreen Juniperus communis. Dried and used in marinades, stews and sauces, they boast a flavor somewhat reminiscent of a mild green peppercorn. Look for them in the spice section of specialty shops or larger grocery stores.

2 tablespoons juniper berries, divided

4 pork tenderloins (about 3 pounds total) well trimmed (There are 2 in a package.)

• salt and pepper

2 tablespoons butter

1 tablespoon vegetable oil

½ cup dry white wine

½ cup vegetable broth plus 2 tablespoons, divided

1½ cups heavy cream

APPLE STUFFING:

2 tablespoons butter

⅓ cup diced onion

⅓ cup diced celery

2 Granny Smith apples, peeled and diced

½ teaspoon sage

1 cup coarse, fresh dark rye break crumbs

⅓ cup vegetable broth

• salt and pepper

Make Apple Stuffing. Put juniper berries in heavy skillet over high heat for about 2 minutes, stirring frequently to toast. When cool slightly crush by using a mortar and pestle, or between sheets of wax paper with a rolling pin. Set aside.

Make a slit down the length of each tenderloin, not cutting quite all the way through. Open out like a book. Put between 2 sheets of wax paper and pound to even thickness. Sprinkle with salt and pepper. Put half of stuffing down middle of one of the tenderloins. Top with a second, putting thin end over the fatter end for even thickness throughout. Shape lightly into a round and tie with butchers' string at 1½ inch intervals. Repeat with remaining 2 tenderloins.

Preheat oven to 375°. Heat butter and oil in large heavy skillet over medium-high heat.

Add tenderloins and brown on all sides. Remove to roasting pan. Sprinkle with 1 tablespoon of toasted juniper berries. Bake 40-45 minutes until meat thermometer registers about 155°. Be sure to test the temperature of the meat, not the stuffing.

Meanwhile pour excess grease from browning pan. Put over high heat; add wine and ½ cup broth, stirring in brown bits from pan. Reduce liquid to a few tablespoons. Add cream and boil to thicken slightly. Add remaining 1 tablespoon juniper berries and season with salt and pepper. Set aside.

When meat is done, transfer to cutting board and let sit at least 10 minutes. Add remaining 2 tablespoons broth to pan, stir and add to sauce. If serving right away, remove string and slice pork. If making ahead, cool meat and refrigerate; remove string and slice cold. Arrange in casserole and cover tightly with foil. Heat in preheated 350° oven about 20-25 minutes. Reheat sauce and serve on side. Garnish meat with fresh sage, if desired. Serves 8-10.

APPLE STUFFING: Heat butter in medium skillet over moderate heat. Sauté onion and celery until soft, about 3-4 minutes. Add apples and sage and sauté 4-5 minutes more until just tender. Add bread crumbs, broth and salt and pepper. Toss to combine. Cool completely. Yields about 3 cups stuffing.

Grilled Maple Pork Chops

An excellent marinade made of walnut oil, real maple syrup and fresh rosemary makes these pork chops come alive.

4 ½-inch thick pork chops, boneless or bone in

2 cloves garlic, chopped

½ cup walnut oil

½ cup Worcestershire sauce

½ cup real maple syrup

1 tablespoon fresh rosemary, roughly chopped

Place pork in a glass container.

In a separate bowl, whisk together the remaining ingredients. Pour over chops. Marinate overnight. Grill until desired doneness. For extra flavor, baste with marinade while grilling. Serves 4.

The son of a brewer, and a tavern keeper himself, Jan Steen is best known for his pictures of unruly merrymakers in humorous situations, but he was, above all, a storyteller. Whether he was painting proverbs, scenes from the theater, the battle between the sexes or religious narratives, his talent to describe and animate a scene was unmatched among his contemporaries. As one of Steen's largest and most ambitious works, *The Worship of the Golden Calf* clearly attests to his extraordinary ability to tell a story.

JAN STEEN (Dutch), *THE WORSHIP OF THE GOLDEN CALF,* c. 1671-72

FROM FAUNA TO FOWL

PAN-SEARED STEAKS WITH MADEIRA & MUSHROOMS

A dash of Madeira turns rib-eyes into fast, gourmet food.

- olive oil
- 2 rib-eye steaks
- salt and pepper
- 2 tablespoons minced shallots or green onions
- 8 ounces sliced mushrooms, any variety
- 4 tablespoons Madeira

Heat a heavy sauté pan over medium-high heat. Brush bottom with olive oil. Place steaks in hot pan. Sprinkle with salt and pepper, and cook over medium-high heat about 3-4 minutes per side. Remove steaks; keep warm.

Sauté shallots or green onions in pan drippings. Add mushrooms, and cook until lightly browned, about 4-5 minutes. Stir in Madeira. Return steak to pan and heat a minute or two. Serves 2.

ROASTED BEEF TENDERLOIN WITH A MUSTARD CAPER SAUCE

A delicious preparation for beef, and perfect for feeding a large group. The Mustard Caper Sauce is a winner.

- 1 5-6 pound beef tenderloin
- 2 cloves garlic, peeled
- 1 teaspoon salt
- 2 teaspoons peppercorns
- 2 tablespoons butter, at room temperature
- 1 tablespoon dry mustard
- 2 teaspoons paprika

MUSTARD CAPER SAUCE:

- ½ cup red wine
- 1 cup plus 2 tablespoons canned beef broth, divided
- ½ cup heavy cream
- 4 teaspoons cornstarch
- 2 tablespoons Dijon Mustard
- ¼ cup small capers, rinsed and drained
- accumulated juices from meat
- salt and pepper

Trim beef discarding large pieces of fat. Tuck the thin end under to make a fairly even thickness.

With a mortar and pestle crush peeled garlic cloves with salt until it becomes a paste. Add peppercorns and crush. Place butter in a small bowl, and add garlic mixture. Stir in dry mustard and paprika. Rub over the entire surface of beef tenderloin. Cover and refrigerate overnight.

Bring tenderloin to room temperature. Preheat oven to 425°. Put tenderloin on a rack in a heavy roasting pan. Roast 45-60 minutes or until meat thermometer inserted in thickest part of meat registers about 135-140° for medium rare. Remove from roasting pan and cover loosely with foil. Let rest 20 minutes before slicing. Reserve drippings for Mustard Caper Sauce. Serves 8-10.

MUSTARD CAPER SAUCE: Put roasting pan over burner (if heat proof) and deglaze pan with red wine by boiling and stirring in any brown bits from roasting. Reduce wine by about half. Transfer to a saucepan, scraping in any flavorful bits. Add 1 cup beef broth and bring to a boil. Add cream and return to boil.

Dissolve cornstarch in remaining 2 tablespoons beef broth. Add to saucepan and boil until slightly thickened, 3-4 minutes. Stir in mustard, capers and any accumulated juices from meat. Season with salt and pepper.

STANDING RIB ROAST

The term "prime rib" is attributed to what is actually a rib roast. The key to this elegant dish is cooking the roast on low heat, or 200°, for a longer time than for the higher heat methods. Proportions have not been given for seasoning the meat because you are simply coating the meat. You will find this is one of the easiest recipes you have ever attempted.

1 8 to 10-pound
   standing rib roast
• olive oil
• garlic powder
• dry mustard
• herbes de Provence
• freshly ground pepper
• salt

HORSERADISH CREAM:

1½ cups heavy cream
¾   cup tangy horseradish
•   cayenne pepper
•   salt

Preheat oven to 200°. Trim any excess fat from rib roast. Make 1-inch slits through the silver skin. Generously rub olive oil, garlic powder, dry mustard and herbs de Provence (a spice blend easily found at the supermarket), coating the entire roast. The meat should be well-coated from top to bottom with olive oil and seasonings. Rub in black pepper.

Place roast on a rack in roasting pan. Cook for about 23 minutes per pound (3-3¾ hours). Do not season with salt until 15 minutes before roast is done. Insert a meat thermometer into thick part of the roast. For rare, remove the roast from the oven at 120°. Let the roast sit on a carving board, covered, for 20-30 minutes before carving. The temperature will rise to 130° while is rests. For medium doneness, remove roast at 130°, cover; allow temperature to rise to 140°. We recommend the rare method.

Serve with Au Jus and Horseradish Cream. Serves 10.

AU JUS: While roast is resting, skim excess fat from the roasting pan. Add 2 cups beef stock; place roasting pan directly on burner; bring contents to a boil. As the sauce boils, scrape up cooked bits in pan. Pour liquid into a saucepan; simmer a few minutes. Adjust seasoning; strain through a fine sieve just before serving.

HORSERADISH CREAM: In a medium bowl (chilled before using) whip cream until stiff. Gently fold in horseradish. Season with pepper and salt; adjust taste until your horseradish cream has plenty of kick. Refrigerate. Yields 2½ cups.

FILET MIGNON WITH HERB CRUST

An elegant way to serve beef with make-ahead preparation. Ideal for dinner parties and family entertaining.

4 beef tenderloin steaks
   (6-7 ounces each)
• salt and pepper
1 tablespoon olive oil
3 slices white bread
⅓ cup chopped fresh parsley
2 cloves garlic, minced
½ cup butter, melted
1½ tablespoons Dijon mustard

Trim fat and membrane from steaks. Season with salt and pepper. Put oil in skillet and on high heat, sear meat about 2 minutes on each side. Remove from skillet to a broiler pan. Next, prepare crust. Place bread in food processor and pulse to make bread crumbs. Transfer to a small bowl and add parsley, garlic and melted butter. Season with salt and pepper.

Preheat oven to 425°. Spread each steak with mustard. Mound bread crumb mixture on top of each steak. Bake for 15-20 minutes. Rest meat for 10 minutes. Flash steaks under a hot broiler for a few seconds to brown the crust before serving. Serves 4.

CHERYL MAUPIN
RALEIGH, NC

$\mathcal{S}$*ucculent* **and tasty, meat** dishes give the cook an opportunity to shine. Spices and marinades, variations in cooking times and temperatures — these secrets are as treasured as the compliments of clean plates and requests for seconds.

Filet Mignon with Herb Crust has the hidden tang of mustard.

Oriental-Style Turkey Breast

Basted with hoisin sauce and accompanied by an Oriental-style stuffing, this recipe brings new flavor and flair to traditional turkey. The hoisin sauce turns the skin a very rich dark brown color with extra crispness.

1   6-8 pound turkey breast
•   salt and pepper
¼   cup hoisin sauce
2   tablespoons melted butter
2   tablespoons flour
2   cups chicken stock

....

ORIENTAL RICE STUFFING:

2   tablespoons sesame oil
1½ cups chopped onion
1   bunch bok choy, washed and chopped (2 cups)
2   cups chopped napa (Chinese) cabbage, see note
1   15-ounce can straw mushrooms, drained
1   cup chopped almond slivers, toasted, see note
1½ cups cooked brown rice
3   tablespoons dry sherry
2   tablespoons soy sauce
½   teaspoon salt
¼   teaspoon white pepper

Make Oriental Rice Stuffing.

Preheat oven to 350°. Rinse turkey breast under cold water. Fill cavity and neck pocket with stuffing. Secure flaps with toothpicks or skewers, and salt and pepper turkey. Combine hoisin and butter in a small bowl, and brush the outside of turkey with sauce. Place in oven and reduce to 325°. Roast according to the bird's weight, basting every 30 minutes with hoisin sauce. When done remove from pan and cover with a foil tent. Serves 6-8.

To make a pan gravy: Place roasting pan directly over a medium high burner and add flour to drippings. Whisk to make a roux, scraping all the sticky brown bits from pan. Cool 3-4 minutes before adding chicken stock. Continue whisking until thickened. Season to taste.

To toast almonds: Cook 2-3 minutes over medium high heat in nonstick pan until lightly brown.

NOTE: Similar to bok choy, the thickly veined leaves of napa cabbage variety are cream-colored with green tips. Milder than round heads of cabbage, choose firm, tightly packed heads.

ORIENTAL RICE STUFFING: In a large skillet heat oil over medium high; sauté onion and bok choy 5 minutes. Stir in cabbage, mushrooms, almonds, and rice; cook 3-4 minutes more. Season with sherry, soy sauce, salt and pepper. Cool before stuffing turkey breast. Any leftover stuffing may be heated in the oven at 325° for 30 minutes and served on the side.

Grilled Venison Tenderloin

The tenderloin is the "filet mignon" of venison. A good substitute is the backstrap cut of venison.

1   whole venison tenderloin (2½-3 pounds)
1   cup olive oil
4   cloves garlic, minced
¼   cup balsamic vinegar
½   cup oyster sauce
2   teaspoons thyme
1   tablespoon coarsely ground pepper
1   teaspoon salt

Trim any fat and silver skin from tenderloin. In a glass dish large enough to hold tenderloin, mix oil, garlic, vinegar, oyster sauce, thyme, pepper and salt. Add tenderloin and turn to coat. Cover and refrigerate 2-4 hours.

Grill over hot coals. When one side is seared, baste, turn and baste again with marinade. Do this on all sides for a total of 14 minutes. Meat should be medium rare inside and crispy outside. Remove from grill and slice into medallions.

If using the backstrap, slice thinly as you would a flank steak. Serve with the juices spooned over, a Béarnaise sauce, or top with sautéed mushrooms kissed with a little sherry. Serves 5-6.

GRILLED QUAIL WITH SHALLOT SAUCE

A perfect meal for a small family's holiday dinner or anytime. A Cranberry Conserve shared by Director Lawrence J. Wheeler, page 210, accents the succulent flavor of grilled quail.

8   quail
2   cloves garlic, minced
½   cup olive oil
½   teaspoon thyme
½   teaspoon rosemary
½   teaspoon basil
•   salt and pepper

SHALLOT SAUCE:

¼   cup minced shallots
¼   cup butter
1½ cups chicken stock
½   cup white wine
2   teaspoons Dijon mustard
2   teaspoons lemon juice
•   dash Worcestershire sauce

Butterfly the quail, by splitting each quail down the backbone and removing the neck. Combine minced garlic with olive oil, thyme, rosemary, basil, salt and pepper. Rub seasoned oil over quail and marinate in the refrigerator for 2 hours.

Make the Cranberry Conserve while quail marinate. Make Shallot Sauce before finishing quail.

Grill butterflied quail, breast side first on high heat for 3 minutes while basting with oil marinade. Turn, continuing to baste, every 2 minutes until quail are cooked, about 10 minutes. Serve on warm plates with Shallot Sauce spooned over quail and Cranberry Conserve on the side. Delicious with an exotic rice or roasted new potatoes. Serves 4.

SHALLOT SAUCE: In a small sauce pan sauté shallots in butter over medium heat 2-3 minutes. Add remaining ingredients, bring to a boil and simmer, stirring occasionally until sauce is reduced by half.

DARIUS PAINTER WORKSHOP (South Italian, Apulian), *RHYTON*, c. 360-340 BC

PIETER AERTSEN (Netherlandish), *A MEAT STALL WITH THE HOLY FAMILY GIVING ALMS*, 1551

Aertsen's *Meat Stall* is considered to be the earliest still-life painting of foodstuffs, and the precursor of a type of painting known as a market-piece, a work that combines still-life and genre elements. In addition to the superabundant display of meats and other foods, the artist has depicted two widely different background scenes which represent a contrast between earthly food for the body and spiritual food for the soul.

Sage-Roasted Cornish Hens

The hens are split down the middle and an herb butter is tucked under the skin. Aromatic and flavorful, this is an easy entrée to serve dinner guests.

4   Cornish game hens

½   cup unsalted butter, softened

1   tablespoon sage leaves

1   teaspoon thyme

1   teaspoon salt

¼   teaspoon freshly ground pepper

2   tablespoons melted butter

Wash Cornish hens and using kitchen shears, cut down the center of each breast, then the center of the back to split in two. Cut out backbone and excess skin. Set aside.

In small bowl combine softened butter with sage, thyme, salt and pepper. With your fingers, carefully loosen the skin of one of the hen halves and tuck about 1 tablespoon of herb butter evenly under the skin. Repeat with remaining hens. Put into large flat roasting pan in one layer. Brush with melted butter. Hens may be prepared ahead to this point. Cover and refrigerate several hours or overnight. Remove about ½ hour before baking.

Preheat oven to 400° Roast 30-35 minutes until brown and crispy and juices run clear when pierced with a fork. Serves 6-8.

Pan-Roasted Chicken with Crispy Potatoes over Arugula

A one-pan dish quickly cooked in a very hot oven is served over dressed fresh arugula, a salad green with a peppery mustard flavor.

1   3-3½-pound chicken

2   large Idaho potatoes

1   pound arugula

•   salt and pepper

•   lemon juice

2-3   tablespoons extra virgin olive oil

2   rosemary sprigs for garnish

Remove back from chicken. Split bird in half by cutting through the sternum. Separate the two legs from breast pieces.

Wash potatoes and cut off ends. Cut in quarters lengthwise and then each piece in half again. Wash and drain arugula. (A salad spinner works well.) Set aside.

Preheat oven to 450°. Generously salt and pepper chicken pieces and potatoes. Heat a large heavy skillet on high with 1-2 tablespoons oil and remove. Place chicken skin-side-down and potatoes with a cut-side-down into hot skillet. Roast in oven 10 minutes. Remove pan and turn potatoes on the other cut-side-down. Do not turn chicken. Return skillet to oven for 7-10 minutes more. Remove and let rest 10 minutes.

While chicken is resting, dress arugula lightly with lemon juice and remaining olive oil. Salt and pepper to taste.

Arrange potatoes in a circular pattern around the plate. Place arugula in center. Place leg piece and breast on top of each serving. Garnish with rosemary sprig. Serves 2.

Michael Haynes
Raleigh, NC

Chicken Breasts in Parchment Bundles can add a festive touch to an easy weekday dinner.

CHICKEN BREASTS IN PARCHMENT BUNDLES

A "signature" dish that is easily prepared ahead, and makes a fun presentation for family and friends.

4   boneless chicken breast
    halves

6   small red potatoes

2   medium onions, sliced
    thinly

1   tablespoon mayonnaise

1   tablespoon Dijon mustard

4   small carrots, julienne

4   celery stalks, julienne

•   paprika

•   tarragon

•   garlic powder

•   Lawry's seasoned salt

•   pepper

2   tablespoons butter

4   sheets 12-inch x 20-inch
    parchment paper

•   butchers twine

Remove skin from chicken if necessary and pound each breast to ¼-inch thick. Quarter the new potatoes and boil 10-15 minutes until just tender. Drain and set aside.

Preheat oven to 450°. Spray one side of parchment paper with cooking oil and divide sliced onions among the four. Lay chicken breast on top of onions. Mix mayonnaise and mustard together and spread on top of each chicken breast coating well. Divide carrots, celery and cooked potatoes and place on and around chicken breasts. Season each packet to taste with paprika, tarragon, garlic powder, seasoned salt and pepper. Dot each with ½ tablespoon butter.

Gather parchment paper together closely around ingredients and tie tightly with twine. Trim excess twine and cut off ragged edges of parchment to form a "top-knot". Place bundles directly on the rack of oven and bake 25 minutes.

To serve, place in center of dinner plate and have each guest cut off their "top-knot" with scissors. Serves 4.

BARBARA SISK LANDON
NORTH WILKESBORO, NC

Delicious **and easy to** prepare, chicken is a popular entrée at any time of the year. For a striking presentation, serve a meal in a "bag" — Chicken Breasts in Parchment Bundles include portions of potatoes, onions, carrots and celery. Cheesy Crusted Chicken, seasoned with a garlic-flavored oil, is destined to become a family favorite, and Chicken Elizabeth, cooked to tender perfection with a hint of prosciutto, can be on your table in less than an hour.

CHEESY CRUSTED CHICKEN

An easy preparation for baked bone-in chicken breasts that develop a delicious crust as they bake.

3	cloves garlic, sliced
½	cup oil
1	cup bread crumbs
1	teaspoon salt
½	teaspoon pepper
½	cup finely grated sharp cheddar cheese
½	cup finely grated Parmesan cheese
4	chicken breasts, bone in

Mix garlic and oil, in a medium bowl; let stand at least 20 minutes or longer. Remove garlic.

Preheat oven to 350°. In a separate bowl, mix together bread crumbs, salt, pepper and cheeses. Dip chicken pieces in garlic oil, then in crumb mixture.

Place crusted chicken on rack in shallow baking pan. Pour remaining oil over chicken pieces. Bake uncovered about 45 minutes. Serves 4.

GILDA MCKINNEY
RALEIGH, NC

CHICKEN ELIZABETH

A crowd-pleasing entrée that you make ahead. Cook, sauce and serve to order. Serve with Roasted Rosemary Potatoes, page 207.

1	8-ounce cream cheese, softened
½	cup butter, softened
1	teaspoon pepper
1	teaspoon basil
1	teaspoon minced garlic
1	teaspoon oregano
1	teaspoon thyme
1	teaspoon tarragon
1	teaspoon parsley
4	boneless chicken breast halves
12	cherry tomatoes, halved
4	thin slices prosciutto, about 4 ounces
¼-⅓	cup white wine

Make cheese filling by mixing together cream cheese, butter, pepper, basil, garlic, oregano, thyme, tarragon and parsley, blending thoroughly.

Pound chicken breasts with a mallet to ¼-inch thickness. Line each breast with 1 slice prosciutto, 6 cherry tomato halves and ¼ cup dollop herb cheese mixture. Roll up the chicken breast and place seam side down in a baking pan. Top each breast with a dollop of cheese mixture and sprinkle generously with white wine. The recipe can be made ahead to this point.

Preheat oven to 375°. Bake for 30 minutes. Serve immediately. Serves 4.

ADAM DAVID LOPEZ
GREENBELT, MD

GRILLED BUTTERFLIED LEG OF LAMB

A boned, butterflied leg of lamb is an easy way to prepare lamb for a festive dinner because there is no waste and it's very easy to carve. This lamb is great hot off the grill, even served cold at a picnic. Make sure to whip up the Garlic Herb Mayonnaise.

1   butterflied leg of lamb, well trimmed, see note

2   unpeeled cloves garlic, cut in half

•   salt and freshly ground pepper

½   teaspoon thyme

½   teaspoon marjoram

½   teaspoon oregano

2   tablespoons olive oil

....

GARLIC-HERB MAYONNAISE:

½   cup mayonnaise

1-2   cloves garlic, finely minced

2   tablespoons mixed fresh herbs (lemon thyme, marjoram and oregano)

½   teaspoon freshly ground pepper

Preheat a gas grill to medium-low. Cut the meat into 2 pieces and flatten; make gashes in the thickest sections and pound to even the thickness. Rub the meat with the cut side of the garlic cloves. Sprinkle with salt and pepper. Combine thyme, marjoram and oregano. Crush, then sprinkle over meat, rubbing in lightly. Rub the meat with olive oil.

Put onto gas grill and cover. Cook 10 minutes per side. Then turn every 3-4 minutes until desired doneness. The whole process will take a total of 25-35 minutes (150° will be medium rare.) Let meat sit for 5-10 minutes before carving. Slice thinly. Pour over the meat any juices that accumulate. Serves 8.

To roast in the oven: Preheat oven to 325°. Cook 10-12 minutes per pound until the meat thermometer reaches 130° for rare, 135° for medium rare and 140° for pink medium. If you wish, add salt a few minutes before taking the roast out of the oven. Adding salt in this manner still flavors the outside, along with the marinade and pepper, but does not penetrate the meat during the long cooking process.

NOTE: Have your butcher bone a leg of lamb. Open it out flat and cut into 2 pieces to "butterfly" it. Make a gash in the thickest parts and flatten to approximately the same thickness. For a big group, prepare both pieces; for a small group grill just one piece and freeze the other for later. One of the halves is slightly bigger than the other, but each will serve 4-6 people.

GARLIC-HERB MAYONNAISE: Combine all ingredients and refrigerate for an hour or 2 or overnight. Adjust garlic to your taste. A little of this pungent sauce is delicious with lamb. Use real mayonnaise.

LEMON LAMB SHANKS

Lamb shanks provide an easy and economical method to enjoy the best of lamb flavor cooked on the bone at half the cost. Aurora Gregory cooks her lamb shanks in a pressure cooker, but in testing, a simple Dutch oven method was developed in case the first is unavailable. Perfect for a small dinner party when served over hot rice.

3   tablespoons olive oil

4   lamb shanks

½   cup white wine

1   cup chicken stock

1   tablespoon grated lemon rind

1   teaspoon salt

½   teaspoon pepper

½   teaspoon sugar

1   clove garlic, minced

½   cup chopped fresh parsley

8   thin lemon slices

Heat oil in a 6-8 quart pressure cooker or Dutch oven. Brown lamb shanks on all sides. Add wine, stock, and grated lemon. Sprinkle meat with salt, pepper and sugar. Cover and lock pressure cooker. Place on high heat and set at 15 pounds pressure. When pressure is reached, reduce heat and cook for 20-25 minutes. Release pressure and carefully remove lid. If using a Dutch oven, cover and cook on high heat until stock boils. Reduce heat and cook for 45-50 minutes until meat starts to fall away from bone.

Remove lamb to serving platter. Add garlic to pot, raise heat and boil sauce rapidly, uncovered, to thicken. Add parsley and spoon over lamb shanks. Garnish with lemon slices. Serves 4.

AURORA K. GREGORY
RALEIGH, NC

$\mathcal{H}ere$ **are two recipe** jewels featuring lamb. Grilled Butterflied Leg of Lamb will easily accommodate a dinner party of eight people, and sophisticated palates will appreciate the addition of a Garlic-Herb Mayonnaise. Delicious Lemon Lamb Shanks, with hints of garlic and citrus, would make a fireside supper a most memorable affair.

Lemon Lamb Shanks melt in your mouth.

BLUE RIDGE THE MUSEUM RESTAURANT

*A*rtistic expression takes many forms: visual, written, performing and culinary. While the focus of the North Carolina Museum of Art is primarily devoted to the visual arts, it provides Museum visitors and guests with an intricate balance of other art forms that make going to the Museum a true sensory experience. What reception or exhibition opening would be complete without music, food and beverages carefully chosen to heighten the visual experience? Such is the concept behind Blue Ridge, the Museum's critically acclaimed full-service restaurant.

Using only the freshest ingredients, Executive Chef and General Manager ANDY HICKS and Pastry Chef JENNIFER HICKS combine skill and experience with imagination, creativity and instinct to design menus tailored to the Museum's specific needs. Be it a Museum function, special event, daily luncheon or one of Blue Ridge's highly touted Friday dinners, this husband-and-wife chef team express themselves through food preparation and presentation.

Skillful practitioners of the culinary arts, Andy and Jennifer have spent the last decade perfecting their craft. A graduate of UNC-Chapel Hill and an avid gardener, Andy served as the Museum's executive chef from 1992 until May 1999. Prior to that he honed his skills in some of the Triangle's most respected kitchens, including Chapel Hill's La Residence, when it was run by Executive Chef Bill Smith of Crook's Corner. The couple met at the Museum where Jennifer worked as a prep cook, line cook and, eventually, as head pastry chef. A graduate of the Culinary Institute of America and the N.C. State University School of Design, Jennifer gained experience at top Triangle restaurants such as Fearrington House in Pittsboro, The Magnolia Grill in Durham and the Governor's Club in Chapel Hill. Today the two manage the Museum's dining operations, which includes Museum event catering and Blue Ridge, the Museum Restaurant.

Andy's passion for gardening translates into exotic creations in the Blue Ridge kitchen where the menu changes seasonally to reflect the availability of fresh fruits, herbs and vegetables. His culinary interpretations illustrate the range of his talent.

Ever mindful that a diner's palate is as varied as his taste in art, the two chefs design Blue Ridge's menu selections to include an eclectic array of culinary fare that ranges from soups, salads and sandwiches to gourmet appetizers, entrées and exquisite desserts. Their culinary expertise and understanding of the Museum's clientele help them transcend the ordinary. A veggie burger took on a new identity as "Hoppin' Jacques" when the Rodin exhibition inspired Andy to rename a bean burger creation based on a classic Hoppin' John recipe. Jennifer's repertoire includes such delights as Chocolate Cherry & Pear Turnover with Almond Praline Anglaise. Name changes aside, new items are occasionally added to lunch and dinner menus, playing off exhibition themes to tie the Museum experience to its delightful restaurant.

ALBERT BIERSTADT (American), *BRIDAL VEIL FALLS, YOSEMITE* (detail), c. 1871-73

Andy and Jennifer Hicks, the chefs and managers of Blue Ridge, create a unique ambiance with their delicious cuisine at the North Carolina Museum of Art.

Blue Ridge's decor strikes a delicate balance. True to the Museum's mission, the restaurant includes its own art installation and offers a striking view of outside sculptures through its back windows, most recently one by North Carolinian Thomas Sayre. The large airy room was artfully designed mindful of those who appreciate both art and food without detracting from the Museum experience. Artist Matt McConnell was commissioned to build special lighting sculptures that dramatically accent the high ceilings and windows in the restaurant.

While food feeds the body, fine dining feeds the soul. On Fridays, the only evening that Blue Ridge is open for dinner, Andy and Jennifer's culinary artistry is showcased. Each week the Hicks present a rotating menu to restaurant patrons who are eager to embrace the taste, feel and smell of the day's special culinary selections.

Appetites ranging from simple to sublime can satisfy their cravings at Blue Ridge. Art lovers and foodies with an appreciation for the fresh and innovative will find that dining at Blue Ridge enhances and completes the Museum experience, adding a new dimension to the sights and textures of one of the nation's premier art museums.

BLUE RIDGE RESTAURANT: Open Tuesday-Friday for Lunch, 11:30 a.m.-2:30 p.m.; Friday Night Dinner, 5:30-10:00 p.m. (last seating at 8:30); Saturday & Sunday Brunch, 11:00 a.m.-3:00 p.m. For reservations and information about special event catering, call (919) 833-2031/(919) 833-3548.

Spiraling out of the landscape, *Gyre* is situated invitingly on the Museum Trail. The sculpture was made by a dramatic earth-casting technique practiced by North Carolina sculptor Thomas Sayre. It brings together recurring themes in his work, such as scale, collaboration and changeable materials. The technique synthesizes form and content: *Gyre*, a work made by man yet born of the earth, explores human interaction with nature.

THOMAS SAYRE (American), *GYRE*, 1999 © Thomas Sayre

A Royal Affair

While nearly half of Blue Ridge's business is attributed to catering Museum functions and special events, preparing a menu for a French princess is not exactly an everyday request.

In 1995, the French Princess Marie-Sol de Latour d'Auvergne traveled halfway around the world to view an elaborate three-panel painting on display in the Museum's European Gallery. More than just a beautiful piece of Renaissance art, *The Annunciation with Saints and Donors* called *The Latour d'Auvergne Triptych*, features the Princess' ancestors, the Count and Countess of Latour d'Auvergne. The triptych was part of the Latour d'Auvernge collection from 1497 until the countess bequeathed it to the town's Franciscan monastery. In 1703, it was returned to the Latour d'Auvergne

The Latour d'Auvergne Triptych, c. 1497

family, before it went into obscurity and resurfaced again in 1957 when Samuel H. Kress purchased it on the art market. The Kress Foundation subsequently donated it to the North Carolina Museum of Art.

In honor of the Princess' Museum visit, Blue Ridge was charged with creating a menu fit for royalty. An elaborate, yet intimate dinner hosted by Museum Director Lawrence J. Wheeler followed a cocktail reception inside the Greek and Roman sculpture gallery. As an opening to an unforgettable meal, Andy prepared his Tomato and Tarragon Bisque made with fresh ripe tomatoes, leeks and fresh herbs. Turban of Sole garnished with spinach mousseline, poached shrimp and salmon caviar provided the meal's elegant main attraction, followed by a salad of fresh mesclun greens with black currant and champagne dressing. Jennifer's piéce de résistance was a decadent White Chocolate Mandarin Mousse with raspberry and passion fruit sauces, accented by her recipe for thin and crispy vanilla almond tuiles.

The royal dinner was indeed an auspicious affair thanks largely to the talented staff at Blue Ridge and the grand gallery settings provided by the North Carolina Museum of Art.

TOMATO AND TARRAGON BISQUE
The mellow aromas of fresh tarragon infuse fresh tomatoes in this delicious soup by Andy Hicks. Goodness teases the palate.

8	fresh ripe tomatoes
½	cup unsalted butter
2	cups chopped leeks
2	cloves garlic, minced
¼	cup all-purpose flour
2	cups chicken stock
1	cup heavy cream
1	tablespoon salt
1	teaspoon fresh ground black pepper
2	tablespoons chopped fresh tarragon

Blanch tomatoes by plunging them into boiling water for 15 seconds, cool, then remove the skins, seeds and roughly chop.

In a heavy-bottomed saucepan, melt butter and cook leeks until they are translucent. Add garlic and cook 5 minutes more, stirring occasionally. Stir in flour and continue to cook, stirring constantly an additional 5 minutes. Add tomatoes and chicken stock and cook on medium-low for 15 minutes until tomatoes are soft and juicy.

Puree soup in a blender or food processor. Return to pot and add cream, salt and pepper and heat through. Just before serving, stir in tarragon. Serves 8.

FIELD GREENS WITH CASSIS VINAIGRETTE

Fresh mesclun greens or baby lettuces are draped lightly with sweet black currant flavor and champagne vinegar zest.

1   shallot, minced
1   clove garlic, minced
½   tablespoon Dijon mustard
¼   cup champagne vinegar
¾   cup pure olive oil
1   cup cassis (black currant liqueur) reduced to ¼ cup
•   salt and pepper
1½   pounds mixed baby greens

Combine shallots, garlic and mustard in a bowl and whisk in champagne vinegar. Slowly drizzle in olive oil while constantly whisking, creating an emulsion. When all of oil is added whisk in reduced cassis, and salt and pepper. Toss greens with vinaigrette and serve. Serves 6-8.

The main course was fresh sole adorned with a delightful lemon chervil beurre blanc followed by a salad course featuring Field Greens with Cassis Vinaigrette.

TURBAN OF SOLE WITH SPINACH MOUSSELINE AND POACHED SHRIMP

A classic preparation of fish surrounded by a dance of colorful morsels — poached shrimp, seasoned spinach, even salmon caviar.

- 8   sole fillets, trimmed
- •   parchment paper
- •   butter
- •   string or butcher's twine
- 24   shrimp, peeled, with tails intact and deveined
- •   salmon caviar

....

COURT BOUILLON:

- 2   quarts water
- 2   tablespoons salt
- 2   cups dry white wine
- 3   stalks celery, chopped
- 1   head garlic, sliced in half horizontally, root removed)
- 4   sprigs Italian parsley
- 2   sprigs thyme
- 1   bay leaf
- 2   lemons, halved
- 1   tablespoon whole peppercorns

....

SPINACH MOUSSELINE:

- 1   pound spinach, cleaned and blanched
- ½   tablespoon salt
- 1   pinch fresh ground pepper
- 1   cup heavy cream
- 2   egg yolks
- 1   whole egg

....

LEMON CHERVIL BEURRE BLANC:

- 3   shallots, thinly sliced
- 1   cup white wine
- 2   lemons, juiced and zest
- 1   pound butter, cubed
- ¼   cup chopped fresh chervil
- •   salt and pepper

Prepare Court Bouillon. To prepare sole, stand each fillet on its long edge, form each into a cylinder leaving as much room as possible in the center while maintaining its form. Encircle fillet cylinder with a buttered strip of parchment paper the same height as the fillet and tie with butcher's twine. Place in a shallow, buttered baking pan. The pan should be at least 1-inch taller than height of fish.

Prepare Spinach Mousseline. Using a spoon or piping bag fill each center of the encircled sole.

Preheat oven to 350°.

Pour hot court bouillon carefully around fillets until ½-inch below the top of fillets. Place a buttered piece of parchment paper over tops of fillets. Reserve some of court bouillon to poach shrimp garnish. Cover the pan in aluminum foil. Poach in oven for 25 minutes or until mousseline is set.

Prepare Lemon Chervil Beurre Blanc.

Bring reserved Court Bouillon to a boil and drop in shrimp. When water comes to a boil again, drain.

To plate: Spoon Beurre Blanc around the plate. Remove paper collar from fillets and place in center of a plate. Garnish perimeter with poached shrimp. Spoon caviar, if available, over the top of fillets. Serves 8.

COURT BOUILLON: Place water, salt and white wine in a large soup pot. Place all other ingredients in a cheesecloth bundle. Tie off with twine and add to liquids. Bring to a boil and simmer 30 minutes. Remove cheesecloth bundle and keep court bouillon hot.

SPINACH MOUSSELINE: Squeeze excess water from spinach. Place spinach, salt, pepper & cream into food processor or blender. Puree. In a separate bowl whisk the eggs together. Add puree to egg mixture. Fill each fillet center with mousseline.

LEMON CHERVIL BEURRE BLANC: In a saucepan reduce shallots, white wine and lemon juice to ¼ original volume. Strain reduction into top of a double boiler. Over medium heat slowly whisk in butter, one cube at a time, only adding the next after the previous has been incorporated. When all butter has been added, add chopped chervil, salt and pepper. The sauce should be kept warm, not hot, or it will break.

$\mathcal{Q}uiet$ and subtle or bold and exciting, celebrations always make a statement. At the North Carolina Museum of Art, celebrations are an integral part of daily operations. From exhibition openings to VIP dinners, cocktail parties to wedding receptions, the Museum provides an auspicious setting for any celebration. Tradition mandates that desserts underscore every celebration. Jennifer Hicks' talent delivers, with her sweet treats running the gamut from simple to elaborate — from Rodin White Chocolate Cherry Oatmeal Cookies to her White Chocolate Mandarin Mousse served in *tuile* cups, the crowning touch for Princess de Latour d'Auvergne's visit to Raleigh.

WHITE CHOCOLATE MANDARIN MOUSSE

A medley of rich fluffy mousse adorned with two fresh fruit sauces and served in Jennifer's Tuiles, page 151, shaped into either cups or as cookies on the side.

6	egg yolks
½	cup sugar
1	cup half-and-half
2½	cups heavy cream, divided
•	grated zest of 1 orange
¼	cup water
¼	cup Grand Marnier
1	tablespoon gelatin

RASPBERRY SAUCE:

2	pints fresh raspberries (or 4 cups frozen raspberries)
½	cup sugar
¼	cup orange juice
⅛	teaspoon ground cloves
¼	teaspoon cinnamon
1	tablespoon orange liqueur
1	teaspoon cornstarch
2	tablespoons water

PASSION FRUIT SAUCE:

1	cup passion fruit puree (or juice)
½	cup sugar
2	tablespoons lime juice
1	tablespoon cornstarch
2	tablespoons water

Make custard base by whisking together egg yolks and sugar in a heat-proof bowl. Put half-and-half, ½ cup of heavy cream and orange zest in a saucepan. Heat over medium-high heat until it just begins to boil. Remove from heat and pour ¼ of liquid into egg mixture. Whisk immediately. Add egg mixture back into remainder of the cream in saucepan and put back on stove over medium heat. Stir constantly with a wooden spoon until it thickens but don't over cook. The mixture should coat the back of a wooden spoon but still be smooth. Strain this mixture into another container and chill.

Lightly oil gelatin molds, ramekins or even sections of PVC pipe… whatever you want your form to be.

Put water and Grand Marnier into a metal bowl and sprinkle gelatin over it. Allow to bloom for at least 10 minutes. Meanwhile, whip remaining 2 cups of heavy cream to medium peaks, refrigerate until ready to assemble.

Over a hot water bath, warm gelatin mixture until it becomes liquid and clear. Whisk briskly into chilled custard and then quickly fold in whipped cream. (You must work quickly during the assembly period because gelatin sets rapidly). Portion into molds. Tap each portion before refrigerating to remove air bubbles, then cover and refrigerate.

To plate: Make concentric circles with sauces on each plate. To create a pattern in the sauce, draw a toothpick back and forth throughout the sauces. Unmold mousse into center of tuile cup, if desired, or place directly on plate and garnish with tuile cookies. Serves 8.

RASPBERRY SAUCE: Combine berries, sugar, juice, cloves, cinnamon and liqueur in a stainless steel saucepan. Put on stove over high heat and cook until boiling. In a small bowl stir cornstarch into water until dissolved. Add to boiling raspberry mixture and stir immediately. Let mixture continue to boil for about 30 more seconds then remove from stove. Press through a fine sieve to remove seeds and cool.

PASSION FRUIT SAUCE: Combine passion fruit puree, sugar and lime juice in a stainless steel pan. Heat on high and cook until boiling. In a small bowl combine cornstarch with water until dissolved. Add to boiling fruit and stir. Let boil 30 more seconds. Remove from heat and cool.

Roasted Chicken Salad Three Ways

Chicken salad has been a standard company dish in the South ever since the 1700s when Thomas Jefferson popularized a cold salad called salma gund, made of cold chicken or turkey, grapes, onions, anchovies, capers and sometimes ham, celery and parsley. From the 18th century forward, chicken salad became a favorite party food served at luncheons, teas and on buffets preceding an evening's ball. With this recipe, Andy Hicks provides a basic recipe which the cook can spice up in one of three ways. Enjoy!

BASIC RECIPE:

- 3 pounds boneless chicken breasts, cooked and fat removed

  (or 1 whole chicken)
- 4 stalks celery, diced
- 1 sweet bell pepper (preferably red, yellow, orange), chopped
- 1 bunch green onions, diced

BASIC RECIPE: In a large baking dish, toss chicken breasts in a bit of olive oil. Roast covered for about 25 minutes at 375° or until done.

Cool and dice into bite-size pieces. Stir in celery, bell pepper and green onions. Finish the Basic Recipe off in one of the following three ways.

Chicken Salad á La Provence

- 2 ripe tomatoes, seeded and diced
- ¼ cup chopped black olives
- ¼ cup chopped fresh Italian parsley
- 2 tablespoons chopped fresh rosemary
- • zest of 3 lemons
- 2 tablespoons extra virgin olive oil
- 1 tablespoon balsamic vinegar
- ½ teaspoon salt
- ¼ teaspoon pepper

CHICKEN SALAD Á LA PROVENCE: Prepared Basic Recipe. Stir in diced tomatoes, olives, parsley, rosemary and lemon zest. In a small bowl, combine olive oil, vinegar, salt and pepper. Stir into chicken salad. Adjust seasonings to taste. Serve in a baked puff pastry shell. Serves 8-10.

Barbecue Chicken Salad with Grilled Corn and Cilantro

- 3 ears fresh corn (2 cups)
- ¼ cup chopped cilantro
- ¼ cup thick barbecue sauce
- 2 tablespoons mayonnaise
- • salt and pepper

BARBECUE CHICKEN SALAD WITH GRILLED CORN AND CILANTRO: Prepare Basic Recipe. Brush corn with olive oil and grill. Cool, then cut off the cob. Add to Basic Recipe along with cilantro, barbecue sauce, mayonnaise, salt and pepper. Adjust seasonings to taste. Roll in a torilla. Serves 8-10.

Chicken Salad with Mango Chutney and Pistachio:

- ½ cup mango chutney
- 1 tablespoon mayonnaise
- ½ cup toasted pistachios
- • salt and pepper

CHICKEN SALAD WITH MANGO AND PISTACHIO: Prepare Basic Recipe. Toast pistachio nuts in at 350° for 10 minutes; roughly chop nuts. Add to Basic Recipe. Stir in chutney and mayonnaise. Season with salt and pepper. Serve on lettuce or toasted sourdough bread. Serves 8-10.

VERSATILE TUILE CUPS

French for "tile," a tuile is a thin crisp cookie that is placed over a rounded object (like a rolling pin) while still hot from the oven. Once cooled and stiff, the cookie resembles a curved roof tile. The classic tuile is made with crushed almonds but the cookie can also be flavored with orange, lemon, vanilla or other nuts. Larger tuiles may be made into cups by using ramekins as molds to cradle the mousse. Smaller tuiles are curled around rolling pins and served as accompaniments to this decadent dessert.

5	tablespoons butter, softened
½	cup confectioners' sugar
5	tablespoons sugar
¼	teaspoon vanilla extract
¼	teaspoon almond extract
⅛	teaspoon salt
2	egg whites
½	cup plus 1 tablespoon flour

Combine softened butter, sugars and extracts in a mixing bowl. Using paddle attachment, cream together until light and fluffy. Add salt and continue to mix. Add whites, mix just until incorporated, add flour, and mix until batter is smooth.

Preheat oven to 350°. Line a sheet pan with parchment paper.

Make template from a plastic lid or a thin piece of cardboard and cutting out a circular shape 1-inch larger than the bottom of ramekin or mold that holds mousse. Spread batter over template on parchment paper. Smooth batter to the level of template then gently remove the template, leaving the desired shape. Repeat this as many times as needed (8 for cups, 16 for sides).

Bake for 2 minutes, rotate the pan 180° then continue to bake, checking every 2 minutes until edges are golden. Since tuiles are very thin, and oven temperatures vary, it's best to stay close by while baking. When they are done, remove from oven and quickly lift from parchment paper, using small offset spatula and drape over a rolling pin or other desired form to shape the tuile. You can also allow the cookies to simply cool flat on the sheet pan. Store airtight for up to 1 day.

RODIN WHITE CHOCOLATE CHERRY OATMEAL COOKIES

White Chocolate and dried cherries, readily available at grocery stores, turn the ever popular oatmeal cookie into something even more delicious. These creations became very popular during NCMA's Rodin exhibition.

2½	cups old-fashioned oats, divided
2	cups flour
½	teaspoon salt
½	teaspoon baking powder
½	teaspoon cinnamon
1	teaspoon baking soda
1	cup white chocolate chunks
1	cup dried cherries
1	cup chopped pecans
1	cup butter
1	cup brown sugar
1	cup granulated sugar
2	eggs
2	teaspoons vanilla extract

Preheat oven to 375°. Lightly grease cookie sheet or line with parchment paper.

In a food processor grind to a powder 1 cup of oats. In a large bowl, sift together flour, salt, baking powder, cinnamon, and soda. Stir in ground oats along with remaining 1½ cups oats, white chocolate chunks, dried cherries and pecans.

In a large mixing bowl, combine butter and both sugars. Cream together on medium speed using paddle attachment. Slowly add eggs, then vanilla. Add flour mixture to butter mixture all at once; pulse machine until it is almost incorporated. Turn machine on first speed and mix for 30 seconds. Turn dough with a spoon to be sure all butter from the bottom is mixed in.

Using an ice cream scoop for large cookies or a tablespoon for small cookies, scoop and round into balls and place at least 2 inches apart on cookie sheet. Bake for 8-16 minutes, depending on size. Remove when edges are brown and centers still seem a little light. Makes 48 2½-3-inch cookies.

TROPICAL ANGEL CAKES WITH COCONUT MASCARPONE SHERBET

The basis for this exotic dessert is a light vanilla bean angel food cake. Coconut Mascarpone Sherbet and a fresh Caribbean Pineapple Confit cooked with allspice give this dessert a hint of the tropics. This stacked dessert is a knockout. It's even garnished with homemade Macadamia Nut Toffee. This dessert has a lot of steps, but Jennifer's methods are very friendly to the home cook.

8-9	large eggs
1	cup flour
1¼	cups sugar, divided
1½	teaspoons cream of tartar
1	vanilla bean
½	teaspoon vanilla extract
½	teaspoon almond extract

CARIBBEAN PINEAPPLE CONFIT:

1	ripe pineapple
1½	cups sugar
½	teaspoon ground allspice
½	cup water
½	cup Reisling or other sweet white wine
2	tablespoons brandy
•	pinch salt

Separate eggs to yield 1½ cups whites. Reserve yolks for another use.

Preheat oven to 325°. Sift flour 3 times. Add ¼ cup sugar to flour and sift once more; set aside.

In bowl of mixer, whip egg whites on high until they begin to foam. Add cream of tartar and continue to whip to soft peaks. With machine running slowly, add remaining 1 cup sugar. Scrape vanilla bean, and add to egg whites; reserve pod for garnish. Continue to beat up to 3 minutes more until egg whites form glossy stiff peaks.

Remove bowl from machine and gently fold in vanilla and almond extracts. Gently fold in flour until just incorporated. Spoon into a large 9-cup greased tube pan or pipe with a pastry bag into small mini-angel food pans. Bake for 30 minutes for large pan and about 9 minutes for minis.

When cake tops are dry and springy remove from oven. Invert large pan onto a thin necked bottle to cool; for mini-pans, invert onto ramekins or teacups. When completely cool, right pans and gently remove cake with a small metal spatula. Yields 1 large or 12 mini cakes.

To plate: Place mini-angel food cakes on the center of each plate. Spoon the confit around the cake. Form a generous scoop of Coconut Mascarpone Sherbet and gently place it on top of cake. Garnish with a shard of Macadamia Nut Toffee, a sliver of the vanilla bean pod, a slice of starfruit, some toasted flakes of fresh coconut (if available), and an edible leaf such as mint or lemon balm for a hint of green.

CARIBBEAN PINEAPPLE CONFIT: Peel and core pineapple and cut into small ¼-½-inch pieces. Combine in a heavy stainless steel saucepan with sugar, allspice, water, wine, brandy and salt. Bring to boil; reduce heat and simmer 30 minutes. When liquid is syrupy and pineapple translucent, remove from heat and cool to room temperature.

MACADAMIA NUT TOFFEE

The secret to toffee is caramelizing the sugar. The easy method yields a candy that may be eaten before it can ever be used as a garnish for Jennifer's Tropical Angel Cakes.

½	cup water
2	cups sugar
¾	cup chopped macadamia nuts

Line a cookie sheet with parchment paper. Coat lightly with baking spray and smear around with hands to create a thin film.

In a heavy saucepan over high heat bring water and sugar to a boil. Watch carefully and wash down sides of pans with water and a pastry brush, as needed to prevent sugar crystals from forming. Do not stir or disturb mixture as it cooks. When syrup turns a light amber color remove from heat. Gently stir in chopped nuts and pour out onto parchment paper.

Spread toffee out evenly with the back of a spoon or metal spatula. Let cool to room temperature. Break apart into large pieces and/or chop some to sprinkle over dessert.

COCONUT MASCARPONE SHERBET

Earmark this recipe to make and share with special friends. Yum!

SIMPLE SYRUP:

2   cups water

2½ cups sugar

2   tablespoons light corn
    syrup

MASCARPONE SHERBET BASE:

1   pound mascarpone cheese

1   14-ounce can coconut milk

1   cup milk

2½ cups simple syrup

1   tablespoon vanilla extract

1   tablespoon rum

Make Simple Syrup by combining water, sugar and corn syrup in a small saucepan. Bring to a boil and stir until sugar dissolves. Remove from heat and cool to room temperature before using. Store in refrigerator. Makes 3 cups.

To prepare Mascarpone Sherbet Base: In a large bowl gently stir mascarpone with a rubber spatula until it is softened and creamy. Fold coconut milk into cheese ½ cup at a time until smooth. Stir in milk, simple syrup, vanilla and rum, whisking until smooth and blended. Chill and then freeze according to ice cream maker's directions. Makes 2 quarts.

THE
BREAD BASKET

L.M.

BANANA NUT BREAD

This recipe makes one large loaf with good banana flavor and nutty richness.

½   cup vegetable oil
1   cup sugar
2   eggs, beaten
3   bananas, mashed
2   cups flour
1   teaspoon baking soda
½   teaspoon baking powder
½   teaspoon salt
3   tablespoons milk
½   teaspoon vanilla extract
½   cup chopped walnuts

Preheat oven to 350°. Grease a 9-inch x 5-inch loaf pan.

In a large bowl, beat oil and sugar together. Add beaten eggs and mashed bananas. Sift flour, baking soda, baking powder and salt together and add to batter along with milk and vanilla. Beat well. Stir in walnuts and pour into a greased loaf pan. Bake for 1 hour. Cool and store airtight. Makes 1 loaf.

SUSAN MCVEIGH
CARY, NC

FETA-DILL FLAT BREADS

These breads are so easy to prepare, you will make them again and again!

1   package frozen Bridgford White Rolls, defrosted
•   olive oil
•   coarse salt
•   crumbled feta cheese
•   fresh dill, chopped (dried dill may be substituted)

Preheat oven to 375°. Brush 2 large baking sheets with olive oil.

On a lightly floured surface, flatten each roll with a rolling pin to make a 5-inch circle. Place circles on oiled pans and brush with olive oil. Sprinkle with salt, feta cheese and dill. Bake in oven for 10-15 minutes. Breads should be browned and slightly puffed. Makes 16 breads.

SARAH'S HERB BREAD

Great with pasta dinner, grilled steaks or chicken or even by itself as a hearty snack. Deeelicious!

1   loaf French bread
1   cup butter or margarine, softened
2   tablespoons finely chopped green onion
2   tablespoons finely chopped black olives
2   tablespoons finely chopped parsley
1   teaspoon dried basil
½   teaspoon thyme
½   teaspoon marjoram
½   teaspoon tarragon

Preheat oven to 350°

Slice French loaf diagonally into ¾-inch slices, almost through to bottom crust. Blend softened butter with remaining ingredients; combine well. Spread sliced surfaces of bread with butter mixture. Place on a baking sheet. Bake at 350° for 15 minutes. Serve warm. Makes 1 loaf.

SARAH ALMBLAD
CARY, NC

AFTER **LUIS EGIDIO MELÉNDEZ** (Spanish), *STILL LIFE WITH BREAD, A JUG, AND A NAPKIN* (detail), after c. 1830

SWEDISH RYE BREAD

This light rye bread makes beautiful aromatic loaves.

2 packages yeast

3¼ cups warm water, divided

¼ cup vegetable shortening plus more for brushing on loaves

¼ cup molasses

⅓ cup brown sugar

2-3 teaspoons anise seed

2-3 teaspoons caraway seed

1 tablespoon grated orange rind

2-3 teaspoons salt

1 cup rye flour

5-6 cups white bread flour, see note

Dissolve yeast in ¼ cup water and let sit 5 minutes. In mixer bowl, place remaining water, shortening, molasses, brown sugar, anise seed, caraway seed, orange rind, salt and rye flour. Mix well. Stir in yeast and gradually add bread flour mixing until dough clings to beater or dough hook and comes away from sides of bowl. Place dough in large greased bowl in a warm place and let rise until double in bulk.

Preheat oven to 375°. Punch dough down, turn out on lightly floured surface and knead about 6-8 minutes, adding flour as needed. Place in 3 (3-inch x 7-inch) or 2 (9-inch x 5-inch) greased pans. Brush with shortening and let rise until dough is about 1-inch above pan. Bake for 20-30 minutes, then lower heat to 350° and bake for 15-20 minutes more. The bread will slip effortlessly from pans. Makes 3 loaves.

NOTE: For variety, 1 cup whole wheat flour may be substituted for one cup of white bread flour.

BETH CUMMINGS PASCHAL
RALEIGH, NC

CHALLAH BRAID

This flavorful bread is a snap to make in the food processor. The golden braid adds a festive touch to your Easter menu.

1 package yeast

½ cup warm water (105°-115°)

• pinch of sugar

2½ cups high gluten flour or bread flour

1 teaspoon salt

2 teaspoons fresh chopped rosemary

¼ cup olive oil

2 eggs, at room temperature

• egg wash, 1 egg mixed with 1 teaspoon water

Combine yeast, warm water and sugar; stir to dissolve. Let sit 5 minutes until it bubbles up.

In bowl of food processor fitted with metal blade, combine 2 cups flour, salt and rosemary. Add olive oil and yeast mixture; pulse a few times to combine. Add eggs and remaining ½ cup flour. Process until dough forms a ball. If dough feels sticky, add a tablespoon or so of flour until smooth to touch.

To knead in processor, let dough ball process for about 45 seconds. Remove from processor and knead a few times to form a smooth ball. Place in oiled bowl turning to coat.

Cover and let rise in a warm place until double in bulk, about 1 hour. Punch down; divide into 3 equal parts. Roll each into a 16-inch rope. Place side by side on lightly greased baking sheet. Starting in middle, braid toward one end, then braid toward the other. Pinch ends to seal and tuck under. Cover loosely and let rise for about 30 minutes.

Preheat oven to 400°. Brush lightly with egg wash. Bake about 25 minutes until golden brown and bottom sounds hollow when tapped. Makes 1 loaf serving 6.

Serve one of these three breads at almost any occasion — from top left: Swedish Rye Bread, Rosemary Mini-Muffins and Challah Bread.

ROSEMARY MINI-MUFFINS

Wonderful with a salad for lunch or with a cup of tea for an afternoon break.

2	teaspoons finely chopped fresh rosemary
½	cup golden raisins
¾	cup whole milk
5	tablespoons butter
1½	cups flour
½	cup sugar
¼	teaspoon salt
2	teaspoons baking powder
1	large egg

Preheat oven to 350°. Grease mini-muffin pans.

In a small saucepan, simmer rosemary, raisins and milk 2 minutes. Do not boil. Remove from heat, add butter, stir to melt, then cool. Sift flour, sugar, salt and baking powder together. Beat egg into milk mixture and stir into flour until just blended. Spoon into pans. Bake 15-20 minutes. Makes 30 mini-muffins.

CHERYL MAUPIN
RALEIGH, NC

MUFFIN TIN DONUTS

These delicious little cakes are a Pope family favorite.

⅓ cup shortening
1 cup sugar, divided
1 egg
1½ cups flour
1½ teaspoons baking powder
½ teaspoon salt
¼ teaspoon nutmeg
½ cup milk
6 tablespoons butter
1 tablespoon cinnamon

Preheat oven to 325°. Mix together shortening, ½ cup sugar and egg in a medium bowl. Sift together flour, baking powder, salt and nutmeg and add to batter alternating with milk.

Spoon batter into small muffin tins, filling cups ⅔ full. Bake for 8-10 minutes.

Melt butter in microwave in a small bowl. In a large plastic bag mix remaining ½ cup sugar and cinnamon. When muffins are cooked and cool enough to handle, dip in melted butter, then shake in sugar mixture to coat. Finish cooling. Makes 30-36.

CONNIE POPE
RALEIGH, NC

CALIFORNIA COFFEE CAKE

A healthy blend of dried fruits and nuts, certain to warm the hearts and tummies of family and friends.

1 cup dried figs
1½ cups dried apricots
½ cup butter
1 cup sugar
3 eggs
1 teaspoon vanilla extract
1¾ cups flour
1½ teaspoons baking powder
1 teaspoon baking soda
1 cup sour cream
1 cup slivered almonds, finely chopped
• juice of ½ lemon
2 tablespoons confectioners' sugar

Preheat oven to 350°. Grease a standard Bundt or tube pan.

Cut stems from dried figs if necessary and chop into small pieces. Chop apricots into small pieces. In a medium mixing bowl cream butter with sugar. Beat in eggs and vanilla. In a separate bowl combine flour, baking powder and soda. Add to butter mixture alternately with sour cream. Stir in figs, apricots and almonds. Pour batter into pan. Bake for 50 minutes. Remove and let cool 10 minutes before turning out.

Make a simple glaze by combining lemon juice and confectioners' sugar in a small bowl. Heat in microwave until bubbly and has a creamy texture. Pour over cake and let sit 10 minutes. Slice and serve warm. Serves 8.

MONKEY BREAD

An older recipe revived for younger generations. An easy quick way to make a sticky bun cake for overnight guests.

3 cans instant biscuits
⅔ cup sugar
2 teaspoons cinnamon
½ cup chopped nuts
½ cup raisins
½ cup butter
⅔ cup brown sugar

Preheat oven to 350°. Greaes a standard Bundt or tube pan.

Open 1 biscuit can at a time and cut dough into quarters. Put sugar and cinnamon into a paper or a resealable plastic bag. Add biscuit squares 1 at a time and shake to coat. Toss randomly into pan. Repeat with other cans layering cubes with nuts and raisins.

In a small saucepan melt butter. Stir in brown sugar and cook until sugar has dissolved but not boiling. Pour over biscuits. Bake for 25 minutes. Turn out onto a serving plate carefully as melted butter and syrup may run over plate. Serves 4-6.

VICKY TEMPLE HUBAND
RALEIGH, NC

CHERRY COFFEE CAKE

A breakfast or afternoon treat that will make a group of friends feel treasured. The moist cake is absolutely delicious.

2	cups flour
½	cup sugar
1	teaspoon baking powder
1	teaspoon baking soda
½	teaspoon salt
1	cup coconut
2	eggs
½	cup sour cream
½	cup milk
¼	cup butter, melted
½	teaspoon vanilla extract
1	12-ounce jar Smucker's cherry preserves

TOPPING:

¼	cup flour
¼	cup coconut
2	tablespoons sugar
2	tablespoons butter, softened

Preheat oven to 375°. Grease a 10-inch springform pan with cooking spray.

In large bowl combine flour, sugar, baking powder, soda, salt and coconut. Set aside. In separate medium bowl whisk together eggs, sour cream, milk, melted butter and vanilla. Add to flour mixture and stir just until combined. Pour into prepared pan, smoothing surface. Spread top with cherry preserves. Sprinkle topping on top of cherry preserves.

Bake for about 40 minutes, until toothpick in center comes out clean. Cool in pan 5 minutes. Remove pan sides. Serves 8-10.

TOPPING: In small bowl combine topping ingredients with a fork.

PECAN SWEET POTATO MUFFINS

A muffin sweetened with maple syrup and applesauce that's chock full of moist goodness. In addition to the sweet potatoes and pecans, they feature grated coconut and currants. Eat for breakfast or serve with an entrée like grilled pork.

1	cup whole wheat flour
1	cup flour
1	tablespoon baking powder
1¼	teaspoons cinnamon, divided
1¼	teaspoons ginger, divided
½	teaspoon salt
½	teaspoon nutmeg
¼	teaspoon ground cloves
2	eggs
½	cup milk
½	cup real maple syrup
1	cup applesauce
2	tablespoons vegetable oil
2	cups shredded, raw sweet potato
1	cup chopped pecans, divided
1	cup currants
½	cup flaked coconut

Preheat oven to 375°. Grease muffin pans.

In medium bowl combine whole wheat flour, flour, baking powder, 1 teaspoon cinnamon, 1 teaspoon ginger, salt, nutmeg and cloves. Set aside.

In separate bowl, whisk together the eggs, milk, maple syrup, applesauce and oil. Stir in the shredded sweet potatoes. Add to flour mixture and stir just to combine. Fold in ¾ cup of pecans, currants and coconut. Divide among prepared muffin cups filling each about ⅔ full.

In small bowl combine remaining ¼ cup pecans, ¼ teaspoon cinnamon and ¼ teaspoon ginger. Sprinkle over top of batter in pan.

Bake for 30 minutes until lightly browned and a toothpick inserted in center comes out clean. Cool in pan 5 minutes then remove. Serve warm. Makes 18.

BLUEBERRY CREAM SCONES

Fresh blueberries and a hint of lemon peel make these moist scones come to life.

2	cups flour
½	cup finely chopped pecans
¼	cup plus 2 tablespoons sugar, divided
1	tablespoon baking powder
½	teaspoon salt
¾	cup fresh blueberries, see note
1	tablespoon grated lemon peel
1¼	cups whipping cream
½	teaspoon cardamom
3	tablespoons unsalted butter, melted

Preheat oven to 425°.

Mix flour, chopped pecans, ¼ cup sugar, baking powder and salt in a large bowl. Stir in blueberries and lemon peel. Add whipping cream and stir just until dough forms. Do not over mix. Turn dough out onto a lightly floured surface; knead gently about 6 turns. Form dough into a 10-inch diameter, ½-inch thick round. Cut dough into 12 wedges. Transfer wedges to a lightly greased baking sheet, spacing evenly.

Combine remaining 2 tablespoons sugar with cardamom in a small bowl. Brush scones with melted butter, then sprinkle tops with sugar mixture. Bake until light golden brown, about 15 minutes. Cool slightly before serving. Makes 12.

NOTE: Frozen (unthawed) or even dried blueberries can be substituted for the fresh ones if desired.

BLUEBERRY OATMEAL MUFFINS

The perfect start to your day — blueberries and oatmeal.

1	cup fresh blueberries
2	tablespoons flour
¾	cup quick-cooking oats
1½	cups flour
¾	cup sugar
2	teaspoons baking powder
½	cup butter or margarine, melted
⅔	cup milk
1	egg

Preheat oven to 400°. Grease standard muffin cups.

Toss blueberries with 2 tablespoons flour and reserve. Mix oats, 1½ cups flour, sugar and baking powder together in large bowl. In small bowl, combine butter, milk and egg; mix into dry ingredients. Fold in reserved blueberry flour mixture. Do not overmix. Spoon into muffin cups, filling ¾ full. Bake for 20 minutes. Makes 12 muffins.

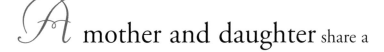

A mother and daughter share a peaceful moment in the late afternoon. Inspired by Primrose McPherson Paschal's *Beulah's Baby,* this repast of Pecan Sweet Potato Muffins (page 159) and Blueberry Cream Scones is perfect fare for both adults and children. The ceremony of serving tea provides a chance to applaud a child's company manners.

PRIMROSE MCPHERSON PASCHAL (American), *BEULAH'S BABY*, 1948

A North Carolina native, Primrose McPherson Paschal was much sought after for her discerning portraits and still lifes profuse with flowers in full bloom. This dignified portrait of a mother and child includes a still-life detail — a handsome bouquet that is a blessing of beauty in rather constrained circumstances. The artist uses the paired generations to poetically reflect on the segregated South of the mid-twentieth century.

PENNSYLVANIA BROWN BREAD

Devour this delicious bread right out of the oven. The unusual molasses flavor is complemented by a Maple Walnut Butter developed during testing of the cookbook's recipes.

½   cup sugar

1   rounded tablespoon shortening

1   egg

½   cup molasses

1   cup flour

1   cup whole wheat flour

1   teaspoon baking soda

1   teaspoon salt

1   cup buttermilk

....

MAPLE WALNUT BUTTER:

1   cup butter, softened

¾   cup real maple syrup

½   cup walnuts

Preheat oven to 350°. Grease an 8-inch loaf pan.

Cream sugar and shortening. Add eggs and molasses. In a separate bowl sift together flours, soda and salt. Add alternately with buttermilk. Pour into pan and bake 1 hour.

MAPLE WALNUT BUTTER: Put softened butter into food processor. Process a few seconds to whip. Slowly add maple syrup through feed tube with motor running, scraping down sides as needed, until well-combined. Add walnuts; pulse and process until chopped. Store in refrigerator for a few days, or freeze for longer storage. (Flavored butter freezes well when rolled into a log in wax paper. It can then be cut off as needed and the rest remains frozen.)

DORIS FREEMAN
RALEIGH, NC

BLACK WALNUT BREAD

Black walnuts are rich in oil; that is why there is no oil in the recipe. A wonderful texture and flavor for a tea sandwich toasted with butter.

1   cup black walnuts

4   cups flour

4   teaspoons baking powder

1   teaspoon salt

1   cup sugar

1   egg

2   cups milk

....

GINGERED ORANGE SPREAD:

1   3-ounce cream cheese

2   teaspoons crystallized ginger

1   tablespoon orange juice

•   sugar

Preheat oven to 350°. Grease two 9-inch x 5-inch loaf pans.

Place black walnuts in a ziploc bag and pound with a rolling pin until well crushed. Sift flour, baking powder, salt and sugar together. Beat egg with milk and pour into flour mixture. Blend well, then stir in nuts. Pour into 2 loaf pans and bake for 1 hour.

GINGERED ORANGE SPREAD: Let cream cheese come to room temperature until softened. Finely chop ginger. Combine both with orange juice until smooth. Sweeten to taste with touch of sugar.

HANNAH SCOGGIN
RALEIGH, NC

CLASSIC FOCACCIA

This focaccia is made on a cookie sheet although it's easily adapted to a round baking ban. It makes a great base for Genoa Shrimp, page 17, for an appetizer or for any food requiring a bread base, and the rectangular shape makes it easier to portion out.

1	envelope dry yeast
1	cup lukewarm water
⅓	cup olive oil
1	tablespoon fresh chopped rosemary
3	cups unbleached flour
1	teaspoon salt

In a small bowl, dissolve yeast in water; let stand 5 minutes. Heat olive oil with rosemary for 3 minutes on medium. Set aside to cool. In a large bowl combine flour, salt, yeast and olive oil until dough forms a ball. Turn out onto a floured board and knead 10 minutes, dusting with more flour as needed. The texture should be very smooth and elastic.

Oil bottom and sides of bread bowl with olive oil. Turn dough over in bowl to coat; cover and let rise in a warm place until doubled in size, 45-60 minutes.

Preheat oven to 375°. Dust a large cookie sheet 11½-inches x 17-inches with flour. Stretch dough out with your hands to form a rectangular shape and press out evenly with your fingertips to the pan's edges, leaving dough about ¼-inch thick overall. Bake 20 minutes or until lightly browned. Remove from pan with a spatula; cut into 16 squares, then cut squares in half diagonally to create finger food wedges.

THYME, ONION AND GARLIC MUFFINS

This savory muffin is easy to prepare and adds variety to a bread basket.

5	tablespoons butter
½	cup finely chopped onion
2	cloves garlic, minced
½	teaspoon dried thyme
1½	cups flour
½	cup whole wheat flour
1	tablespoon baking powder
¾	teaspoon salt
⅛	teaspoon pepper
1	large egg
1	cup buttermilk

Preheat oven to 400°. Grease muffin tins or use foil/paper baking cups.

Melt butter in small saucepan. Add onion and garlic and cook, stirring a few times until tender. Remove from heat and add thyme. Mix flours, baking powder, salt and pepper in large bowl. In small bowl beat egg and whisk in buttermilk. Add onion/thyme mixture. Make a well in dry ingredients and pour in egg mixture. Mix gently just until dry ingredients are moistened.

Fill muffin tins. Bake for 20-25 minutes until light brown. Cool in pans 15 minutes before turning out onto a rack. Makes 12-14.

NOTE: An easy, consistent way to fill standard muffin tins is by using an ice cream scoop.

CORNMEAL ANGEL BISCUITS

One batch of these may only serve the cook!

1	package dry yeast
¼	cup warm water (105°-115°)
1	cup buttermilk
1½	cups self-rising flour
1¼	cups self-rising cornmeal
½	cup vegetable shortening
1	tablespoon molasses

Dissolve yeast in warm water and set aside. Microwave buttermilk about 45 seconds to take off chill. Place flour, cornmeal and vegetable shortening in mixer bowl. Using lowest speed, blend. Mix buttermilk, yeast and molasses together; add to flour mixture. Blend, then increase speed and beat on high about 10 seconds. Scrape into a clean bowl, cover with plastic wrap and refrigerate overnight.

Preheat oven to 400°. To bake, turn dough out onto a well-floured board. Knead lightly, making several turns to smooth out dough. Roll to a thickness of ½-inch and cut into small 2-inch rounds with a floured biscuit cutter. Bake on a lightly greased cookie sheet for 12-14 minutes. Makes 15.

NOTE: This recipe can easily be doubled. Use only 1 package of yeast, but double everything else.

A symbol of hospitality, baked goods flourish in Southern kitchens where bread-making is an art form. New neighbors are taken gifts of muffins or freshly baked biscuits. There isn't a more welcoming gift than a warm loaf tied with a bow.

HERB BISCUITS
Flaky and light, bursting with herbal highlights.

2	tablespoons butter, divided
¼	cup chopped onion
½	teaspoon oregano
½	teaspoon thyme
½	teaspoon chopped rosemary
1½	cups flour
2	teaspoons baking powder
½	teaspoon salt
¼	cup shortening
1	egg, lightly beaten
¼	cup milk
2	tablespoons Parmesan or Romano cheese

Preheat oven to 450°. In a small pan, melt 1 tablespoon butter of medium heat. Sauté onion, oregano, thyme and rosemary.

In a medium bowl, blend flour, baking powder and salt. Cut in shortening. Combine onion herb mixture with egg and milk and add to flour all at once. Stir lightly until dough just comes together.

Turn out onto a floured surface, knead lightly, just enough to make dough workable. Roll out to ¼-inch thickness. Cut with a floured 3-inch biscuit cutter and place on a greased baking pan.

Melt remaining 1 tablespoon butter and brush tops of biscuits. Sprinkle cheese over the tops. Bake for 12-15 minutes. Serve warm. Makes 12-15.

HEYWARD H. MCKINNEY, JR.
RALEIGH, NC

MADEIRA FRUIT BREAD
If you enjoy panettone, this bread is for you. Toast slices for fuller flavor.

¾	cup unsalted butter, softened
1	cup sugar
4	eggs
3	tablespoons Madeira
2	teaspoons vanilla extract
•	pinch of salt
1¾	cups flour
⅓	cup diced dried dates
⅓	cup diced dried apricots
⅓	cup diced dried figs
1	cup chopped walnuts

Preheat oven to 350°. Grease and flour a 9-inch x 4-inch loaf pan.

Cream butter and sugar until well combined. Add eggs 1 at a time, beating well after each addition. Beat in Madeira, vanilla and pinch of salt. Add flour, diced dates, apricots, figs and walnuts and mix well.

Pour batter into prepared loaf pan. Bake about 1 hour, or until golden. Let stand for 10 minutes, invert onto rack and cool. Makes 1 loaf.

DESSERTS
TO
CELEBRATE

ANGEL BAVARIAN CAKE

This heavenly concoction made with a prepared angel food cake may be made richer still by frosting with more whipped cream. Just as good less the fat calories, the cake may also be covered with toasted coconut.

4	eggs
1	cup sugar
2	tablespoons flour
•	pinch salt
2	cups milk
2	packages plain gelatin
½	cup cold water
½	teaspoon almond extract
2	cups heavy cream
1	angel food cake
2	cups toasted coconut, optional

Beat egg yolks with sugar until light; add milk, flour and salt. Transfer to a small saucepan and cook over medium heat until custard coats spoon, stirring constantly. (It will still be thin.)

Sprinkle gelatin over cold water; let sit 2 minutes to soften. Add to the hot custard, stirring well until gelatin is completely dissolved. Stir in almond extract. Set aside to cool.

Beat egg whites until stiff peaks. In a separate bowl, beat heavy cream to firm peaks. When custard is cool, fold in whipped cream and egg whites.

Cut the angel food cake into thirds, crosswise, to make 3 layers. Grease a standard 9-cup tube pan and line bottom with ⅓ cake. Spoon ⅓ custard cream over cake and repeat with remaining cake layers and custard. Cover and refrigerate cake overnight.

To toast coconut: Spread out on a baking sheet and bake in a 300° oven for 15-20 minutes. Turn after 8-10 minutes, and keep a watchful eye to not overcook.

Loosen cake gently with knife, carefully lift out and transfer to a serving plate. Press toasted coconut over top and sides of cake before slicing. Serves 12-16.

JEAN LADD
CARY, NC

CRANBERRY BUTTERMILK CAKE

A delicious cake to have on hand to slice for dessert or breakfast. It has the texture of a fruit cake with the moisture of a simpler spice cake.

2½	cups flour
1	cup sugar
1	teaspoon salt
1	teaspoon baking soda
1	teaspoon baking powder
1	cup chopped pecans
1	cup chopped dates
2	cups fresh cranberries, see note
•	grated rind of two oranges
2	eggs
1	cup buttermilk
¾	cup oil

ORANGE GLAZE:

¾	cup orange juice
¾	cup sugar

Preheat oven to 325°. Sift flour once, then measure and sift again with sugar, salt, baking soda and baking powder. Fold in pecans, dates, cranberries and orange rind.

Beat eggs with buttermilk and oil. Add to dry ingredients and blend well. Pour into a greased and floured 9-cup tube pan. Bake 1 hour or until done.

Pour Orange Glaze over hot cake in pan, and let stand 30 minutes. For best results, gently prick a few holes with a fork or a skewer to help glaze seep into cake. Remove cake from pan, cool and serve with whipped cream.

NOTE: If cranberries are not in season, plump 2 cups dried cranberries by pouring boiling water just enough to cover and let set a few minutes. Drain when ready to fold into cake. Serves 12.

ORANGE GLAZE: Heat juice and sugar together until dissolved. Do not boil.

SHARON ROHRBACH
RALEIGH, NC

PREVIOUS PAGES: **POMPEO GIROLAMO BATONI** (Italian), *THE TRIUMPH OF VENICE* (detail), 1737

BROWN SUGAR POUND CAKE

A recipe published in NCMA's original cookbook, this classic was a regular State Fair winner 25 years ago. Too good not to pass on to a new generation of Museum fans.

1 cup butter

½ cup solid vegetable shortening

1 pound light brown sugar

¾ cup white sugar

5 eggs

3 cups flour

½ teaspoon baking powder

1 teaspoon salt

1 cup milk

1 cup chopped walnuts

Preheat oven to 325°. Grease and flour a standard tube pan.

Cream shortenings and sugar together in large mixer bowl. Add eggs 1 at a time, beating well after each addition. Sift flour, salt, and baking powder together, and add alternately with milk. Stir in walnuts. Pour into pan. Bake for 1½ hours. Cool on rack and gently remove from pan. Serves 10-12.

HELEN BARNES CHAMBLISS
ROCKY MOUNT, NC

NANCIE'S CARROT CAKE

This popular cake is baked in a Bundt pan for the ultimate ease, great for serving a crowd.

1⅓ pounds carrots or a 1-pound bag peeled baby carrots

2 cups sugar

1½ cups corn oil

4 eggs

2½ cups flour

2 teaspoons baking powder

2 teaspoons baking soda

1 teaspoon salt

1½ teaspoons cinnamon

1½ teaspoons nutmeg

1 cup raisins

1 cup chopped pecans or walnuts

CREAM CHEESE FROSTING:

1 8-ounce package cream cheese, softened

4 tablespoons butter, room temperature

2 cups sifted confectioners' sugar

2 teaspoons vanilla extract

Preheat oven to 325°.

Grate carrots to measure 4 cups. Combine sugar and oil in mixer bowl and beat. Add eggs 1 at a time, beating well after each. Sift flour, baking powder, baking soda, salt, cinnamon and nutmeg together. Gradually add to oil mixture while beating. Fold in carrots, raisins and nuts. Pour into greased and floured Bundt pan and bake for 1 hour. Remove from oven and let cool 10 minutes before turning out on a rack. Once cool, ice with Cream Cheese Frosting.

For a layer cake, grease and flour three 8- or 9-inch pans or line the bottoms with greased wax paper circles. Bake for 25-30 minutes. Remove from pan and cool. Ice with Cream Cheese Frosting. Serves 12.

CREAM CHEESE FROSTING: Place cream cheese and butter in mixer bowl and beat well. Stir in sugar and vanilla. Beat until smooth.

NANCIE A. WAGNER
RALEIGH, NC

*D*essert **is the ultimate** comfort food. Cookies and milk after school, a moist slice of cake or a piece of pie after a holiday feast, a yummy pudding or custard after a home-cooked meal, the sweetness of summer fruits, and anything chocolate — these are the foods that stir memories.

SOUTHERN COMFORT CAKE
A wonderful stand-by cake to serve with tea or to finish a holiday meal. Serve with or without ice cream for any occasion.

1 box yellow cake mix
1 3.4-ounce box instant vanilla pudding
4 eggs
½ cup vegetable oil
½ cup Southern Comfort whiskey

SOUTHERN COMFORT GLAZE:

4 tablespoons butter
½ cup sugar
2 tablespoons water
¼ cup Southern Comfort whiskey

Preheat oven to 325°. Grease and flour a standard Bundt pan.

In medium bowl combine cake mix, pudding, eggs, oil and Southern Comfort. Beat at medium speed for 2 minutes. Put into prepared pan and bake for 1 hour. Cool and invert onto plate.

Prick top with toothpick or fork. Brush cake on top and sides with half the Southern Comfort Glaze. Cool. Reheat glaze and brush top and sides with remaining glaze. Serves 8.

SOUTHERN COMFORT GLAZE: In a small saucepan, heat all ingredients over medium heat. Stir to dissolve sugar and brush over tops and sides of cake.

EVELYN (EVIE) DURBIN
CARY, NC

RUMMED WREATH CAKE
This moist cake is akin to a savarin, a rum-flavored cake named after Brillat-Savarin, a famous 18th-century food writer. Baked in a large ring mold, the center of the cake can be filled with fresh fruit or whipped cream.

½ cup butter
½ cup sugar
3 eggs, separated
¼ cup milk
1 cup sifted all-purpose flour
1½ teaspoons baking powder

RUM SYRUP:

1 cup water
½ cup sugar
¼ cup dark rum

Preheat oven to 375°. Grease and flour a 1-quart ring mold. In medium bowl, blend butter and sugar until light and creamy. Beat in egg yolks and milk. Combine flour and baking powder and gradually add to mixture, stirring well. In small bowl, beat egg whites until stiff and fold into batter. Pour into pan. Bake 20 minutes. Make Rum Syrup and pour over cooled cake. Serves 6.

RUM SYRUP: Bring water and sugar to a boil. Remove from heat and stir until sugar has dissolved. When syrup has cooled to lukewarm, stir in the rum (add more if you like).

MRS. FORREST GETZEN
RALEIGH, NC

MOTHER'S GINGERBREAD LAYER CAKE

Moist layers of gingerbread are sandwiched by creamy lemon icing.

1 cup honey
1 teaspoon ginger
1 teaspoon cinnamon
½ teaspoon ground cloves
2½ cups sifted flour
1 teaspoon baking powder
½ teaspoon salt
½ cup butter
1 teaspoon baking soda
½ cup light brown sugar, firmly packed
• zest of 1 lemon
1 egg
1 cup buttermilk

LEMON ICING:

½ cup butter, softened
1 pound confectioners' sugar
• juice of one lemon
1 tablespoon milk

Preheat oven to 350°. Grease two 8-inch cake pans. Line with waxed paper.

In a small saucepan, combine honey, ginger, cinnamon and cloves; bring to a boil. Remove from heat and cool.

Sift flour with baking powder and salt.

In a medium bowl, cream butter, baking soda and sugar. Add honey mixture and beat well. Add lemon zest and egg; beat well. Alternately stir in flour and buttermilk. Pour into cake pans. Bake about 35 minutes.

Cool in pans 5 minutes, then turn out on racks to cool. Cool completely before icing. Serves 10-12.

LEMON ICING: In a bowl, beat together butter, sugar and lemon juice. Add milk to achieve spreadable consistency.

DRIED PLUM SPICE CAKE WITH BUTTERMILK GLAZE

Prunes have had a facelift and are now being called dried plums on new packaging. Whatever they're called, they're delicious. Destined to be a crowd pleaser, take this to your next covered dish gathering.

2 cups flour
1 teaspoon baking soda
1 teaspoon cinnamon
1 teaspoon allspice
3 eggs
1 cup vegetable oil
1½ cups sugar
1 teaspoon vanilla extract
1 cup buttermilk
1 cup chopped dried plums (prunes)
1 cup chopped nuts

BUTTERMILK GLAZE:

4 tablespoons butter
1 cup sugar
½ cup buttermilk
1 tablespoon white corn syrup
1 teaspoon vanilla extract
½ teaspoon baking soda

Preheat over to 350°. Grease a 9-inch x 12-inch baking pan.

Sift flour, baking soda, cinnamon and allspice together in a medium bowl.

In a mixing bowl beat eggs, oil, sugar and vanilla. Add sifted ingredients alternately with buttermilk. Do not beat just blend. Fold in dried plums and nuts. Pour into pan and bake 40-45 minutes.

While cake is baking, prepare Buttermilk Glaze. Pour over cake while both are hot. Serves 12.

BUTTERMILK GLAZE: Combine butter, sugar, buttermilk, corn syrup, vanilla and baking soda in deep saucepan over medium heat. Stir until it comes to a boil. Adjust heat to maintain a low boil. Boil until 220° is reached on candy thermometer.

PEGGY ALLGOOD
CARY, NC

GREEK COCONUT LEMON CAKE

This unique cake is easily made in the food processor, baked then soaked with rich lemon syrup.

½   cup butter
1   cup sugar
4   eggs
1   cup self-rising flour
2   cups flaked coconut

LEMON SYRUP:

1   cup sugar
½   cup water
•   juice and grated rind of 2 lemons

Preheat oven to 375°. Grease an 8-inch x 8-inch glass baking dish.

In a food processor, cream butter and sugar until fluffy. Add eggs, blending well after each addition. Add flour and coconut, then pulse to combine. Pour into baking dish. Bake for 10 minutes, then lower heat to 300° and bake another 40 minutes.

Make Lemon Syrup while cake is baking.

Remove cake from oven and let cool for 5 minutes. Pour syrup over top. Serve with whipped cream, ice cream or lemon curd. Serves 6-8.

LEMON SYRUP: Place sugar, water, lemon juice and grated rind in small saucepan. Bring to boil, stirring only until sugar has dissolved. Reduce heat and simmer 5 minutes.

CHERYL MAUPIN
RALEIGH, NC

OLD-FASHIONED POUND CAKE

A rich, moist, lemon-flavored pound cake.

1   cup butter, softened
½   cup solid shortening
3   cups sugar
5   eggs
2   teaspoons lemon extract, see note
3   cups all-purpose flour
½   teaspoon baking powder
½   teaspoon salt
1   cup milk
•   confectioners' sugar, optional

Preheat oven to 350°. Grease and flour a standard 9-cup tube pan.

In mixer bowl, cream butter, shortening and sugar together. Add eggs one at a time, beating well after each addition. Stir in lemon extract.

Sift flour, baking powder and salt together. Add alternately with milk to batter. Pour into tube pan and bake for 1 hour and 20 minutes or until toothpick comes out clean. Cool in pan 5-10 minutes, then turn out onto rack to cool completely. When cool, cake may be dusted with confectioners' sugar. Serves 12.

NOTE: As a variation, orange extract may be substituted for lemon extract, or use fresh lemon juice if you have neither on hand.

BERTIE STEVENS
RALEIGH, NC

*A*unt **Pauline's White Chocolate** Coconut Cake is three layers of lacy perfection. At your next book club or bridge party, volunteer to bring dessert and be prepared to rake in the compliments.

AUNT PAULINE'S WHITE CHOCOLATE COCONUT CAKE

White chocolate and buttermilk give the cake layers added dimension before being frosted by a frothy coconut icing.

4	ounces white chocolate
½	cup water
1	cup softened butter
1¾	cups sugar, divided
4	eggs, separated
2¼	cups cake flour
1	teaspoon baking soda
1	cup buttermilk

COCONUT ICING:

1¼	cups sugar
1	tablespoon light corn syrup
⅓	cup plus 1 tablespoon water
3	egg whites
1	teaspoon vanilla extract
2	3.5-ounce cans coconut, divided

Preheat oven to 350°. Grease and flour three 9-inch cake pans.

In double boiler, melt chocolate with water, stirring frequently; cool.

In mixer bowl, place butter and 1½ cups sugar, beat well (5-10 minutes). Add egg yolks 1 at a time, beating well after each. Add cooled chocolate mixture. Sift flour and baking soda together and add to creamed mixture alternating with buttermilk, beginning and ending with flour.

In separate clean bowl beat egg whites until soft peaks. Add remaining ¼ cup sugar, about 1 tablespoon at a time, beating until stiff. Fold egg whites into batter. Pour into cake pans. Bake for 25-30 minutes, until a toothpick inserted in middle comes out clean. Cool 5 minutes, then remove from pans and cool completely before icing. Serves 12.

COCONUT ICING: Combine sugar, syrup and water in heavy saucepan. Stir over low heat until sugar dissolves. Boil gently for 5-7 minutes until syrup spins a thread when dropped from a spoon or forms a ribbon when dropped in cold water. Beat egg whites to soft peaks and add hot syrup in a thin stream while still beating. Add vanilla. Beat until stiff and glossy, about 2 minutes more. Fold 1 can coconut into icing. Reserve other can for sprinkling over top and sides of cake.

LAWRENCE J. WHEELER
CHAPEL HILL, NC

COOKY SHORTBREAD WINKS

A family favorite for holiday treats. They may be formed into a variety of shapes, dipped into chocolate and then again into nuts, coconut or colored sugar. Be creative!

1	cup butter or margarine
¾	cup confectioners' sugar
1	tablespoon vanilla extract
2	cups flour
¾	teaspoon salt
½	cup old-fashioned oats
½	cup semi-sweet chocolate chips
¼	cup milk
•	chopped nuts
•	coconut
•	colored sugars

Preheat oven to 325°.

In a mixing bowl, cream butter, sugar and vanilla. Stir in flour, salt and oats. Chill slightly. Form teaspoonfuls of dough into shapes with your fingers: balls, crescents, triangles, bars, stars and disks. Bake on ungreased cookie sheets for 20-25 minutes. Watch carefully so as not to over bake. Cool on racks.

In a double boiler or microwave melt chocolate in milk stirring until smooth. Dip the rounded sides of the cooled cookies into chocolate and then into nuts, coconut or colored sugar. Place on waxed paper until chocolate has set. Store in an airtight container. Makes 48 cookies.

CAROLYN STIDHAM
RALEIGH, NC

ZUCCHINI BROWNIES

Moist, rich, easy to make brownies.

1	cup flour
1	teaspoon baking powder
½	teaspoon salt
½	teaspoon baking soda
1	cup grated zucchini
½	cup butter
1	tablespoon water
1	cup sugar
1	egg
1	teaspoon vanilla extract
1	cup mini semi-sweet chocolate chips
•	confectioners' sugar

Preheat oven to 350°. Grease a 9-inch x 9-inch square baking pan.

Sift together flour, baking powder, salt and baking soda; set aside. Grate zucchini and measure. Place in paper toweling, press to remove moisture and set aside.

Melt butter with water. In a small bowl, combine sugar, egg and vanilla. Add to melted butter. Beat well. Slowly add flour mixture. Stir in zucchini and pour into pan. Sprinkle chocolate chips on top. Bake for 35 minutes. Before serving dust with confectioners' sugar. Makes 16.

EMILY S. ROSEN
RALEIGH, NC

NEIMAN-MARCUS BARS

A coveted recipe as outstanding as the retail name.

1	box pound cake mix
½	cup butter
3	eggs, divided
1	cup chopped pecans
1	pound confectioners' sugar
1	8-ounce cream cheese

Preheat oven to 350°. Grease a 9-inch x 13-inch pan with butter.

In medium bowl with electric mixer combine cake mix, butter, 1 egg and pecans. Press mixture into pan bottom.

In another bowl, beat with mixer to combine sugar, cream cheese and 2 remaining eggs. Spread over cake mixture. Bake for 35-40 minutes or until golden brown. Cool and cut into bars. Makes 16 bars.

SUE HENDRIX
RAEFORD, NC

ACCORDION SWEETS

This unusual shaped cookie is made in an "accordion" created by aluminum foil. Almost like a pound cake "cookie", these would be pretty with a dish of fruit or ice cream.

¾ cup butter, softened
¾ cup sugar
2 eggs
1 teaspoon vanilla extract
½ teaspoon salt
1¼ cups sifted flour
• roll of heavy-duty aluminum foil

Make two aluminum foil "accordions". To make accordion, fold 1 yard (36-inches x 18-inches) of aluminum foil in half lengthwise to double thickness. Fold foil into 1-inch accordion pleats. Repeat process for second accordion.

Preheat oven to 325°. Cream butter and sugar. Add eggs, vanilla and salt and beat well. Gradually add flour.

Place accordions on baking sheet. Spray generously with baking spray. Allowing two cookies per fold, drop dough by teaspoonfuls about 6 inches apart into folds. Bake 25-30 minutes until golden on edges. Cool completely before removing from foil. Flip foil and use other side when making next batch. Makes 48 cookies.

HANNAH SCOGGIN
RALEIGH, NC

MACADAMIA RASPBERRY SHORTBREAD

Classic shortbread becomes even more decadent with hints of macadamia nuts, raspberry jam and chocolate.

½ cup macadamia nuts
¼ cup sugar, divided
¾ cup unsalted butter
½ teaspoon vanilla extract
1 cup flour
¾ cup raspberry jam (with seeds)
⅓ cup chocolate chips

Preheat oven to 350°. Grease an 8-inch or 9-inch square baking pan.

Put nuts and 2 tablespoons of the sugar into bowl of food processor fitted with metal blade. Process until well ground. In mixer bowl, cream butter with remaining 2 tablespoons sugar. Add nut/sugar mixture and continue beating until light and fluffy. Beat in vanilla. Stir in flour just until well-combined. Press into baking pan. Bake 30-35 minutes until lightly browned. Cool.

Spread top of shortbread with raspberry jam.

Melt chocolate chips in small pan or microwave, stirring frequently. Drizzle over shortbread using a small cone made from parchment paper, or simply use a spoon. Let set. Cut into 16 squares.

MARBLE SQUARES

Rich cookie bars, brimming with nuts and marbled with chocolate.

2½ cups sifted flour
1 teaspoon baking soda
1 teaspoon salt
½ cup butter, room temperature
¾ cup sugar
¾ cup packed brown sugar
1 teaspoon vanilla extract
½ teaspoon water
2 eggs
1 cup chopped pecans or walnuts
1 12-ounce package chocolate chips

Preheat oven to 350°. Grease a large baking pan or cookie sheet (15-inch x 10½-inch).

In a small bowl, blend flour, baking soda, and salt; set aside. In a large bowl, cream butter and sugars, vanilla and water. Beat in eggs. Gradually stir in flour mixture and then nuts.

Press the dough into pan. Sprinkle chocolate chips over top. Bake for 5 minutes. Open oven door and with a knife marble the chocolate into mix. Continue baking 20 minutes. Cut into squares when cool. Makes 25.

MARY LIB TRENT
CARY, NC

CLASSIC LEMON BARS

Lemon bars spread on a crust akin to a shortbread are a legacy recipe that must be passed on from the Museum's first cookbook.

1 cup butter or margarine
½ cup confectioners' sugar
2 cups flour

. . . .

LEMON FILLING:
4 eggs, well-beaten
½ teaspoon salt
2 cups sugar
½ tablespoon grated lemon rind
½ cup lemon juice
4 tablespoons flour
1 teaspoon baking powder
• confectioners' sugar for topping

Preheat oven to 350°. Cream together butter, sugar and flour. Spread into an ungreased 9-inch x 13-inch x 2-inch pan. Cook for 15 minutes or until brown. Remove from oven and lower temperature to 325°.

Meanwhile prepare Lemon Filling. In a medium bowl, beat eggs. Blend in salt, sugar, lemon rind and juice, flour and baking powder. Spread on top of cooked pastry. Bake for 30 minutes. Remove from oven and sprinkle with confectioners' sugar. Cool thoroughly before cutting. Store in refrigerator. Makes 30-40 bars.

MRS. FEREBEE TAYLOR
CHAPEL HILL, NC

SPICY DATE COOKIES

These cookies are crunchy and delicious, and destined to be frequently made.

½ cup butter, softened
1¾ cups light brown sugar, packed
1 egg
¼ teaspoon baking soda
2 tablespoons hot water
1¾ cups sifted flour
2 teaspoons baking powder
¼ teaspoon salt
¼ teaspoon ginger
¼ teaspoon cinnamon
¼ teaspoon nutmeg
¼ teaspoon ground cloves
½ teaspoon vanilla extract
1 cup finely chopped dates
1 cup chopped walnuts

Preheat oven to 350°. Lightly grease a cookie sheet

In a mixing bowl, cream butter and brown sugar. Beat in egg. Dissolve baking soda in hot water. Add to butter along with flour, baking powder, salt, ginger, cinnamon, nutmeg and cloves. Add vanilla.

Put finely chopped dates and walnuts together in a separate small bowl. Form dough with hands into small balls about 1-inch in diameter. Roll in date nut mixture. Place on cookie sheet 3 inches apart. Using the base of your hand, press until flattened. Bake 10-12 minutes. Remove from oven when light brown. Transfer to wire rack to cool. Makes 36.

KARLA ARUNDEL
RALEIGH, NC

Three tiers of fabulous finger foods — from top left: Spicy Date Cookies; Cooky Shortbread Winks; Zucchini Brownies; Sarah's Double Chocolate Cookies; Accordion Sweets.

VIENNESE CRESCENTS

A Christmas favorite from Austria. The crescent shape is a commemorative symbol, taken from the Turkish flag, when the Turks invaded Vienna in 1500 and were defeated by Austria. This recipe works well in a food processor.

1   cup ground almonds
1   cup butter
½   cup sugar
2   cups flour
1   teaspoon vanilla extract
•   XXX confectioners' sugar

Preheat oven to 300°.

When using a processor, first grind almonds finely. Remove from bowl and measure. Using same bowl, cream butter and sugar well. Add almonds, flour, and vanilla; process until dough forms a ball.

When using a mixer, cream butter and sugar well, add nuts (which have been finely ground), flour and vanilla, mix well.

Mold dough into cylinders about 3-inches long, 1-inch wide and ½-inch thick. Roll in confectioners' sugar, place on lightly sprayed cookie sheet and shape into crescents. Bake 30-35 minutes, checking bottoms to be sure they do not brown too much. When cooled, roll in confectioners' sugar again. Makes 36 cookies.

LILLIAN MAXWELL
RALEIGH, NC

ANONYMOUS (Spanish), A MAN SCRAPING CHOCOLATE, c. 1680-1780

Spanish conquistadors brought chocolate from the New World to Europe in the early sixteenth century. During the seventeenth and eighteenth centuries, hot chocolate was a favorite drink of people of all social classes in Spain. This engaging image shows a young man kneeling as he scrapes a large slab of chocolate paste on a *metate*, a stone tool used by natives of Mexico and Guatemala for grinding corn and probably, like chocolate, introduced into Spain from the New World.

SARAH'S DOUBLE CHOCOLATE COOKIES

Fudgy chocolate treats are easily made in the food processor — no beating or stirring required.

5	ounces semi-sweet chocolate
½	cup dark brown sugar, packed
½	cup sugar
½	cup unsalted butter, room temperature
1	egg
2	teaspoons vanilla extract
¾	cup plus 2 tablespoons unbleached flour
½	teaspoon baking soda
•	pinch salt
1	cup chocolate chips
½	cup chopped pecans, toasted

Preheat oven to 350°.

Break chocolate into small pieces and combine with sugars in bowl of food processor fitted with metal blade. Chop using on/off turns and then process 1-2 minutes until chocolate is as fine as sugar.

Cut butter into 4 pieces, add and blend 30 seconds. Add egg and vanilla and process 1 minute stopping as necessary to wipe side of bowl. Add flour, baking soda, salt, chocolate chips and pecans. Mix with 2-3 on/off turns. Run spatula around sides to loosen dough. Blend again with 2 on/off turns.

Drop by rounded teaspoons on ungreased cookie sheet 1½ inches apart. Bake on center rack of oven for 8 minutes. Remove and cool in pans for 3 minutes before transferring to rack to cool completely. Makes 36 cookies.

Sarah J. Warden
Wilson, NC

FRENCH SILK PIE

A light meringue crust with a taste of crunchy nuts holds a rich chocolate filling.

MERINGUE CRUST:

3	eggs whites
¼	teaspoon cream of tartar
⅛	teaspoon salt
¾	cup sugar
½	teaspoon vanilla extract
1	cup finely chopped nuts

CHOCOLATE FILLING:

4	ounces sweet baking chocolate
3	tablespoons water
1	tablespoon brandy
2	cups heavy cream, divided
¼	cup confectioners' sugar

Preheat oven to 350°. Grease a 10-inch pie plate.

To make meringue crust, beat egg whites with cream of tartar and salt until foamy. Gradually add in sugar and vanilla. Beat until peaks form; fold in nuts. Pour into pie plate and mold into shape. Bake for 1 hour. Let cool.

To make Chocolate Filling: Melt chocolate with water. Cool. Add brandy. Whip 1 cup cream and fold into chocolate. Spread on cooled crust.

Whip remaining 1 cup cream and sweeten with confectioners' sugar. Spread on top of pie. Serves 8.

Gilda McKinney
Raleigh, NC

Chocolate, **the most beloved** food, makes other foods taste even better — pretzels, nuts, strawberries, even zucchini. Bake a batch of Sarah's Double Chocolate Cookies (page 179), a pan of Chocolate Temptation Squares (page 182) or Zucchini Brownies (page 174), wrap them up and deliver them to a friend with a smile.

INTENSE CHOCOLATE CAKE

Heads up! Chocolate lovers will add this recipe to their list of favorites.

6	ounces German sweet or imported chocolate
¾	cup unsalted butter
4	eggs, separated
¾	cup sugar, divided
¼	cup flour
2	tablespoons ground almonds
¾	teaspoon cinnamon
1	teaspoon vanilla extract
¼	teaspoon cream of tartar

GLAZE:

3½	ounces chocolate
3	tablespoons unsalted butter
3	tablespoons coffee
1-2	teaspoons sugar (optional)

Preheat oven to 375°. Butter an 8-inch springform pan. Line with wax paper; butter and flour pan.

In microwave or double boiler, melt chocolate and butter together and cool. Beat egg yolks until yolks ribbon when beater is lifted. Gradually beat in ½ cup sugar. Add chocolate mixture, flour, almonds, cinnamon, vanilla. Beat well. Beat egg whites with cream of tartar. Gradually beat in ¼ cup sugar until peaks form. Fold into chocolate mixture and pour into prepared pan. Bake for 30-35 minutes. Cool in pan. Remove from pan to glaze. Serves 10.

GLAZE: Slowly melt chocolate and butter together. Stir in coffee and sugar (if desired). Cook until thickened. Spread over cake.

GILDA MCKINNY
RALEIGH, NC

NO-DAIRY DELICIOUS CHOCOLATE CAKE

A moist chocolate cake made with no dairy products. Pretty when dusted with powdered sugar and served with fruit.

3	cups flour
2¼	cups sugar
2	teaspoons baking soda
⅔	cup cocoa
2	cups water
1	tablespoon vanilla extract
2	tablespoons white vinegar
⅔	cup plus 2 tablespoons canola oil

Preheat oven to 350°. Grease a 9-inch x 13-inch baking pan.

Sift together flour, sugar, baking soda and cocoa. In another bowl mix water, vanilla, vinegar and oil. Whisk both mixtures together by hand for 1 minute. Pour in baking pan. Bake 35-40 minutes or until toothpick inserted comes out clean. Serves 8 to 10.

JEAN-MARIE MILLER
RALEIGH, NC

Cocoa Profiteroles with Espresso Sauce — a delightful choclate puff to serve with after dinner coffee.

COCOA PROFITEROLES WITH ESPRESSO SAUCE

Use a good quality cocoa such as Ghiradelli or Drôste and the flavor will shine through in these small chocolate cream puffs. This is a very special dessert. Make this!

2	cups water
1	cup butter
½	cup cocoa
1¾	cups flour
⅓	cup sugar
½	teaspoon salt
8	eggs
1	pint vanilla ice cream

ESPRESSO SAUCE:

¾	cup brown sugar
½	cup sugar
2	tablespoons instant coffee (or 1 tablespoon instant espresso)
⅓	cup light corn syrup
⅓	cup water
3	tablespoons unsalted butter
2	tablespoons Tía Maria or Kahlúa

Preheat oven to 450°. Grease a standard baking sheet.

In a large saucepan, bring water and butter to a boil. Sift cocoa, flour, sugar and salt together in a medium bowl. Add the dry ingredients to saucepan all at once. Beat vigorously with a wooden spoon until dough pulls away from sides of the pan. Remove from heat and let cool slightly. Beat in eggs 1 at a time, blending well after each addition. The dough will become slick and glossy.

To bake: Spoon dough by the heaping teaspoonfuls onto baking sheet. Space profiterole dough 2 inches apart. Bake for 10 minutes, then lower heat to 375° and bake 30-40 minutes more. Remove profiteroles from pan and cool. Cut in half, not slicing all the way through so they are hinged. Store in an airtight container.

To serve: Fill profiteroles with a spoonful of vanilla ice cream. Arrange three puffs on each dessert plate and ladle Espresso Sauce over the tops. Makes 24 profiteroles, serving 8.

ESPRESSO SAUCE: In a medium saucepan bring the sugars, coffee, corn syrup and water to a boil, stirring constantly. Lower heat to a simmer and cook 5-10 minutes, stirring frequently. Remove from heat and add butter, in pieces. Stir in liqueur.

CHOCOLATE TEMPTATION SQUARES

These chewy rich bars will tempt anyone with a chocolate craving. They freeze well for early preparation.

FIRST LAYER:

1	cup old-fashioned oats
1	cup flour
½	cup brown sugar
¼	teaspoon salt
½	cup butter, cut up

SECOND LAYER:

3	ounces semisweet chocolate
2	tablespoons butter
3	eggs
¾	cup brown sugar
1½	teaspoons vanilla extract
¼	cup flour
•	dash salt
1	cup chocolate chips
1½	cups chopped pecans, divided
2	cups coconut, divided

Preheat oven to 350°. Lightly grease a 13-inch x 9-inch baking pan.

To make first layer: In medium bowl combine oats, flour, brown sugar and salt. Cut in butter until well-combined. Press firmly into prepared pan. Bake for 10 minutes. Remove and cool 10 minutes.

To make second layer: Melt chocolate and butter together while first layer is baking. Set aside to cool.

In medium bowl, beat eggs and sugar until thickened, about 1 minute. Beat in vanilla, flour, salt, and reserved chocolate mixture. Stir in chocolate chips and 1 cup each of the pecans and coconut.

Spread second layer over first layer. Top with remaining ½ cup pecans and 1 cup coconut. Return to oven and bake 25 minutes. Cool. Cut into 24 squares.

COCOA ROULADE

Firm texture of chocolate glaze complements the soft airy cake and filling. Make for any party; even kids love it. Use Dutch processed cocoa for best results.

5	eggs, separated
1	cup sugar
¼	cup cocoa
¼	cup flour
1	teaspoon vanilla extract
4	tablespoons confectioners' sugar, divided
1	cup heavy cream
4	ounces semi-sweet chocolate
3	tablespoons butter

Preheat oven to 350°. Grease a 10-inch x 16-inch baking sheet.

Separate eggs and beat yolks slightly. Add sugar and beat until yolks ribbon. Stir in cocoa, flour and vanilla.

In a separate bowl, beat egg whites to form stiff peaks. Gently fold into batter. Spread batter evenly into pan. Bake 10-15 minutes.

Sprinkle a clean dish towel with 2 tablespoons confectioners' sugar. Turn cake out onto dish towel and roll up into a log while still warm and cover with a damp cloth. Let cool.

Beat cream and sweeten with remaining 2 tablespoons confectioners' sugar. Unroll cake; spread whipped cream over entire surface. Roll again and chill.

Melt chocolate in a bowl over hot water. Stir in butter; blend well. Cover roulade with melted chocolate and refrigerate until ready to serve. Serves 8.

INGEBORG SAGAN
RALEIGH, NC

POACHED PEARS WITH RASPBERRY AND CHOCOLATE MINT SAUCES

Although this recipe looks complicated, it consists of sauces that may be made ahead and pears that are poached to order. Do not be put off by its length; just read through and give it a try!

6 pears, preferable bosc

2 lemons, divided

2½ cups apple cider or juice

½ cup sugar

1 vanilla bean

1 cinnamon stick

¼ cup heavy cream

RASPBERRY SAUCE:

1 10-ounce package frozen raspberries in syrup

⅓ cup orange juice

3 tablespoons superfine sugar

¼ cup cassis (currant liqueur)

CHOCOLATE MINT SAUCE:

4½ ounces bittersweet chocolate, such as Ghiradelli

2 ounces unsweetened chocolate

⅓ cup hot water

¼ cup light corn syrup

¾ teaspoon peppermint extract

Make both Raspberry Sauce and Chocolate Mint Sauce and set aside.

Peel pears, leaving stem intact. Cut a lemon in half and rub over surface of pears to prevent discoloration. Trim bases of pears slightly so they will stand up. Remove peel from remaining lemon in one continuous strip and combine with apple cider, sugar, vanilla bean and cinnamon stick in a large non-reactive saucepan. Bring to a boil over medium high heat.

Add pears in a single layer upright and space evenly, preferably not touching. Reduce heat to low and simmer about 30 minutes until just tender. Transfer pears to a warm platter and bring poaching liquid back to a boil. Cook on high until liquid is syrupy.

Whip heavy cream to stiff peaks and keep chilled.

To serve: Place 2 tablespoons of reduced syrup in middle of dessert plate. Lightly baste pear with syrup and place in middle of puddle. Spoon Raspberry Sauce on one side of pear, and Chocolate Mint Sauce on the other. Spoon a large dollop of whipped cream on stem and let it drape down the side of warm pear. Serves 6.

RASPBERRY SAUCE: Place thawed berries with syrup in blender. Add orange juice and blend until smooth. Strain through a fine sieve. Stir in sugar and cassis.

CHOCOLATE MINT SAUCE: Chop both chocolates into pieces and melt in top of double boiler with hot water and corn syrup. Whisk until smooth. Add peppermint extract. Cool slightly. May be made ahead and refrigerated then reheated before serving.

SARAH J. WARDEN
WILSON, NC

OCEANIC, MICRONESIAN, CAROLINE ISLANDS, *COCONUT GRATER,* 20th century

Lemon **Berry Trifles star** in this afternoon celebration. Finger sandwiches feature Pennsylvania Brown Bread (page 163) spread with maple butter, Black Walnut Bread (page 163) with an orange ginger cream cheese, and Frances' Fresh Garden Spread (page 65) on sourdough rounds. *The Garden Parasol* by Frederick Carl Frieseke inspires a setting for the perfect summer pick-me-up, to be enjoyed *al fresco* with good friends or a good book.

LEMON BERRY TRIFLES

This quick and easy dessert will be a hit with children as well as adults. It is a feast for the eye as well as the palate. Mixed berries have been used, but almost any fruit would suffice. Use small parfait glasses, champagne flutes or small wine glasses.

2-3 cups mixed berries
      (blueberries, raspberries,
      blackberries, strawberries)
1   cup lemon curd (an 11¼-
      ounce jar), chilled
½   cup whipped cream (about
      ⅓ cup before whipping)
•   Mint leaves for garnish
•   Parfait glasses

Wash berries and drain very well on paper towels. Cut strawberries if large.

Stir together lemon curd and whipped cream. Shortly before serving, put a bit of lemon curd mixture into bottom of each glass. Add a layer of berries and then another layer of lemon curd. Continue until glass is full. Garnish with a berry and a sprig of mint. Serves 6-8.

GRAND MARNIER FRUIT

Jars of fruit found in the produce section of many grocery stores are a true convenience food, especially when you wish to serve fruit to a crowd. The large 4-pound jars can be found at warehouse stores. Drain off the syrup and soak the fruit overnight in this special mixture of grapefruit juice and liqueur .

1   64-ounce (4-pound) jar
      mangos in light syrup
1   64-ounce (4-pound) jar
      pink grapefruit
1   cup grapefruit juice, freshly
      squeezed or from carton
½   cup Grand Marnier
2   cups sliced strawberries
•   whole strawberries
•   raspberries
•   blackberries

Drain mangos and pink grapefruit and set aside in a large bowl.

In separate bowl or measuring cup, mix grapefruit juice and Grand Marnier. Add sliced strawberries. Pour over mangos and grapefruit in large bowl. Marinate several hours or overnight in the refrigerator.

Arrange mango slices, grapefruit sections, whole strawberries, raspberries and blackberries on a large platter or tray. Drizzle remaining juice over mixture. Serves 25.

CASEY'S BREAD PUDDING

According to Dee Cook, many people are often surprised they like this bread pudding. The lemon sauce complements the pudding beautifully in this recipe shared by a neighbor of her mother-in-law in Texas.

6	1-inch slices of French bread
2	eggs, well-beaten
⅔	cup plus 1 tablespoon sugar
2	teaspoons vanilla extract
2	teaspoons baking powder
2	tablespoons grated coconut
¼	cup raisins
2	tablespoons melted butter
½	teaspoon nutmeg

LEMON SAUCE:

•	zest and juice of 1 lemon
¼	cup sugar
1	tablespoon cornstarch
½	cup water
1	egg, well-beaten

Preheat oven to 400°. Grease an 8-inch x 8-inch square glass baking dish.

Soak bread in a flat dish in 2 cups of water for 10 minutes. Drain bread in colander, pressing lightly to remove excess water.

Beat eggs with ⅔ cup sugar, vanilla, baking powder, coconut, raisins and melted butter. Combine with bread and place in baking dish. Mix remaining 1 tablespoon sugar with the ½ teaspoon nutmeg, and sprinkle over top. Bake for 20-30 minutes. Serve pudding warm with Lemon Sauce. Serves 4-5.

LEMON SAUCE: Mix ingredients in a small saucepan and cook on low heat until thickened.

DELORES (DEE) COOK
APEX, NC

DUBLIN BREAD PUDDING

A moist bread pudding with a rich, smooth whiskey sauce. Put it on your list of company desserts.

1	large baguette (6-7 cups, cubed)
¾	cup raisins
2	tablespoons white rum
6	eggs
1½	cups half-and-half
1½	cups sugar
½	teaspoon cinnamon
2	teaspoons vanilla extract
3	tablespoons melted butter or margarine

WHISKEY SAUCE:

½	cup plus 3 tablespoons butter (or 11 tablespoons)
1½	cups confectioners' sugar
2	eggs, beaten
1-2	tablespoons Irish Whiskey

Preheat oven to 350°. Grease an 8-inch x 8-inch baking pan.

Cut baguette into 1-inch cubes. If using fresh bread, leave it out for several hours so it becomes dry or use day old bread.

In a small bowl soak raisins in rum for 30 minutes. In a large bowl beat eggs and whisk in half-and-half, sugar, cinnamon, vanilla and cooled melted butter. Add bread and soak until softened. Stir in raisins with rum.

Spoon into baking pan. Bake for 30-40 minutes until top is golden brown and pudding is set. Let cool and cut into 3½-inch squares. Serve warm with Whiskey Sauce. May be reheated if made ahead. Serves 6-8.

WHISKEY SAUCE: In a stainless steel bowl or double boiler, combine butter, sugar and eggs. Using a hand mixer, beat over simmering water until mixture reaches 155° on candy thermometer. Stir in whiskey.

An American artist who lived most of his professional life in France, Frederick Carl Frieseke embraced a highly decorative impressionist style, remarkable for its intense, rapturous color and vivacity of brushwork. Large and dazzling, *The Garden Parasol* ranks among his finest achievements: a sumptuous confection of light and color, grandly evoking the serene pleasure of taking tea on a summer afternoon. The setting is the garden of the artist's house at Giverny, where Frieseke spent many summers as the neighbor of Claude Monet.

FREDERICK CARL FRIESEKE (American), *THE GARDEN PARASOL*, 1910

SIR WILLIAM BEECHEY (British), *THE ODDIE CHILDREN*, 1789

Prior to the eighteenth century, British artists often portrayed children in family portraits as if they were small adults. In this painting of the children of a London lawyer, Sir William Beechey reflected a new attitude of tolerance for childhood games in the second half of the eighteenth century. Particularly charming is young Catherine Oddie, on all fours and gazing out as if to invite the viewer to join in the fun.

STEAMED CRANBERRY PUDDING

A real homespun recipe, a traditional family dessert for Thanksgiving and other holidays.

1 egg, lightly beaten
½ cup molasses
2 teaspoons baking soda
½ cup boiling water
½ teaspoon salt
1½ cups flour, divided
2 cups cranberries

BUTTER SAUCE:

½ cup butter
1 cup sugar
1 tablespoon flour
½ cup heavy cream
• pinch salt

Grease a 6-cup pudding mold.

In a medium bowl, mix together egg, molasses, baking soda, boiling water, salt and 1 cup flour. Put cranberries in food processor and chop coarsely with 1-2 on/off turns.

Dust with remaining ½ cup flour and stir into pudding. Pour batter into a pudding mold; cover tightly and steam 1½ hours. Make Butter Sauce and serve over hot pudding. Serves 6-8.

BUTTER SAUCE: Combine all ingredients in a small saucepan and heat gently. Cook about 5 minutes until sauce is smooth and thickened. May be made ahead and reheated, but be careful not to scorch.

FRANCES TAYLOR
SANFORD, NC

VANILLA ECLAIRS WITH A CHOCOLATE GLAZE

Just like the bakery makes with an easy vanilla cream filling and chocolate glaze.

½ cup butter
⅛ teaspoon salt
1 cup water
1 cup flour
4 eggs

VANILLA FILLING:

1 package vanilla pudding (instant)
2¼ cups milk
1½ cups Cool Whip (thawed)
½ teaspoon almond extract

CHOCOLATE GLAZE:

4 ounces semi-sweet chocolate
2 tablespoons heavy cream
1 tablespoon unsalted butter

Preheat oven to 450°.

In a heavy saucepan bring butter, salt and water to boil. Add flour all at once, stirring until mixture pulls away from sides of pan. Remove from heat and cool slightly. Stir in eggs 1 at a time, incorporating each egg well before adding the next. Beat until mixture looks satiny.

Drop 2 spoonfuls of batter side by side on an ungreased baking pan and shape into logs. Bake for 15 minutes, then lower heat to 375° and bake 45 minutes more or until puffed and brown. Cool on rack and make Vanilla Filling and Chocolate Glaze.

Cut partway through eclairs and fill with vanilla cream. Chill for 20 minutes before applying glaze. Spread glaze over top of eclairs in a thin layer. Keep refrigerated. Makes 12.

VANILLA FILLING: Mix vanilla pudding with milk and fold in cool whip and almond extract. Chill.

CHOCOLATE GLAZE: Melt chocolate and cream in a saucepan over low heat. Stir in butter until smooth.

PAULA MEHLHOP
CARY, NC

CROWD-PLEASING BANANA PUDDING

The unique addition of sour cream combines with vanilla pudding and whipped cream to make a rich and creamy pudding. Layer into a trifle bowl and take to your next potluck. It would be the perfect dessert geared to children at a holiday open house.

3   small packages instant French vanilla pudding

5   cups whole milk

1   8-ounce carton sour cream

1   12-ounce Cool Whip, see note

1   box vanilla wafers

6   bananas, sliced

In a large bowl, mix vanilla pudding with milk and blend thoroughly. Stir in sour cream and fold in Cool Whip. Mix well. In a large rectangular dish, layer vanilla wafers, bananas and cream mixture in three parts. Repeat until dish is full. Chill for at least 1 hour. Serves 20.

NOTE: Cool Whip may be easily replaced with ¾ cup heavy cream combined with 1 tablespoon sugar, whipped to soft peaks. Fold in as directed for whipped topping.

RITA ELLIOTT
APEX, NC

CHILLED PEACH-N-BLUEBERRY PIE

The taste of summer's fruits chilled in a baked homemade pie crust brushed with peach jelly.

5   cups fresh peaches, divided

2½   tablespoons lemon juice, divided

¾   cup sugar, divided

3   tablespoons corn starch

¼   cup cold water

1   tablespoon butter

2   tablespoons Grand Marnier, or other orange liqueur

1   cup fresh blueberries

½   cup peach preserves

....

BASIC PIE CRUST:

1¼   cups all-purpose flour

½   teaspoon salt

¼   cup vegetable shortening

3   tablespoons cold unsalted butter, cut up

2-3   tablespoons ice water

Peel enough peaches to make 1½ cups when sliced. (Dip in boiling water for about 15 seconds or so and then in cold water to facilitate peeling.) Toss slices with 1 tablespoon lemon juice and ¼ cup sugar. Put into blender or processor and puree until smooth.

In saucepan combine remaining ½ cup sugar and cornstarch. Stir in cold water and peach puree. Put over medium heat and cook, stirring, until thick and bubbly. Remove from heat, swirl in butter and then add Grand Marnier. Cool to room temperature.

While peach puree is cooling, make Basic Pie Crust. Peel remaining peaches totaling 3½ cups. Toss with remaining 1½ tablespoons lemon juice and the blueberries.

In small saucepan, bring peach jelly to a boil. Spread or brush entire inside of baked pie shell to coat evenly. (This will prevent a soggy crust.) Cool to set. To hasten process, refrigerate about 5 minutes.

Stir reserved peach puree into sliced peaches and blueberries. Pour into prepared pie shell. Chill several hours. Serves 8.

BASIC PIE CRUST: Combine flour and salt. Cut in shortening and butter until mixture resembles coarse meal. Add just enough water to hold dough together. Form into a ball. Wrap in plastic wrap and chill 20-30 minutes.

Preheat oven to 425°. On lightly floured surface, roll dough into a circle large enough to line a 9-inch pie plate. Put in pan. Double over edges and flute decoratively. Prick bottom and sides all over with a fork. Line with a piece of aluminum foil. Fill with dried beans or pie weights. Bake for 8 minutes. Remove foil and beans. Prick with fork again. Lower oven heat to 375° and bake about 15 minutes more, until golden brown. Set on rack to cool completely.

JUAN BAUTISTA ROMERO (Spanish), *STILL LIFE WITH STRAWBERRIES AND CHOCOLATE*, c. 1775-90

PEANUT BUTTER SILK PIE WITH MOCHA GLAZE

This peanut butter extravaganza is made in a prepared chocolate cookie crumb crust topped with a mocha glaze.

1   8-ounce cream cheese, softened

1   cup sugar

1   cup creamy peanut butter

1   tablespoon melted butter

1   teaspoon vanilla extract

1   cup heavy cream

1   9-inch chocolate cookie crumb crust

MOCHA GLAZE:

1   cup semi-sweet chocolate chips

3   tablespoons strong coffee

In a medium bowl, beat cream cheese, sugar, peanut butter, butter and vanilla until smooth and creamy. In a separate bowl, whip heavy cream until stiff. Gently fold cream into peanut butter mixture.

Make Mocha Glaze and carefully spoon over pie. Chill until firm. Serves 8.

MOCHA GLAZE: Place chips and coffee in a glass bowl. Melt in microwave on high 1-2 minutes until a spreadable consistency.

EVELYN (EVIE) DURBIN
CARY, NC

OATMEAL PIE

Old-fashioned, much like a chess pie but with a little more texture from the cooked oats.

1	10-inch pie pastry
2	eggs, beaten
10	tablespoons butter, melted
⅔	cup sugar
⅔	cup light corn syrup
⅔	cup old-fashioned oats
1	teaspoon vanilla extract
½	teaspoon salt

Preheat oven to 350°. Line a 10-inch pie plate with pastry.

In a medium bowl, combine eggs, butter, sugar, corn syrup, oats, vanilla and salt. Pour into pie shell and bake for 45 minutes. Serve warm with ice cream or whipped cream. Serves 6.

CHARLOTTE NEWBY
CHAPEL HILL, NC

JANET'S PECAN PIE

This pie makes a nice gift because it tastes "freshly made" after two or three days.

3	eggs
1	cup sugar
1	teaspoon salt
1	teaspoon vanilla extract
½	cup melted butter
⅓	cup light corn syrup
1	cup pecans, see note
1	9-inch unbaked pie shell

Preheat oven to 375°.

In a medium bowl, beat eggs. Add sugar, salt and vanilla. Stir in butter, corn syrup and nuts; mix well. Pour into pie shell. Bake for 10 minutes, then reduce heat to 350° and bake for 40 more minutes. Serves 6-8.

NOTE: To give nuts a richer flavor, toast before adding to pie filling.

JANET SIEGFRIED
RALEIGH, NC

CRANBERRY RAISIN TART

The walnut crust brings the seasonal tastes of citrus, cranberry and nuts full circle.

WALNUT CRUST:

3	cups walnuts
½	cup sugar
⅓	cup unsalted butter, melted

CRANBERRY RAISIN FILLING:

3	cups (12 ounces) cranberries
¾	cup orange juice
2	oranges
1	cup raisins
1	teaspoon lemon zest
¾	cup brown sugar plus 3 tablespoons, divided
3	tablespoons dark rum
1½	tablespoons butter
¾	cup chopped walnuts

Place walnuts and sugar in food processor fitted with metal blade. Process until finely ground. Transfer to bowl and toss well with butter until all nuts are moistened. Press firmly into 11-inch tart pan with removable bottom. Chill.

To make Cranberry Raisin Filling: In medium saucepan combine cranberries and orange juice. Peel oranges removing white pith. Cut out sections in between membranes; cut each section in half. Add to pan along with raisins, lemon zest and ¾ cup of the brown sugar. Bring to a boil, then lower heat and simmer 8 minutes until cranberry skins have popped. Remove from heat and stir in rum and butter. Let mixture cool 10 minutes, then stir in chopped walnuts. Stir cranberry filling well to make sure all fruit and nuts are distributed evenly.

Pour cranberry mixture into chilled tart shell, spreading evenly. Sprinkle remaining 3 tablespoons brown sugar on top. Chill 15-20 minutes in refrigerator until set. (Note: Tart can be made ahead to this point and kept in refrigerator overnight. Bake the next day.)

Preheat oven to 375°. Set tart on top of larger baking pan for easier handling, and to prevent butter from crust from leaking through. Bake 35 minutes until pastry is golden and pie has a dark finished glaze. Serve at room temperature with a dollop of whipped cream. Serves 6-8.

APPLE CHARLOTTE WITH VANILLA CUSTARD SAUCE

The preparation of this dessert would be fun for children who would enjoy dipping the bread crusts into melted butter and sugar. It's a very forgiving process with elegant results. The Vanilla Custard Sauce requires constant stirring; enlist an advanced young chef.

6	bread-lined ½-cup ramekins, see below
4	Granny Smith apples, peeled, cored and diced
¼	cup sugar
2	tablespoons unsalted butter
2	tablespoons raspberry jam
2	tablespoons heavy cream
½	cup chopped pecans
6	mint sprigs

BREAD-LINED RAMEKINS:

18	pieces very thin white bread
1	cup sugar
½	cup butter, melted
•	vegetable oil cooking spray

VANILLA CUSTARD SAUCE:

1½	cups milk
6	egg yolks
1	cup sugar
1	teaspoon vanilla extract

Prepare bread-lined ramekins and Vanilla Custard Sauce.

Preheat oven to 400°. In a bowl, toss the apples with the sugar. In a large skillet, melt butter, then sauté apples for 10 minutes. Add raspberry jam, cream and pecans to the skillet and cook for 2 more minutes, stirring constantly. Remove from heat and cool slightly.

Fill each ramekin to the top with apple mixture. Cover with remaining bread circles, sugar side up. Cover each ramekin tightly with foil. Bake for 30 minutes. Just before serving remove foil and broil until tops are golden brown, about 1-2 minutes. These can be baked ahead just before dinner; flash under the broiler just before serving.

To serve: Spoon ¼ cup Vanilla Custard Sauce onto warm plates. Run a knife around ramekin edge, then unmold the charlottes onto the center of each plate. Garnish with mint. Serves 6.

BREAD-LINED RAMEKINS: Spray six ½-cup ramekins with cooking spray. Remove crusts from the bread. Using the ramekin bottom as a guideline, cut circles out of 12 pieces of bread. Cut remaining 6 pieces in half. Dip one side of 6 circles into the melted butter, then the sugar; place into the bottom of each ramekin, sugar side down. Repeat this process with the bread halves, fitting 2 halves along the side of each ramekin. The remaining 6 circles should be held to cover the apple-filled ramekins. Just before topping each ramekin, dip one side of circle in butter and sugar. Place on top of each charlotte, sugar side up.

VANILLA CUSTARD SAUCE: Fill a large bowl with ice and cold water. Place a smaller bowl inside the ice-filled bowl and place a fine mesh strainer over the bowl. Scald milk in a heavy-bottomed saucepan over medium heat; remove from burner. In another heavy-bottomed pot combine yolks, sugar and vanilla and mix well. Pour a small amount of hot milk into egg mixture, whisking constantly. Slowly add the remaining milk continuing to whisk. Place the mixture over medium heat and stir with a wooden spoon until mixture thickens to a creamy consistency and coats the back of a spoon. Pour through the strainer into ice bath to chill. Cover Vanilla Custard Sauce with plastic wrap directly on top of custard, this will keep out any water from condensation. Keep refrigerated until ready to use, up to 4 days.

NOTE: Constant stirring is very important to insure that eggs do not cook on the bottom. If there are bits of curdled egg, they will be removed when mixture is strained.

For an impressive molded dessert, serve Apple Charlotte with Vanilla Custard Sauce.

APPLE HARVEST PECAN TART

This rustic apple tart is made even more decadent by its pecan pie tart shell.

11-INCH FILLING:

- • 11-inch tart shell
- 2-3 large Granny Smith apples
- 2 tablespoons lemon juice
- 6 tablespoons butter
- ¾ cup brown sugar
- ½ cup dark corn syrup
- 2 eggs lightly beaten
- 1 teaspoon vanilla extract
- ¼ teaspoon salt
- 1½ cups plus 2 tablespoons coarsely chopped pecans

PECAN TART SHELL:

- 1½ cups flour
- ½ teaspoon salt
- 8 tablespoons cold butter, cut up
- 1 egg
- 2 tablespoons sugar
- 2 tablespoons ice water

9-INCH TART FILLING:

- 2-3 small Granny Smith apples
- 1 tablespoon lemon juice
- 4 tablespoons butter
- ½ cup brown sugar
- ⅓ cup dark corn syrup
- 1 egg, preferably jumbo
- ½ teaspoon vanilla
- • pinch of salt
- 1 cup plus 1½ tablespoons coarsely chopped pecans

Make Pecan Tart Shell. While it's chilling, prepare filling.

Preheat oven to 375°. Peel and core apples. Cut into quarters, and then slice into neat slices. Toss with lemon juice.

Melt butter in medium saucepan. Remove from heat; stir in brown sugar and dark corn syrup. Whisk in lightly beaten eggs, vanilla and salt. Remove and set aside about ¼ cup of the mixture to use later for glazing the apples. Add 1½ cups pecans to the remaining mixture and pour into prepared tart shell. Decoratively arrange apple slices in concentric circles over the pecan mixture. Brush apples with most of the reserved syrup mixture. Add the remaining 2 tablespoons pecans to the rest and sprinkle over the top of the tart. Bake for 45 minutes until set and apples are beginning to brown (about 40 minutes for a 9-inch tart). Cool and serve. Serves 8-10.

NOTE: The tart shell can be made in a 9-inch tart pan using the same quantity of ingredients, but reduce filling ingredients by ⅓. For a more attractive tart, use smaller apples so that there will be room for 2 circles of apples.

PECAN TART SHELL: In bowl of food processor combine flour and salt. Process briefly. Add butter and pulse until mixture resembles coarse crumbs. In separate small bowl whisk together egg, sugar and ice water. With motor running add to processor and run just until mixture comes together into a ball. Do not over process. Shape into a flat cylinder, wrap in plastic wrap and chill 30 minutes.

Roll into circle large enough to line an 11-inch tart pan with a removable bottom with about a ¾-inch overhang. Cut to size if necessary. Fold the ¾-inch overhang to the inside to make a double edge, pressing firmly. Tart may be chilled for 30 minutes while the filling is made, or made the day before and chilled overnight.

APPLE SQUARES

Make for picnics and lunchboxes in the fall.

3   large apples
½   cup raisins
•   juice and zest from one lemon
2   teaspoons cinnamon
1¼ cups sugar, divided
½   cup water
2   tablespoons milk
•   confectioners' sugar

....

PASTRY CRUST:

3   cups flour
1   tablespoon sugar
1   cup butter
½   cup ice water

Prepare Pastry Crust.

Core and cut apples into bite-size pieces. In a large sauté pan combine apples, raisins, lemon juice, zest, cinnamon, 1 cup of the sugar and water. Cook on medium low heat until mixture has thickened, about 10 minutes. Stir occasionally and do not overcook apples. Set aside and cool completely.

Preheat oven to 375°. Divide pastry crust in half and roll out. Line a 9-inch x 13-inch cookie pan with first half, spreading about ½-inch up the sides. Spread cooled filling over bottom crust. Top with remaining pastry and seal edges as if for pie. Brush top pastry with milk and sprinkle with remaining ¼ cup sugar.

Bake until golden brown 40-45 minutes. When cool dust with confectioners' sugar and cut into squares. Makes 12-16.

PASTRY CRUST: Put flour, sugar and butter in food processor. Cut in butter by pulsing until flour has consistency of cornmeal. Slowly add ice water through tube and run until dough just forms a ball. Wrap in plastic wrap and chill.

BETTY GINN
RALEIGH, NC

NORWEGIAN APPLE PIE

For at least 10 years Joanne Dalldorf has been using this recipe from Thru the Grapevine, *a cookbook published by the Junior League of Elmira, New York, and she claims it never fails. What's wonderful about this pie is that it requires no crust. This is destined to be a new family favorite.*

1   cup sifted flour
2   teaspoons baking powder
½   teaspoon salt
1½ cups sugar
½   teaspoon cinnamon
2   eggs
½   teaspoon lemon juice
1   teaspoon vanilla extract
2   cups diced apples
1   cup chopped nuts

Preheat oven to 375°. Grease a 10-inch deep dish pie plate.

In a small bowl, combine flour, baking powder, salt, sugar and cinnamon. Set aside. In a separate bowl, beat eggs. Add lemon juice and vanilla. Add dry ingredients to egg mixture, stirring until just moistened. Stir in apples and nuts and mix thoroughly. Pour into pie plate. Bake for 30-35 minutes. Serves 6-8.

JOANNA S. DALLDORF
CHAPEL HILL, NC

STRAWBERRY RHUBARB CRISP

Sweet strawberries and the tangy tartness of rhubarb strike a delicate balance in this rich fruit tart with an oatmeal pecan topping.

1½	pints ripe strawberries
7	ribs fresh rhubarb
½	cup sugar
½	cup brown sugar
•	juice and zest of 1 lemon
2	teaspoons cinnamon
1	teaspoon ginger
½	cup unbleached flour

CRISP TOPPING:

1	cup unbleached flour
1	cup brown sugar
⅔	cup quick-cooking oats
⅔	cup chopped pecans, toasted
•	pinch salt
½	cup butter, divided

Wash hull and halve berries. Remove stringy fibers from rhubarb with a potato peeler and cut into ½-inch pieces.

In a large bowl combine strawberries, rhubarb, sugars, lemon, cinnamon and ginger. Let rest to dissolve sugars. Make Crisp Topping.

Preheat oven to 425°. Grease an oval 9-inch x 13-inch baking dish. Sprinkle flour over fruit mixture and stir until a smooth syrup appears. Pour fruit mixture into baking dish. Cover with topping. Bake in top ⅓ oven for 10 minutes, then reduce heat to 375° and bake 20 minutes more or until topping is golden brown and juices are bubbling over. Serves 6-8.

CRISP TOPPING: Combine flour, brown sugar, oats and pecans in a small bowl. Cut chilled butter in small pieces and work into flour mixture with fingertips until crumbly.

BILL BLAAUW
SWEPSONVILLE, NC

BLACKBERRY COBBLER

Old-fashioned cobbler, with sweet summer berries in a butter golden crust, is a fantastic way to end any celebration. Golden Honey Ice Cream, page 197, gives crowning glory to this dessert.

12	cups blackberries or mixture of fresh berries, washed
½	cup sugar
½	cup flour
½	teaspoon salt
1	egg
10	sprigs fresh mint, for garnish

BUTTERY PECAN CRUST:

⅔	cup chopped pecans
2	cups flour, plus extra for rolling out dough
⅓	cup sugar
3	teaspoons baking powder
1	teaspoon salt
12	tablespoons cold butter, in small pieces
1	teaspoon vanilla extract
⅔	cup cold milk

Preheat oven to 350°. Grease a 9-inch x 13-inch baking dish with cooking spray.

In large bowl combine berries with sugar, flour and salt, stirring gently. Spoon berry mixture into dish. Set aside.

Make Buttery Pecan Crust, and arrange over berry filling. Don't worry if it breaks; just piece it together on top of the fruit, lightly pressing to seal edges. Prick with a fork. Bake cobbler for 40-45 minutes, or until fruit is bubbling.

Meanwhile, in a small bowl, prepare an egg wash by beating an egg with 2 tablespoons water. Remove cobbler from oven and preheat the broiler. Using a pastry brush, glaze crust with egg wash. Flash under the broiler for 1-2 minutes, or until the crust is deep golden. Cobbler may be refrigerated for up to 24 hours or tightly covered and frozen for up to 2 months.

Serve warm with Golden Honey Ice Cream and garnish with springs of fresh mint. Serves 10.

BUTTERY PECAN CRUST: Place nuts in the work bowl of food processor. Grind into a coarse meal. Add flour, sugar, baking powder and salt; pulse to combine. Add butter to bowl and pulse the machine 5 times. In a small bowl, combine milk and vanilla. With motor running, add milk in a fine stream. Process until dough is combined. Remove dough from bowl; turn out onto floured board and knead 6 turns. Pat and lightly roll into 9-inch x 13-inch rectangle.

GOLDEN HONEY ICE CREAM

The creamy sweetness perfectly accents any cobbler or fruit pie.

16 egg yolks
1 cup honey
2 tablespoons vanilla extract
4 cups milk

Prepare an ice bath by filling a large bowl with ice and water. Set a second small bowl into the ice water. Set aside.

In mixing bowl combine yolks, honey and vanilla. Whisk to blend ingredients.

In 2-quart saucepan, bring milk to a simmer over medium heat. Remove from heat. Slowly add milk to yolk mixture while constantly whisking. Pour mixture back into saucepan. Place over medium heat. Using a wooden spoon, constantly stir the mixture until it coats back of the spoon, about 5 minutes. Do not boil.

Pour mixture through a fine mesh sieve into the smaller bowl of the ice bath. Allow to cool to room temperature, stirring occasionally and adding more ice to the large bowl as necessary. Transfer mixture to ice cream freezer and freeze according to manufacturer's instructions. Makes 1 quart.

Blackberry Cobbler need only be dolloped with Golden Honey Ice Cream.

HAL'S ICE CREAM

Heyward, alias Hal, McKinney is well known for periodically sharing a big batch of ice cream with the NCMA staff. This delightful recipe can provide the base for your favorite ice cream. The rich and creamy custard will fill a four-quart ice cream maker. It may be increased by half for a six-quart freezer. For best results make the base (excluding fruit) the day before.

8	eggs
2	cups sugar
4	cups milk
1	quart heavy cream
2	teaspoons vanilla extract
3-4	cups prepared fruit

In a large heavy saucepan, blend eggs, sugar and milk. Stir and cook slowly over medium low heat until it just thickens. The custard is done when it coats a spoon. Remove from heat. Continue to stir to cool and prevent curdling. Set aside to cool completely. When cooled, stir in heavy cream and vanilla and mix well. Store in a non-metal or glass container in the refrigerator at least overnight. The base will keep for several days.

NOTE: Don't worry if your base tastes too sweet. It will taste less sweet after being frozen.

When ready to turn the base into ice cream, prepare fruit, strawberries, blueberries, peaches or whatever. Fruit should be chopped fine or pureed, then sweetened. Bananas are sweet enough on their own and need no extra sugar.

Put custard in ice cream maker. Add fruit (or nothing for vanilla ice cream). Churn according to manufacturer's instructions. For better texture, after churning, remove dasher, pack down ice cream in fresh ice and salt and let flavors develop 4-5 hours in freezer. Makes 3 quarts.

HAL'S VARIATIONS: For Butter Pecan ice cream, roast pecan pieces in butter in 350° oven for 20-30 minutes. Freeze before adding to custard. For chocolate ice cream, add a little extra sugar to the base and sift cocoa powder into custard after it has cooked.

HEYWARD H. McKINNEY, JR.
RALEIGH, NC

BANANA RUM SUNDAE

This is a variation on Bananas Foster. Serve in sorbet glasses or small bowls.

3	tablespoons butter
4	small firm bananas, cut on the diagonal into 6 petal-shaped pieces
½	cup light brown sugar, packed
3	tablespoons Myers Dark Rum
3	tablespoons banana-flavored liqueur
•	vanilla ice cream

Melt butter in a large skillet over moderate heat. Sauté bananas quickly on both sides just to warm them; do not overcook. Carefully transfer banana pieces, dividing between 4 dishes or glasses. Reserve pan.

In same pan, make a sauce by quickly cooking brown sugar, rum and liqueur until sugar melts.

Place 1 large scoop of ice cream in center of bananas. Spoon sauce over bananas and ice cream. Serve immediately. Serves 4.

CAROLYN R. BOOTH
CARY, NC

ZESTY LIME SORBET

Refreshingly light for a good intermezzo or to eat with your favorite cookie.

3	cups water
1½	cups sugar
2	egg whites
1	cup fresh lime juice (8-10 limes)
2	tablespoons lemon juice
¼	cup Cointreau (orange liqueur)

To make a simple syrup: Dissolve sugar in water in a saucepan over medium high heat. Set aside.

In a medium bowl, beat egg whites until stiff. Slowly whisk in syrup. Add juices and Cointreau. Mix well. Let cool and refrigerate several hours until cold.

Place mixture in an ice cream freezer and process 45 minutes, stopping to turn and blend sorbet from bottom after 20 minutes. Transfer to another container if desired and freeze until ready to serve. Makes 1 quart.

BITE-SIZE CHEESECAKES

Rich and creamy without a crust, these cheesecakes may be made in regular or mini-muffin tins. They freeze very well and may be topped with fresh strawberries, blueberries or any garnish of your choice.

3	8-ounce packages cream cheese, softened
5	eggs
1	cup sugar
1½	teaspoons vanilla extract

SOUR CREAM TOPPING:

3	cups sour cream
½	cup sugar
1	teaspoon vanilla extract

Preheat oven to 350°. Line muffin tins with paper muffin cups.

In a large bowl, beat cream cheese until smooth. Add eggs 1 at a time. Mix in sugar and vanilla and blend well. Fill cups ¾ full. Bake for 20-25 minutes. Do not be alarmed if cakes fall slightly when removed from oven.

Spoon topping over each cake and return to oven for 5 minutes. Cool, chill and garnish each with a berry before serving. Makes 50-60.

SOUR CREAM TOPPING: Mix all ingredients together until smooth. Chill until ready to use.

Mrs. Charles M. Johnson, Jr.
Raleigh, NC

KEY LIME CHEESECAKE TARTS

These tarts are made to order for any summer buffet. Light creamy and flavorful, they may be made the day before and finished with a dollop of whipped cream at serving time. Tart shells are found in the freezer section of the grocery store near puff pastry and pie crusts. They come eight to a package.

16	pre-baked 3-inch tart shells in foil liners
2	8-ounce packages cream cheese, at room temperature
¾	cup granulated sugar
2	large eggs, room temperature
½	cup Nellie and Joe's Key Lime Juice
•	whipped cream, optional

Preheat oven to 325°.

Beat cream cheese and sugar together in bowl until smooth, scraping sides of bowl often. Add eggs, 1 at a time beating well after each addition. Add key lime juice.

Place tart shells on a baking pan with sides. To fill shells, place filling into a 4-cup measuring cup and pour slowly into shells. Bake for 20 minutes. Turn off oven and let sit for another 20 minutes.

Refrigerate at least 4 hours. Serve chilled with a dollop of whipped cream. Makes 16.

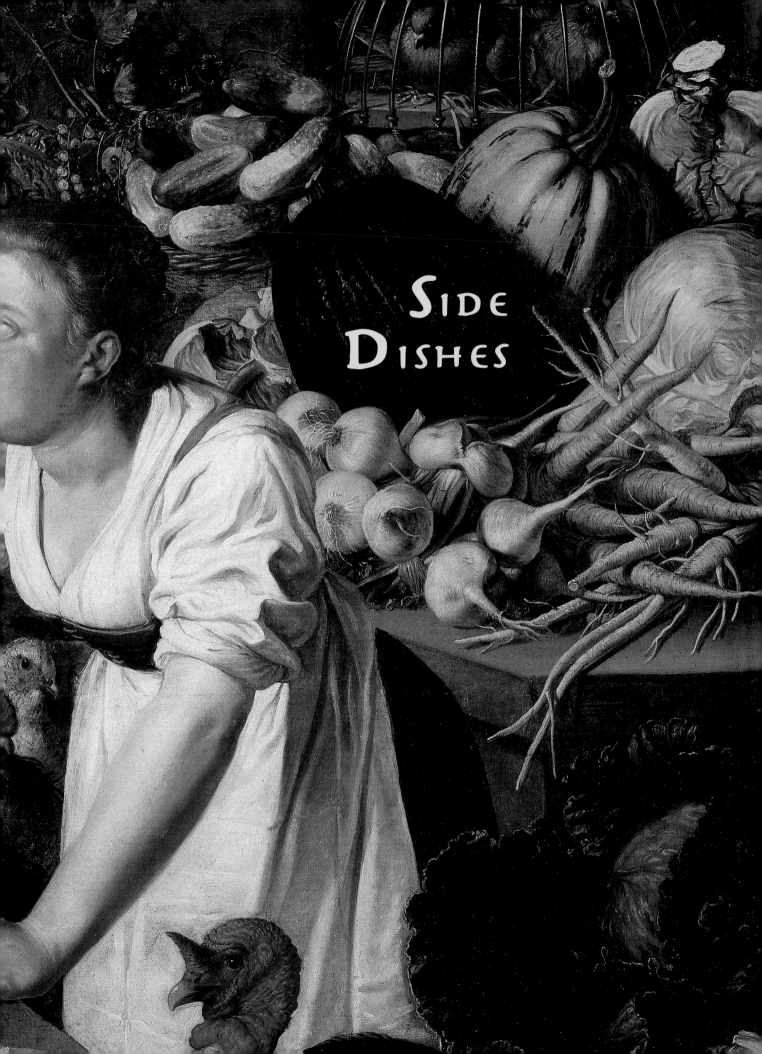

SIDE
DISHES

YUMMY DEVILED EGGS

Rice vinegar adds an interesting bite to these delicious deviled eggs.

1	dozen large eggs
½	cup mayonnaise
2	tablespoons heavy cream
1	teaspoon sugar
1	tablespoon rice vinegar
•	salt
1-2	teaspoons chervil for garnish

Place eggs in a large pan with water to cover. Boil eggs 2 minutes, remove from heat, cover and let stand 11 minutes. Pour off hot water and add cold water to stop cooking.

Once cooled, remove shells and cut eggs in half lengthwise. Separate yolks and press through a coarse strainer. Put whites on a plate.

To yolks, add mayonnaise, cream, sugar, vinegar and salt. Stir to blend.

Fill egg whites with yolk mixture. Sprinkle with chervil. Makes 24. Serves 8-10.

DELORES (DEE) COOK
APEX, NC

CAROLINA OYSTER & SAUSAGE STUFFING

Great combination of flavors make this stuffing outstanding; you could feast on it alone. This must be baked separately, not stuffed in bird, as the oysters need just a little time to cook. For best results, use a real country pork sausage like Neese's, a popular North Carolina brand.

1	pound pork sausage
2½	cups chopped onion
2½	cups chopped celery
½	cup butter
1	16-ounce package herbed stuffing
1	pint oysters, with liquid
3	cups chicken stock
1	teaspoon salt
1	teaspoon pepper
2	eggs, lightly beaten

In a large skillet over medium heat, brown sausage and crumble. Remove from pan and drain off fat. Set aside.

In same skillet, sauté onion and celery in butter until soft, about 5 minutes.

Preheat oven to 350°. In a 3-quart casserole combine celery and onion

with sausage stuffing, oysters with liquid and chicken stock. Season with salt and pepper. Stir in eggs. Bake for 30 minutes. Serves 8.

OYSTER PIE
IN A POTATO CHIP CRUST

An oyster pie in a potato chip crust is a popular side dish at holiday meals in the Gregory household.

6	cups potato chips
½	cup butter, melted
2	teaspoons minced dried onions
1	teaspoon paprika
1	pint oysters
1	can cream of mushroom soup
3	eggs, beaten
½	teaspoon celery salt
•	salt and pepper

Preheat oven to 375°. Finely crush potato chips by hand or in a plastic bag with a mallet, yielding 1½ cups. In a bowl combine chips, butter, dried onions and paprika. Press firmly into sides and bottom of 9-inch pie pan. Bake 10 minutes. Cool.

Lower oven temperature to 325°. Chop oysters and mix with undiluted soup, eggs and celery salt. Salt and pepper to taste. Pour into crust. Bake 50 minutes. Serves 6.

AURORA K. GREGORY
RALEIGH, NC

BAKED SAUSAGE & WILD RICE

A good main course for a fall or winter gathering. Prepare with optional chopped chard (or other greens) for added color and flavor.

1	pound bulk hot pork sausage
1	6-ounce package long grain and wild rice
1	8-ounce can sliced water chestnuts
¼	pound mushrooms, sliced
1	tablespoon vegetable oil
4	cups coarsely chopped Swiss chard leaves (optional)

Preheat oven to 350°. Cook sausage and drain off excess fat. Cook rice according to package directions. Drain water chestnuts. In a large sauté pan, heat oil over medium heat and sauté mushrooms briefly to brown lightly. If adding chard, remove mushrooms. Sauté in same pan until just wilted. Combine all

ingredients in a 3-quart casserole dish. Bake for 25 minutes. Serves 4.

BERTI STEVENS
RALEIGH, NC

BULGHUR PILAF

The nutty texture of this dish goes well with lamb, pork or even chicken.

2	cups vegetable broth or chicken broth
¾	cup white raisins
1	teaspoon cumin
2	tablespoons olive oil
1	large onion
1	clove garlic
1	cup coarse bulghur
½	teaspoon salt
½	teaspoon freshly ground pepper

In a large measuring cup or other microwave-safe container, combine broth, raisins and cumin. Cook on high in microwave for about 3 minutes. Set aside.

In a medium-sized heavy saucepan, heat olive oil over medium low heat; add onion and garlic and sauté slowly until tender, 5-8 minutes. Stir in bulghur and sauté 1 minute. Add broth mixture and season with salt and pepper. Bring to a boil; reduce heat, cover and simmer 15-18 minutes until liquid is absorbed. Fluff with a fork. Serves 4.

SAFFRON RICE SALAD

A delicious rice salad that may be served warm or cold. It would pair beautifully with any grilled chicken or pork dish, or try the next time you prepare fish.

1	5-ounce bag Mahatma saffron rice mix
3	tablespoons oil, divided
2½	tablespoons red wine vinegar
•	pepper
¼	cup chopped onion
½	cup chopped seeded tomato
½	cup slivered almonds
¾	cup small diced celery
⅔	cup frozen green peas, thawed
⅓	cup raisins

Prepare rice in a medium saucepan according to package directions using 1 tablespoon oil instead of butter and only 1⅓ cups water. Turn cooked rice into a medium bowl.

Mix in remaining oil, vinegar and pepper to taste; toss to mix. Add onion, tomato, almonds, celery, peas and raisins.

Serve in a bowl lined with cabbage or lettuce leaves. Serves 6.

SALLY HALLIDAY
RALEIGH, NC

CURRIED BASMATI RICE
Rice need never be a ho-hum side dish again with this flavorful recipe featuring chilies, curry, raisins and a little coconut. This would be delicious with the Tangy Tandoori Chicken, page 101.

2	tablespoons olive oil
1	small chopped onion
1-2	green chilies (Anaheim or similar), seeded and chopped
1½	cups basmati rice
1	teaspoon salt
2	teaspoons curry powder
1	cup golden raisins
3	cups vegetable broth or chicken broth
½	cup grated coconut

Heat olive oil over medium heat in heavy saucepan. Add onion and green chilies and sauté until soft, about 5-7 minutes. Stir in rice and sauté about 1 minute. Add salt, curry powder, golden raisins and broth.

Bring to a boil, cover and cook about 10 minutes until tender and liquid is absorbed. Stir in coconut. Serves 6-8.

MARINATED VIDALIAS
This onion recipe would go well with any grilled meat, fish, chicken, or to dress up burgers or sliced tomatoes or anytime you would use raw onion slices.

¼	cup white vinegar
½	cup sugar
1	cup water
2-3	Vidalia onions
¼	cup mayonnaise
1	teaspoon dill weed
1	tablespoon chopped parsley
¼	teaspoon celery salt
½	teaspoon paprika

In a small saucepan, bring vinegar, sugar and water to boil. Stir until sugar is dissolved. Cool slightly. Slice onions in medium to thin slices and separate rings. Pour vinegar over onions in a shallow dish and marinate overnight. Serves 4-6.

Drain onions well. In a medium bowl, mix mayonnaise with dill, parsley, celery salt and paprika. Stir in onions and mix to coat well.

BARBARA SISK LANDON
NORTH WILKSBORO, NC

GRILLED & CHILLED VEGETABLE SALAD
The robust, earthy flavors of the marinated grilled vegetables make this a side dish for many occasions.

2	zucchini
2	yellow squash
1	eggplant
1	green bell pepper
1	red bell pepper
1	large onion
3	whole portobello mushrooms
3	cloves garlic, chopped
3	tablespoons fresh rosemary
3	tablespoons fresh thyme
2	cups balsamic vinegar
½	cup olive oil
•	salt and pepper

Cut zucchini, yellow squash and eggplant lengthwise into strips. Cut peppers in half and remove seeds. Cut onion into rings but do not separate. Leave mushrooms whole. Place vegetables in a bowl.

In a separate bowl, combine garlic, rosemary, thyme and vinegar. Whisk in olive oil. Pour dressing over vegetables. Marinate in refrigerator 8-10 hours.

Grill vegetables until tender on either a stovetop or outdoor grill. Cool, then slice mushrooms and pepper into strips. Salt and pepper to taste. Return to refrigerator and chill until ready to serve. Serves 8.

OVEN STEAMED SUMMER VEGETABLES
These easy summer vegetables are a quick way to prepare a colorful medley. Cut vegetables a similar size so that they will cook in about the same time.

3	tablespoons olive oil, divided
2	small yellow squash, sliced
2	small zucchini squash, sliced
8	ounces mushrooms, cut in quarters
4	cloves garlic, chopped
⅓	cup chopped fresh oregano
⅓	cup chopped fresh basil
•	salt and pepper

Preheat oven to 400°. Grease large baking pan with 1 tablespoon oil.

Arrange yellow squash, zucchini & mushrooms in pan. Strew garlic, oregano, and basil around. Sprinkle with salt and pepper. Drizzle with remaining 2 tablespoons olive oil.

Cover tightly with foil. (May be prepared ahead to this point.) Bake until just crisp tender, 15-20 minutes. Serve immediately. Double recipe as needed for more guests. Serves 4.

"COLD AND TASTY" CARROTS
A simple, provocative salad. Make a day ahead for best results. A great dish for potlucks or picnics.

1	pound carrots, peeled and sliced
1	medium onion, sliced
1	tablespoon water
1	tablespoon cider vinegar
2	teaspoons sugar
1	teaspoon canola oil
¼	teaspoon salt
¼	teaspoon white pepper
¼	teaspoon dry mustard
2	tablespoons diced green pepper

Cook and drain carrots. In a glass measuring cup, combine onion, water, vinegar, sugar and oil. Microwave this mixture 1 minute.

Pour over hot carrots. Sprinkle with salt, pepper and dry mustard and mix.

Chill overnight, stir occasionally. Garnish with diced green pepper before serving. Serves 6.

REBECCA CLAYTON
RALEIGH, NC

MADEIRA CARROTS
An elegant side dish with unique flavor. For best results in appearance and uniform cooking, cut carrots into fairly even-sized pieces, such as a julienne.

1	pound carrots
½	cup Madeira
4	tablespoons butter
¼	teaspoon salt
¼	teaspoon tarragon.

Peel carrots and cut in half and then quarter lengthwise. If larger carrots are used cut into thirds before quartering.

The desired size is approximately ¼-inch x ¼-inch x 3-inch.

Place carrots, Madeira, butter and salt in a 1½-quart saucepan. Cook on low heat until tender, but not limp. Remove from heat and stir in tarragon to taste.

Let stand a few minutes before serving to develop flavors. Serves 4-5.

CONNIE POPE
RALEIGH, NC

CHILLED ASPARAGUS NAPOLI

This is a delicious side salad to serve with a traveling picnic. Pack dressing in a small plastic container.

1	pound asparagus, cut in 3-inch lengths
1	clove garlic, split in half
½	teaspoon salt
⅛	teaspoon freshly ground pepper
½	teaspoon sugar
¼	cup balsamic or red wine vinegar
1	cup olive oil
2	tablespoons minced parsley
2	tablespoons finely chopped red bell pepper
1	tablespoon minced green onion tops
1	hard-cooked egg, chopped fine

Boil 4 quarts of water in a large pot with 2 teaspoons salt. Drop asparagus pieces into boiling water, blanch 1½ minutes and immediately plunge in iced water. Drain and refrigerate.

Rub the inside of a small bowl with garlic. Combine salt, pepper, sugar and vinegar in bowl. Whisk until sugar and salt are dissolved. Whisk in olive oil (or ½ cup olive oil to ½ vegetable oil.) Add parsley, bell pepper and green onion.

To serve: Divide asparagus among plates. Sprinkle with chopped egg, then pour dressing over the top. Serves 4.

ZUCCHINI SQUASH STUFFED TOMATOES

An easy, make ahead assembly will make these a popular recipe when serving friends and festive suppers.

1	medium zucchini
1	medium yellow squash
1	teaspoon salt
4	medium tomatoes
2	tablespoons olive oil
2	cloves garlic, minced
¼	cup chopped fresh basil

Coarsely shred zucchini and yellow squash using a food processor or hand grater.

Place grated squash into a colander and toss with 1 teaspoon salt. Let sit for 20-30 minutes to drain. Dry on paper towels.

Slice a thin piece off the top of each tomato. Gently clean out seeds and juice. Set cut side down on a paper towel to drain for about 10 minutes.

Preheat oven to 450°. Place seeded tomatoes, cut side up, in a baking pan. Bake, uncovered, for about 10 minutes until tender but not falling apart. Do not overcook.

Meanwhile, heat olive oil in a large heavy skillet over medium heat. Add garlic and grated zucchini and yellow squash. Sauté, stirring occasionally, for about 5 minutes until just tender. Stir in fresh basil.

Shortly before serving spoon squash mixture into each tomato. Serve immediately. Serves 4.

TOMATO ASPIC

A congealed side dish with delicious tang.

1	package lemon jello
1	cup boiling water
1	8-ounce can tomato sauce
1	5-ounce jar sliced olives, drained
¾	cup finely chopped celery
1½	tablespoons vinegar
½	teaspoon salt

Dissolve jello in boiling water. Add tomato sauce, olives, celery, vinegar and salt. Stir well.

Pour into an 8-inch x 8-inch dish or into 6 individual 6-ounce molds. Refrigerate until set. Serves 6.

NOTE: Other ingredients may be substituted for olives and celery. Try shrimp, onion, green pepper, artichokes, etc.

MAZIE FROELICH
HIGH POINT, NC

CUSTARDY CORN PUDDING

A little sweet tinged with subtle spice makes this colorful pudding a winner. Add a crock of baked lima beans for a casual veggie meal.

1	tablespoon butter
1	cup chopped white onion
1	cup chopped red pepper
1	cup chopped yellow pepper
3	cups white corn kernels
½	teaspoon nutmeg
½	teaspoon freshly ground pepper
1½	cups water
1	cup white cornmeal
¾	cup milk
⅓	cup sugar
1	teaspoon salt
6	large eggs, lightly beaten

Preheat oven to 375°. Butter a 2-quart baking dish. In a large skillet, melt butter. Sauté onion, peppers and corn with nutmeg and pepper over medium heat 5-7 minutes until onions are translucent. Set aside.

Place water in a small, heavy-bottomed saucepan over medium high heat. Whisk in cornmeal and cook until very thick like polenta, about 5 minutes.

Transfer cornmeal to a medium bowl and stir in milk, sugar, salt and eggs. Add corn/pepper mixture and pour into baking dish. Bake 45-50 minutes or until knife inserted in center comes out clean. Remove from oven and allow to rest 20 minutes before serving. Serves 6-8.

CREAMED SUMMER CORN

Corn becomes an intense delight in this simple sautéed side dish.

6	ears corn
4	tablespoons butter
•	fresh ground pepper
⅓	cup half-and-half

Place corn cobs on a plate and score each row of corn down the middle. Cut corn off cob. Transfer with milky liquid to a sauté pan.

Cook corn slowly in butter until it melts, then add fresh ground pepper and half-and-half. Cook corn just until heated through. Serves 3-4.

LAWRENCE J. WHEELER
CHAPEL HILL, NC

Two festive side dishes — Artichokes Stuffed with Feta Cheese and Twice Baked Squash, page 207.

To serve, drain artichokes, reserving marinade. Place artichoke halves, cut side up, on a serving platter of shredded lettuce. Stir marinade into bulghur mixture. Spoon some of bulghur into each artichoke half. Place any additional bulghur mixture in a bowl and serve with the artichokes. Serves 4 (or 2 if left whole).

FANCY SUCCOTASH

Succotash is a derivative of the Naragansett Indian word msickquatash, *"boiled whole kernels of corn." In the southern United States, this is a popular side dish always featuring corn and lima beans.*

4	tablespoons butter
½	cup chopped scallions
½	cup finely chopped yellow bell pepper
½	cup finely chopped red bell pepper
2	cups cooked corn
2	cups cooked baby limas
1	tablespoon Worcestershire sauce
½	teaspoon salt
½	teaspoon white pepper
1	tablespoon fresh chives

In a large saucepan melt butter and sauté scallions and peppers over medium heat for 5 minutes. Stir in corn, baby limas, Worcestershire, salt and pepper. Heat through. Add fresh chives just before serving. Serves 4-6.

SPINACH-LACED BRUSSELS SPROUTS

Delicious. Pre-steam Brussels sprouts and clean spinach ahead for quick and easy cooking at serving time.

1½	pounds fresh Brussels sprouts
1	pound spinach leaves
1½	tablespoons minced garlic
3	tablespoons olive oil
•	salt and pepper

Choose Brussels sprouts that are relatively similar in size and trim woody ends; cut a small X into the base of the core. Bring 1-inch water to boil in a steamer and add sprouts. Cook smaller sprouts 5-8 minutes, larger ones 8-10. Test with a fork until just tender. Remove from heat and cool to touch. Slice vertically into 2 or 3 parts depending on their size. Set aside. Wash spinach thoroughly, drain and dry. Remove

ARTICHOKES
STUFFED WITH FETA CHEESE

For a side dish, cut the artichokes in half. To serve as a first course or luncheon dish, the artichokes could be left whole, allowing one per person. Remove the choke and prickly inner leaves and stuff the center.

2	medium artichokes
3	tablespoons lemon juice, plus more for rubbing edges
2	tablespoons olive oil
1	tablespoon water
1	tablespoon fresh oregano or 1/2 teaspoon dried
½	cup bulghur
¼	teaspoon salt
1	large tomato, peeled, seeded and chopped (1 ¼ cups)
½	cup crumbled feta cheese
¼	cup fresh parsley

Wash artichokes; trim stems and remove loose outer leaves. Cut off 1 inch from each top; with a scissors snip off the sharp leaf tips. Brush cut edges with a little lemon juice.

Place a steamer basket in a large saucepan. Add water to just below the bottom of the steamer basket. Bring to a boil. Add artichokes. Cover and reduce heat; steam for 30-35 minutes or until a leaf pulls out easily.

Drain artichokes upside down on paper towels. When cool, halve each artichoke lengthwise. Pull out center leaves and scrape out choke and discard. Place artichoke halves in a plastic bag set in a deep bowl.

For marinade: Mix 3 tablespoons lemon juice, olive oil, water and oregano in a small bowl. Pour over artichokes in bag. Close bag and turn artichokes to coat well. Marinate in refrigerator for several hours, turning bag occasionally.

Meanwhile, in a medium bowl combine bulghur, salt and 1 cup hot water; let stand for 1 hour. Drain well, pressing out excess water. Combine the drained bulghur, chopped tomato, feta cheese and parsley. Cover and chill thoroughly.

large stems and chop coarsely. In a large sauté pan, cook garlic in hot oil for 1 minute. Add Brussels sprouts and spinach and stir until spinach wilts and Brussels sprouts are heated through. Season with salt and pepper, then serve immediately.

ITALIAN CHARD
WITH PARMESAN CHEESE
Another delicious vegetable with a quick savory preparation.

1	bunch Swiss chard (with either red or white stems)
2	tablespoons olive oil
2-3	cloves garlic, minced
•	salt and freshly ground pepper
½	cup freshly grated Parmesan cheese

Wash chard well. Cut off stems and slice into ½-inch pieces the same way you would celery. Coarsely chop leaves, leaving separate from stems.

Heat oil in heavy sauté pan or large saucepan over medium heat. Add garlic and sliced chard stems. Sauté about 4 minutes until beginning to be tender, but still crisp.

Stir in chopped chard leaves and sauté 5 minutes more until wilted and just tender.

Season with salt and freshly ground pepper, and toss with grated Parmesan cheese. Serve immediately. Serves 3-4.

SAUTÉED GREEN BEANS
WITH PECANS AND FRESH TARRAGON
Pretty and flavorful with a tang of tarragon and garlic.

2	pounds green beans
¼	cup olive oil
½	cup butter
¼	cup minced shallots
2	tablespoons minced garlic
½	cup chopped pecans
¼	cup chopped tarragon
•	salt and ground pepper

Clean green beans and cook in boiling, salted water until tender about 2-5 minutes. Rinse under cold water and drain.

In a sauté pan, heat olive oil and butter, add green beans, shallots and garlic. Toss. Add pecans, tarragon, and salt and pepper to taste. Serves 8-10.

ILYA SCHOR (American), *PASSOVER SEDER PLATE*, c. 1952-55

BROCCOLI CAULIFLOWER CASSEROLE
A great do-ahead vegetable side dish for a Thanksgiving or Christmas dinner.

1	head broccoli
1	head cauliflower
3	tablespoons butter
3	tablespoons flour
2	cups milk
•	salt and pepper
•	dash nutmeg
½	pound mushrooms, sliced
1	tablespoon olive oil
12	ounces medium sharp cheddar cheese, grated, divided
2	stalks celery, small dice

Preheat oven to 350°. Grease a 9-inch x 13-inch casserole.

Cut broccoli and cauliflower into bite-sized pieces. Blanch in boiling water 3-4 minutes. Drain. Set aside.

In a medium saucepan make a roux with butter and flour. Add milk, cook and stir until thickened. Season with salt, pepper and nutmeg.

In a large sauté pan, toss mushrooms in olive oil until lightly browned.

In a large bowl combine broccoli, cauliflower, cream sauce, sliced mushrooms, ¾ of the cheese and diced celery.

Transfer to casserole. Top with remaining cheese and bake for 40 minutes until bubbly. Serves 8-10.

GUINEVERE D. WILSON
RALEIGH NC

PERFECT PICNIC COLE SLAW
Shared by a college friend of Janet Rand's at the University of Michigan, this tangy cole slaw is especially suited to picnics since there is no mayonnaise.

1	medium head finely shredded green cabbage
2	green bell peppers, sliced
2	medium white onion, sliced
2	tablespoons chopped parsley
•	salt and pepper

WHITE VINEGAR DRESSING:

2	cups white vinegar
1	cup salad oil
1	cup water
1½	cups sugar

Layer cabbage, peppers, onions and parsley in a large non-metallic bowl. Mix and pour dressing over. Do not salt or pepper. Cover and place in the refrigerator overnight. Just before serving, drain slaw. Add salt and pepper to taste. Serves 6-8.

JANET C. RAND
WILSON, NC

MUSHROOMS FLORENTINE
A wonderful accompaniment to any meal. May be served on toast points as an appetizer or with crostinis for an hors d'oeuvre.

2	10-ounce packages frozen spinach leaves
4	tablespoons butter
¼	cup chopped onion
1	pound fresh mushrooms, sliced

1 cup grated mozzarella cheese
1 teaspoon salt
1 teaspoon garlic salt

Thaw and cook spinach; drain well.

In a medium skillet, melt butter over medium heat and sauté onion and mushrooms for 5 minutes. Stir in spinach, cheese, salt and garlic salt and transfer mixture to a greased 9-inch x 9-inch baking dish. Bake at 350° for 20 minutes. Serves 8.

GERRY GILBERT
RALEIGH, NC

TWICE BAKED SQUASH

This colorful vegetable dish combines acorn squash with spinach and Parmesan to make a perfect fall or winter side dish. For a vegetarian dish, use minced garlic instead of bacon.

2 small acorn squash
1¼ cups chopped cooked spinach (1 10-ounce frozen spinach)
3 slices bacon
½ cup grated Parmesan cheese, divided
3 tablespoons butter, melted
2 tablespoons chopped green onion
⅛ teaspoon salt
⅛ teaspoon cayenne pepper
2 tablespoons soft bread crumbs

Preheat oven to 350°. Halve squash crosswise and remove seeds. Place squash cut side down in a baking dish. Bake for 30 minutes.

Turn, placing squash cut side up; cover and bake another 20-25 minutes or until nearly tender. If frozen spinach is used, thaw and drain well.

Cook bacon until crisp; drain and crumble. Scoop out squash pulp, leaving shell intact. Combine in a large bowl with spinach, bacon, ⅓ cup Parmesan cheese, butter, green onions, salt and cayenne pepper. Fill squash shells with this mixture.

Combine the bread crumbs with remaining Parmesan cheese and sprinkle over squash. Return squash to baking dish and bake uncovered 25-30 minutes or until heated through. Serves 4

PAULA MEHLHOP
CARY, NC

SQUASH & POTATO SKEWERS

Roasted "french-fry" cut potatoes, acorn squash and butternut squash will be popular with kids.

8 6-inch wooden skewers
2 large red potatoes
½ acorn squash
½ small butternut squash
¼ cup olive oil
½ teaspoon garlic salt
⅛ teaspoon pepper

Soak skewers in water for 30 minutes. Cut potatoes into 3-inch long by ½-inch thick strips. Peel acorn and butternut squash and scrape out seeds. Cut into approximately 3-inch long by ½-inch thick strips. Combine oil, garlic salt and pepper; toss potatoes and squash in the mixture.

Preheat oven to 400°. Thread potatoes and squash strips alternately on 8 skewers. Place on a baking sheet and roast for 25 minutes or until tender. Halfway through cooking, flip skewers over to brown evenly. Serves 4 to 6.

GREEK POTATO SALAD

Olives give this salad zing while the radishes and pepper provide the crunch. A wonderful side salad for grilled chicken, fish or spicy ribs.

2 pounds red potatoes
1 cup whole Kalamata olives
½ pound Feta cheese
6 radishes
1 cup chopped green pepper
¼ cup chopped parsley

DIJON LEMON DRESSING:
¾ cup olive oil
¼ cup lemon juice
1 teaspoon Dijon mustard
1 clove garlic, minced
1 teaspoon salt
½ teaspoon pepper

Peel potatoes, quarter and drop into boiling water. Cook for 10-15 minutes until just tender. Drain, cool and dice into 1-inch cubes. Remove pits from olives, if necessary, and halve. Crumble Feta cheese and slice radishes. In a large bowl, combine the potatoes with the olives, Feta, radishes, green pepper and parsley. Toss with Dijon Lemon Dressing,

cover and chill in refrigerator for at least 2 hours. Serves 6-8.

DIJON LEMON DRESSING: Whisk ingredients together in a small bowl.

POTATO LATKES

This favorite Jewish dish is prepared at Hanukkah incorporating a little Southern "frying" heritage. These delicious pancakes may be made a few days before and reheated on cookie sheets. They also freeze well.

6 large potatoes, peeled
1 large onion, grated
3 eggs
1 teaspoon pepper
1 teaspoon salt
¼ cup flour
2 teaspoons baking powder
¼ cup chopped fresh parsley
• oil for frying
• applesauce
• sour cream

Grate potatoes. Squeeze excess water from grated potatoes and onions with cheesecloth.

In a large bowl mix ingredients thoroughly. Heat oil in a large skillet and drop in potato mixture by the spoonful. Brown on each side. Drain on absorbent paper. Serve with dollops of applesauce or sour cream. Serves 12.

CONNIE C. SHERTZ
RALEIGH, NC

ROSEMARY POTATOES

These rosemary potatoes were a common dish Adam Lopez often encountered during a trip to Italy. He added the prosciutto.

4 medium red potatoes, cubed
• olive oil
• salt and pepper
1 teaspoon rosemary
½ cup diced prosciutto ham

Preheat oven to 400°. Combine potatoes, salt, pepper and rosemary in a medium bowl. Drizzle olive oil over potatoes, enough to coat. Spread on a cookie sheet and bake uncovered for 10 minutes. Stir in prosciutto. Bake another 10-15 minutes. For crisper potatoes, bake longer. Serves 3-4.

ADAM DAVID LOPEZ
GREENBELT, MD

CREAMED CHESTNUTS

The late Susie Sharp shared her secret for preparing fresh chestnuts, available from September through February. Unless you can find canned peeled chestnuts, this dish will be considered a labor of love.

2	pounds chestnuts
•	boiling water
½	cup butter
2	tablespoons flour
1½	cups milk
½	cup heavy cream
•	cayenne pepper
•	salt
⅓	cup dry sherry

To peel, put chestnuts in a large pot with boiling water to cover. Simmer 15-20 minutes.

With a sharp knife, score each chestnut with an "X" deep enough to cut the outer skin. Shell and skin chestnuts while hot and moist. This is important as the job becomes very difficult once the scored chestnuts have cooled.

In a large saucepan make a sauce by melting butter over medium heat. Stir in flour to make a roux. Add milk and cream. Cook and stir until sauce thickens. Season with cayenne pepper and salt.

About 30 minutes before serving, heat sauce and chestnuts in the top of a double boiler. Add sherry at the last minute. Serves 10.

SUSIE SHARP
RALEIGH, NC

SWEET NOODLE KUGLE

Oodles of noodles mixed with fruit and cottage cheese make this dish an unexpected surprise. It's a side dish that resembles dessert. Always cook it in a shallow pan for best results.

½	pound egg noodles
4	tablespoons butter
⅓	cup apricot preserves
2	eggs
½	cup sugar
½	cup cottage cheese
½	cup sour cream
½	cup raisins
•	cinnamon

Prehat oven to 350°. Cook noodles in boiling water, drain and return to pot. While still hot, stir in butter and preserves mixing until butter has melted.

Preheat oven to 350°. In a separate bowl beat eggs and sugar. Stir in cottage cheese, sour cream and raisins. Mix into noodles. Sprinkle top with cinnamon.

Cover with foil and bake 45 minutes. Remove cover and bake 5-10 minutes more to crisp top.

It may be made a day ahead and refrigerated before baking. Serves 8.

LIZ GOTTLIEB
DURHAM, NC

HORSERADISH POTATOES

This side dish was popular at a special dinner for Thomas P. F. Hoving, Director of the Metropolitan Museum, when he spoke in Greenville in 1968. Easy to prepare ahead.

8-10	potatoes (white or Yukon Gold)
1	cup diced carrots, cooked
1	tablespoon hot horseradish
½	cup milk or sour cream
•	salt and pepper
1	cup butter

Peel and cook potatoes in boiling water until fork-tender.

Preheat oven to 325°. Drain and cream with an electric beater until potatoes are light and fluffy. Stir in carrots, horseradish, milk, salt, pepper and butter. Put into a 3-quart casserole. Bake for 20-30 minutes until brown on top.

If made ahead, bring to room temperature before baking. Serves 8.

MRS. JAMES FICKLEN, JR.
RALEIGH, NC

GRUYÈRE MASHED POTATOES

Comfort food made even more decadent.

2	pounds small red potatoes
½	cup warm milk
¼	cup grainy mustard (preferably mustard with horseradish)
¼	pound Gruyere cheese (1¼ to 1½ cups shredded)
¼	cup snipped chives

Scrub potatoes and cut into chunks. (Do not peel.) Put in a large saucepan with enough salted water to cover. Cover and bring to a boil. Reduce heat and boil gently until tender, about 15-20 minutes. Drain well.

Add milk, mustard and Gruyere cheese. Mash until fairly smooth, adding a bit more milk if needed. Stir in chives. Serves 6-8.

OVEN-FRIED SWEET POTATO CHIPS

The hint of cayenne pepper imparts great flavor to these sweet potato chips. So easy to prepare, they will become a favorite side dish.

4	medium sweet potatoes
⅓	cup olive oil
1	teaspoon kosher salt
⅛-¼	teaspoon cayenne pepper

Preheat oven to 425°.

Peel and slice potatoes ⅛-inch thick. Place in large mixing bowl. Add remaining ingredients and mix to coat potatoes.

Place potatoes on baking sheets in a single layer. Bake in oven for 15 minutes. Turn chips and continue cooking until done, about 15 minutes. To crisp potatoes, slide under broiler for 1 or 2 minutes. Watch carefully to prevent burning. Serves 6-8.

SWEET POTATO PUDDING

Though called a pudding, this recipe has traditionally been served as a side dish for Christmas and Thanksgiving dinners.

6	cups shredded raw sweet potato
⅓	cup sugar
¼	cup syrup (maple or cane)
2	tablespoons corn meal
2	eggs, lightly beaten
½	cup milk
½	teaspoon nutmeg
3	tablespoons melted butter
•	dash salt
1	tablespoon grated orange rind (optional)

Preheat oven to 350°. In a large bowl stir together shredded sweet potato, sugar, syrup, corn meal, eggs, milk and nutmeg. Add melted butter, salt and orange rind if desired and put into a buttered 9-inch x 9-inch baking dish. Bake for 45 minutes. Serves 6-8.

MARY M. BLAKE
RALEIGH, NC

BALTHASAR VAN DER AST (Dutch), *STILL LIFE WITH BASKET OF FRUIT, 1622*

COOK'S PANTRY

• BASIC STOCKS •

VEGETABLE STOCK

1	tablespoon olive oil
¾	cup chopped onion
¼	cup chopped celery
1	leek, sliced
1	clove garlic, chopped
½	cup sliced mushrooms
2	quarts water
•	bouquet of thyme, bay, parsley, peppercorns

Sweat onion, celery, leek and garlic in olive oil about 6-8 minutes. Add remaining ingredients. Bring to boil and simmer 30-45 minutes. Strain and cool. Makes 2 quarts.

CHICKEN STOCK

2-3	pounds chicken bones
1	cup chopped onion
½	cup chopped celery
½	cup chopped carrot
3	quarts water
•	bouquet of thyme, bay, parsley, peppercorns

Combine ingredients in a soup pot. Bring to boil and simmer 2 hours. Strain and skim fat from top. Makes 3 quarts.

FISH STOCK WITH VEGETABLES

1-2	pounds fish bones and heads
6	cups water
1	cup white wine
4	black peppercorns
2	sprigs parsley
1	teaspoon thyme
½	onion, sliced
1	small carrot, sliced
1	rib celery, sliced
1	clove garlic, crushed

Rinse fish bones and heads in cold water. Bring trimmings to a boil in a large pot with all the other ingredients. Turn down the heat and simmer for 30 minutes. Strain stock through a fine sieve. Makes 1½ quarts.

• DRESSINGS •

POTATO SALAD OR COLE SLAW DRESSIONG

Excellent sauce for side salads. Pour over potatoes while still hot, but let cool before adding to cabbage for slaw.

3	eggs
½	cup white vinegar
¾	cup sugar
1	cup water
2	teaspoons salt
½	teaspoon dry mustard
4	tablespoons butter

In a medium saucepan, beat eggs and add vinegar, sugar, water, salt and mustard. Beat until well blended. Place on medium heat and bring to boil stirring constantly. Add butter and allow to melt. Makes 2 cups.

EMILY S. BOWEN
PINEHURST, NC

VEDA STEWART'S ALL PURPOSE DRESSING

A tangy salad dressing reminiscent of one served on hearts of lettuce in yesteryear. The relish may be found at a farmers' market or a specialty grocery with homemade condiments.

½	cup mayonnaise or heavy cream
½	cup chili sauce or ketchup
¼	cup fresh lemon juice
¼	cup pepper and onion relish

Mix ingredients together and chill. Makes 1½ cups.

MARY ALICE JACKSON
SMITHFIELD, NC

STRAWBERRY BASIL DRESSING

Try this over a green leaf salad topped with orange segments and red onion slices

10	whole strawberries, cleaned & hulled
¼	cup raspberry vinegar
½	cup light olive oil
½	cup vegetable oil
1	tablespoon lemon juice
½	teaspoon basil
•	freshly ground pepper

Purée strawberries in a food processor. While still running, slowly add vinegar. Slowly add oils and lemon juice. Season with basil and pepper. Yields 1½ cups.

LEMON TAHINI DRESSING

A versatile dressing with Asian flavors.

½	medium yellow onion, peeled
1	small green pepper, seeded
2	stalks celery
1	teaspoon white pepper
1	teaspoon garlic powder
1	cup tahini (sesame paste)
¾	cup fresh lemon juice
½	cup soy oil
1	cup sesame oil (use light-colored sesame, not dark oriental [s/b Asian] variety)
¾	cup tamari (premium soy sauce)
1	tablespoon honey

Blend ingredients in food processor. Yields 1 quart.

• CONDIMENTS •

MANGO CHUTNEY

This would make a nice Christmas gift for a neighbor because it's quick and easy to make. Peeling the mangoes is made easier with kitchen shears.

6	ripe mangoes, peeled and chopped
¾	cup sugar
½	cup cider vinegar
¼	teaspoon chopped garlic
¾	cup water
2	teaspoons fresh ginger, chopped or grated
⅓	cup crystallized ginger
2	tablespoons lime juice
2	teaspoons curry powder
½	teaspoon red pepper flakes
1	cup chopped onion
1	cup currants

Boil sugar, vinegar, garlic and water. Simmer 5 minutes. Add mangoes and simmer 10 minutes. Remove fruit and reserve syrup.

Add grated fresh ginger, crystallized ginger, lime juice, curry powder red pepper flakes, onion and currants to syrup. Bring to a boil and simmer for 10 minutes. Return fruit to syrup. Cool completely, then pour into jars. Store in refrigerator. Makes 1 quart.

BETTY A. NIZICH
CARY, NC

FIG LIME CHUTNEY

Make for yourself, make for your friends. The zesty sweetness will suit grilled chicken and fish, or simply liven up a roasted vegetable and rice dinner.

6	cups ripe figs
•	zest of 2 limes (about 2 tablespoons)
½	cup lime juice
½	cup cider vinegar
½	cup brown sugar
¼	cup crystallized ginger
1	teaspoon dry mustard
1	teaspoon salt
1	Granny Smith apple, peeled and chopped
1	medium onion, quartered, then thinly sliced
1	jalapeño pepper, finely chopped

Wash figs and remove stems. Cut into 1-inch pieces. In large saucepan stir together lime zest, lime juice, vinegar, brown sugar, ginger, dry mustard and salt. Add figs, apple, onion and jalapeño pepper. Bring to a boil; reduce heat and simmer, uncovered, stirring occasionally, until very thick, about 30-35 minutes. Fruit should be tender, but not mushy. Store in airtight container or jars in refrigerator. it will keep for several weeks. Makes 5 cups.

CRANBERRY CONSERVE

Brandy and ginger deepen the flavor of cranberries cooked in this unique conserve.

¾	cup sugar
¾	cup water
•	grated rind of half an orange
3	pieces crystallized ginger, chopped
1	pound fresh cranberries
½	cup chopped walnuts
⅓	cup brandy

In a large heavy saucepan bring sugar, water, orange rind and ginger to a boil. Simmer 10 minutes.

Add cranberries and nuts. Return to boil, lower heat and simmer 2-3 minutes or until cranberries burst. Add brandy. Makes 3-4 cups.

LAWRENCE J. WHEELER
CHAPEL HILL, NC

CRANBERRY ORANGE RELISH

This sauce works well with turkey, but is equally delicious served over waffles or ice cream. The recipe is adapted from Craig Claiborne's New York Times Cookbook *to have a more intense orange flavor.*

1	12-ounce bag cranberries (3 cups)
1	tablespoon grated orange rind
1	cup orange juice
2	cups sugar
½	cup slivered almonds

Wash and pick over cranberries. Combine with orange rind, juice and sugar in a large saucepan. Cook over medium heat about 10 minutes or until cranberries pop open. Skim foam from surface. Add almonds and cool. Serves 8-10.

This recipe may also be made with frozen cranberries and is easily halved (use 1½ cups cranberries).

SALLY HALLIDAY
RALEIGH, NC

SPICED CRANBERRY SAUCE

Serve at holiday dinners or spread over turkey sandwiches. So good, you could grab a spoon and eat it solo.

1	12-ounce bag cranberries
2	cups sugar
2	cups port
½	teaspoon cinnamon
½	teaspoon nutmeg
½	teaspoon ground cloves

Wash and pick over cranberries. In a 3-quart saucepan, heat cranberries, sugar and port on high, stirring until sugar is dissolved. Boil, uncovered, 4-5 minutes or until cranberries have popped and liquid has a good red color. Remove from heat and stir in cinnamon, nutmeg and cloves. Cool and serve. Makes 3-4 cups.

CAROLYN HERGENROTHER
DURHAM, NC

MOM'S GREAT CUCUMBER PICKLES
Crisp with a little bite.

7	pounds unwaxed cucumbers washed and sliced
8	ounces pickling lime

Use enamel, crockery or stainless steel container when soaking cucumbers. Mix lime with enough water to cover cucumbers. Let soak for 12 hours or overnight. Rinse thoroughly and soak in ice water for 2 hours.

Prepare brine by placing all ingredients in large stainless or enamel pot. Add sliced cucumbers. Bring to a boil and boil five minutes. Remove from heat and let stand overnight.

Pack in sterilized jars and immerse in boiling water to seal. Makes 8 pints.

BRINE:

8	cups sugar
½	gallon apple cider vinegar
1	tablespoon salt
1½	tablespoons pickling spices
2-3	tablespoons whole cloves
1	teaspoon mustard seed
½	teaspoon turmeric
•	garlic cloves to taste
•	cinnamon stick for each jar

DALE PIXLEY
WENDELL, NC

FIREY EGGPLANT VIDALIA KETCHUP
A tangy, spicy Thai-style concoction that contrasts delightfully with vegetarian and fish entrees.

2	small eggplant
1	large Vidalia onion
2	tablespoons peanut oil
2	tablespoons sesame oil
1	cup apple juice
1	cup rice vinegar
1	cup honey
¼	cup hoisin sauce, see note
¼	cup soy sauce
1	tablespoon garlic/chili paste
1	3-inch piece fresh ginger root, peeled and minced

Peel and finely chop eggplant and onion to yield approximately 3 cups each. Heat peanut oil and sesame oil in a heavy-bottomed sauté pan over medium high. Add eggplant and onion, stirring often to prevent sticking. Cook until onions are translucent, about 3 minutes. Deglaze pan with apple juice. Add remaining ingredients, bring to a boil and cook for 2-3 minutes. Reduce to simmer, cover and cook for 1 hour. Cool and store in refrigerator for up to 4 weeks, or process in a water bath to put away. Makes 1 quart.

NOTE: Widely used in Chinese cooking, hoisin sauce is a mixture of soybeans, garlic, chili peppers and various spices. Its flavor is sweet and spicy. Look for it in oriental markets and many large supermarkets.

DILLY HONEY MUSTARD
Delicious. Pour into jars and share with all your friends.

32	ounces Dijon mustard
⅓	cup honey
½	cup dill weed
3	tablespoons mustard seeds
1	tablespoon Worcestershire sauce
1¼	teaspoons paprika
1¼	teaspoons freshly ground pepper

In medium bowl stir together all of the ingredients. Store in refrigerator. Put into jars or containers of choice.

This mustard is best when made at least a week ahead of time to let flavors develop. Makes 5 cups.

• BEVERAGES •

PINK LADY PUNCH

4	cups cranberry juice
4	cups pineapple juice
1	cup sugar
2	quarts chilled ginger ale

Mix cranberry and pineapple juices with sugar. Add ginger ale. Mix well and chill. Serve over ice. Makes 20 cups.

MARIAN B. CHASE
BURLINGTON, NC

OLD-FASHIONED EGG NOG

6	eggs, separated
1¾	cups sugar
1	cup apple brandy
2	quarts whole milk
2	cups whipping cream

Beat eggs yolks with sugar in a large bowl. Beat in brandy and then add milk. In separate bowls beat egg whites and heavy cream until stiff. Gently fold each into egg nog and refrigerate. Makes 12 cups.

JEAN LADD
CARY, NC

SPANISH SANGRIA
A delightful refreshing cocktail to serve on a summer's eve or for a winter gathering. Keep well chilled and serve over ice.

1	bottle (25 ounces) burgundy
¼	cup brandy
2	tablespoons Cointreau or Grand Marnier
3	cups red Hawaiian Punch
3	oranges
2	lemons
2	bananas

In a large 3-quart pitcher combine wine, brandy, orange liqueur and punch; mix well. Thinly slice oranges, lemons and slice bananas. Add fruit to wine stirring gently. Cover and refrigerate at least 4 hours before serving over ice. Makes 3 quarts.

GLORIA B. PERRY
MORRISVILLE, NC

MULLED CRANBERRY CIDER
This warm drink is refreshing and not too sweet. Tag for your Christmas open house.

½	gallon cranberry apple cider
1	3-inch cinnamon stick
3	whole allspice
3	whole cloves
4	1-inch strips lemon zest
4	whole black peppercorns
1½	cups dry white wine, see note

Place cider in medium saucepan. Tie spices into a piece of cheesecloth or place in a tea ball. Add to pan and bring to a boil. Reduce heat and simmer 20-30 minutes. Stir in white wine and heat through. Serve immediately or chill in refrigerator and reheat shortly before serving. Serves 12.

NOTE: If the cider is preferred without alcohol, simply add 1½ cups more cider.

BASIC COOKING GUIDELINES

BREADS AND PASTRIES

•*Muffins and other quick breads:* When making quick breads such as muffins, banana bread, etc. stir sparingly, just enough to combine the ingredients. This rule is true for pancake and waffle batter as well.

• *Pie Crust:* When making a pie crust, handle as little as possible. Have the butter or shortening cold, cut it into pieces, then incorporate. Blend the shortening using a fork, pastry blender or your fingers just until the mixture looks like crumbs. Use just enough ice water or other cold liquid for the dough to hold together and form a ball. If a food processor is used, be careful not to over mix. Incorporate the butter or shortening with a few short pulses of the machine. For best results using either method, wrap the dough in plastic wrap and chill for about 30 minutes before rolling.

•*Yeast Breads:* In contrast to making quick breads and pie crusts, when making yeast breads, stir vigorously, knead well, and use warm ingredients. The water for dissolving the yeast should be between 105° and 115°. (An instant-read thermo-meter is a very handy tool for measuring water temperature.) A food processor or large mixer with a dough hook makes the production of yeast breads quicker and easier.

BAKING/COOKING

•*Baking and cooking times:* Baking and cooking times called for in a recipe may vary somewhat. There is such a variance in ovens and cook tops, that it is difficult to be absolutely exact. Often a recipe will give an alternate guideline. For instance, many cakes will say to "bake until a toothpick comes out clean." Insert a toothpick or thin metal skewer into the center of the cake. If liquid clings to the pick, the cake no doubt needs a longer baking time. Check frequently around the recommended baking time. Another helpful guide is to look at the edges of a cake; they often begin to separate from the edges of the pan when done. For roasting meats, the best solution is to use a good meat thermometer. Cooking time will varies according to the temperature of the meat when it goes in the oven, for example, it will take a bit longer if it was just removed from the refrigerator.

• *Pan size* also affects baking and cooking times. Try to use the pan size called for in the recipe. If the correct size is not available, then get as close as possible to the volume of the recommended size. For instance, if the recipe calls for a 9-inch round pan, then the closest square pan would be an 8" square. (Remember there are no corners in a round pan.) Use your basic mathematical skills (Volume = length x width x height, or for circles, Volume = 3.14 x radius squared). Find a good chart that lists pan sizes.

• *Deglaze:* When a recipe says to "deglaze a pan," it means to add a liquid to the pan that, usually, has been used for browning, sautéing or roasting meat. The liquid is then brought to a boil over fairly high heat while stirring in all the little brown bits clinging to the sides and bottom. This process transfers all of the flavor goodies from the pan to the sauce or gravy.

• *Pan Gravies* - The simplest way to make a sauce is right in the pan used to cook the meat or poultry. Remove cooked item to a warm platter and add enough flour to drippings to make a roux. Stir and cook over medium heat for 1-2 minutes. Add stock, water, milk or cream ½ cup at a time. Bring to simmer and stir until sauce thickens. Continue to add liquid a little at a time and cook through until sauce reaches desired consistency. Season with salt, pepper and herbs or spices of your choice.

• *Preheat:* For optimal baking, always preheat an oven to recommended temperature for at least 10 minutes.

• *Reduce:* When a recipe says to "reduce" a liquid, it means to boil it moderately so that the volume will decrease through evaporation. The purpose is to concentrate the flavor of the liquid and/or to thicken it. The technique is used frequently for sauces and gravies. The resulting liquid is sometimes called a reduction.

• *Roux:* (pronounced roo as in kangaroo) A roux is a mixture of equal parts fat and flour. The fat could be butter, shortening, bacon fat or even oil. The fat is first melted or heated, then flour is added to it. The mixture is then stirred over low heat for a minute or two to cookout the raw flour taste. If the roux is for a white sauce this short cooking is all that is required. If the roux is for a brown sauce or gravy, it should be cooked longer until it is golden brown (the darker the roux, the darker the resulting sauce).

INGREDIENTS

• *Eggs:* When a recipe calls for raw eggs (such as in a mousse), use pasteurized eggs, now available in many large grocery stores. In rare cases, unpasteurized eggs can cause salmonella poisoning. Eggs for a cake batter should be room temperature - egg whites whip better when room temperature.

• *Pasta:* When cooking pasta, add a tablespoon or so of oil to the water. The oil helps keep the pasta from boiling over, and also helps keep it from sticking together when drained.

MEASURING PITFALLS

• *Measuring dry ingredients:* For dry ingredients such as flour, sugar, cornmeal, etc., use metal nesting measuring cups (the kind where the ingredients go clear to the top). Spoon the ingredient into the cup and level with a knife or spatula.

• *Measuring liquids:* Use glass measuring cups for liquids (the kind in which the marks can be seen through the container), so that the contents won't get spilled on the way to the bowl.

• *Weight vs. Volume:* Our cumbersome measuring system uses ounces for both volume and weight. Therefore, notice whether an ingredient is packaged by weight or volume. For example, 16 ounces of sour cream means it weighs 16 ounces or 1 pound. It does not mean that it will measure 2 cups (16 ounces by volume). It will, in fact, measure only between 1¾ and 1⅞ cups. The key is to look at the package amount. Sour cream says, "net wt 16 oz." That means, that it has been weighed rather than measured. Under serving size in the nutrition area of the label, it says 2 tablespoons. The number of servings is pegged at "about 15," which means "about" 30 tablespoons, not the 32 tablespoons that are in 2 cups. For some recipes, this small difference will not matter very much, but for baked goods, accuracy is much more important. (The pastry chef is often called the chemist of the kitchen, because accuracy is essential.)

• *Measuring pasta:* Dry pasta: Estimate 1 pound serves 4-5 people. Fresh pasta: 1 pound serves 3-4 people.

• *Package or can size:* Another pitfall when accuracy is important is can size. Many companies have changed the sizes of their containers (sometimes instead of raising the price), so watch carefully. For instance, if a recipe calls for 2 cups of chicken broth, be sure and measure. Most canned broth now comes in 14-ounce or 14.5-ounce cans rather than 16-ounce, meaning that a can contains only about 1¾ cups of liquid rather than 2 cups. (Hint: Water can be used to fill the cup instead of opening another can.)

• *Measuring "sticky" ingredients:* When measuring peanut butter, corn syrup, molasses and other sticky ingredients, first rinse the measuring cup with cold water. Shake out the excess

MEASURING EQUIVALENTS

1 tablespoon	=	3 teaspoons
½ tablespoon	=	1½ teaspoons
2 tablespoons	=	1 fluid ounce
4 tablespoons	=	¼ cup
16 tablespoons	=	1 cup
⅓ cup	=	5 tablespoons + 1 teaspoon
½ cup	=	8 tablespoons
1 cup	=	16 tablespoons
1 cup	=	8 fluid ounces
2 cups	=	1 pint
4 cups	=	1 quart
2 pints	=	1 quart
1 pint	=	16 fluid ounces
1 quart	=	32 fluid ounces
4 quarts	=	1 gallon

water leaving the cup moist, and then add the ingredient. It will slip out of the cup like magic.

LAST MINUTE REPAIRS

• *Cakes:* If part of a cake sticks to the pan, put it back together with icing. For layer cakes it is easy to hide with icing. For a tube or bundt cake, carefully put the parts together and make a quick icing or glaze to hide the damage. A little powdered sugar mixed with any liquid (water, milk, cream, lemon juice) and a bit of vanilla or other flavoring will hide many flaws. If it still shows too much try adding something bulky such as coconut, mini chocolate chips, chopped nuts, etc. to the top.

• *Sauces, Soups, and Stews:* If too thin, mix a teaspoon or two of cornstarch with a tablespoon of water. Add to the sauce and bring to a boil. For thickening a soup or stew, a few of the soft "bulky" ingredients (potatoes, vegetables, etc.) can be removed and pureed in a blender or food processor and stirred back into the liquid. If too thick, thin it a bit with hot water or broth. Sometimes the easiest way to mix in the broth is to remove a small amount of the "too thick liquid," add broth or water to it, and stir it back in. It will then be easier to incorporate into the stew.

• *Too Salty:* Cut a potato into large chunks and add to the stew or soup. Simmer for 10-15 minutes and remove if it doesn't fit with the other ingredients. The potato will absorb some of the excess salt.

TIPS ON PAIRING WINES
by Paul Gilster

There has never been such a variety of wine available in this country. And because so many of today's wines are labeled by type of grape, it's fun to match different foods with them to see what goes best with which variety. In general, be careful to match the weight of the wine with the desired entrée; full-bodied wines demand heavier dishes. Here are some pointers on good pairings to get the wine buyer started; a list of personal favorites will grow with experience.

RED WINES

Barbera: Famous in Italy's Piedmont region. Serve with grilled meats, especially when using spicy sauces; pasta featuring meat sauces; and game birds such as pheasant or quail.

Cabernet Sauvignon: The principal grape of Bordeaux. Best with rare beef, especially steak; rack or shank of lamb, duck, venison. For a more laid-back evening, Cabernet works nicely with pizza, hamburgers or a meaty lasagna.

Gamay: The classic grape of Beaujolais. Serve slightly chilled with seafood stews, grilled chicken, or hamburgers. Ideal with Parmigiano Reggiano and other hard cheeses.

Merlot: Velvety on the palate, Merlot is wonderful with lamb shanks or grilled duck, or consider beef in béarnaise sauce. A classic match with grilled salmon or rare tuna.

Malbec: Considered nondescript in France, Malbec soars in Argentina and is rapidly making waves in the United States market. Matches include: roast beef, leg of lamb or spicy sausage dishes and more.

Mourvedre: Normally found in the Rhône, usually blended with grapes like Grenache, Syrah and Cinsault. Mourvedre is superb with roasted salmon, or paired with game. Full-bodied Rhones like Chateauneuf-du-Pape are ideal with lamb.

Nebbiolo: The powerful grape of Lombardy, where it appears in Barolo and Barbaresco, among others. Matches: rustic stews, especially lamb, or beef roasts. A superb counterpoint to mushrooms, or pair it with aged cheeses.

Petite Syrah: An aggressive and dense wine that works with spare ribs or pork chops. It's weighty enough to stand up to Beef Wellington and dense game dishes like venison.

Pinot Noir: The great grape of Burgundy goes with salmon or tuna (perhaps its greatest match), or try light chicken dishes. Excellent with game, especially pheasant or quail, venison, rabbit. Beef short ribs work exceptionally well.

Sangiovese: The signature grape of Tuscany (think Chianti and Brunello di Montalcino). The lighter Chianti makes a great pizza wine. Try Sangiovese also with pork tenderloin, seafood etouffée or jambalaya. And it's ideally matched with pasta in tomato-based sauces, even spicy ones.

Syrah: A Rhône grape, known in Australia as Shiraz. Fine with Stilton and other blue cheeses. Other matches: grilled lamb chops, duck, liver, heavy soups (especially minestrone), or for a classic combination, try cassoulet.

Tempranillo: The grape of northern Spain's Rioja region. Try duck with a fruit glaze, or quail. Barbecued ribs or lamb chops also make a fine match.

FRA VITTORE (GUISEPPE) GHISLANDI (Italian),
PORTRAIT OF A YOUNG MAN WITH A TURBAN, c. 1720-30

Zinfandel: Ripe and peppery, Zinfandel brings out the best in Cajun dishes with blackened spices or sausages. Or try pork tenderloin, pork or beef roasts, or leg of lamb.

WHITE WINES

Champagne and other sparkling wines: Pair with shellfish or grilled seafood, but also consider duck in medium sauces and spicy sausage dishes. Excellent with stir-fried chicken or even turkey.

Chardonnay: Avoid overly-oaked California wines for the best food pairings. Oily dishes like salmon and roast duck are ideal. Shellfish, especially scallops or clams. Other possibilities: lighter meats, especially pork; chicken in light or cream-based sauces; grilled poultry.

Gewürztraminer: This Alsatian specialty matches with spicy sausage and pork dishes. Excellent to accompany Asian cuisines, or try it with pungent blue cheeses.

Marsanne: Grapefruit and honey notes make this grape ideal with grilled fish. Try shellfish and particularly oysters. Also works well with vegetable dishes and fruit.

Pinot Blanc: Subtle and expressive, Pinot Blanc pairs with chicken in light sauces, and is unusually good with chilled dishes such as antipasto. Also a fine match for clams, oysters or smoked trout.

Pinot Gris: A fruity, refreshing, uncomplicated wine. Try with antipasto or raw oysters. Excellent with a quiche.

Riesling: Germany's most famous grape, though remember that sweeter late harvest wines are designed for after dinner. Pair with shrimp, lobster, and seafoods in light sauces or grilled. Others: sautéed or roast chicken, spicy cuisines, especially Thai and Chinese. Superb with an onion tart.

Rousanne: Notes of orange and honeysuckle will go with richer seafood dishes. Nice with ethnic cuisines, from Thai to Mexican. Excellent with shellfish and grilled chicken.

Sauvignon Blanc: Assertive acids allow this wine to pair with smoked cheeses, bell peppers and stronger flavors. Ideal with sole, halibut or shrimp dishes and superb with vegetarian fare. Or try it with Vietnamese or Thai curries.

Viognier: Look for peach, pear and mineral notes. Pair with sautéed tuna or swordfish and other seafood in rich sauces. Works nicely with pork loin or Thanksgiving turkey.

AN ENTERTAINING TIMELINE

2 WEEKS BEFORE THE PARTY
- Make out a guest list
- Plan the menu including wine and other beverages
- Pick the recipes (remember dietary restrictions of guests)
- Invite guests

1 WEEK BEFORE THE PARTY
- Make out grocery list
- Buy nonperishable items
- Make ahead things that can be frozen, if desired
  — Breads: wrap in foil or put in freezer bags
  — Cakes: bake cake, put individual layers on cardboard cake circles (available where cake decorating supplies are sold) and wrap in heavy duty foil. Frost or ice the cake after thawing.
- Do any major cleaning that is needed
- Wash any dishes that have not been used in a long time
- Polish silver if necessary

2 DAYS BEFORE THE PARTY
- Buy the rest of groceries (except very perishable produce or bread)
- Cook anything ahead that will keep
- Clean house

1 DAY BEFORE THE PARTY
- Do final cleaning
- Set table
- Make centerpiece if using
- Get out all serving dishes
- Cook anything that will keep for one day

MORNING OF PARTY
- Cook anything that is possible to cook ahead
- Chop any vegetables, etc.
- Thaw anything that has been frozen
- Ice cake or finish dessert as necessary
- Buy any last minute groceries needed

2 HOURS BEFORE PARTY
- Organize last minute cooking including reheating foods
- Make sure all the prep dishes are washed
- Empty the dishwasher so it's free to load

30 MINUTES BEFORE PARTY
- Get dressed and ready to avoid last minute rush
- Take out any appetizers that need to be room temperature
- Take care of any last minute cooking that is possible
- Put butter dishes, etc. on the table if using

15 MINUTES BEFORE PARTY
- Open appetizer wine and get other hors d'oeuvres ready
- Fill water glasses with ice (water can be added later)

PARTY TIME
- Relax and enjoy your guests

RECIPE INDEX

All recipes contributed by
Museum members, docents and staff
feature the contributor's name.
Other featured recipes were developed by
Taste•Full Publications.

SUGGESTED MENUS

SOUP SUPPER
Caldo Zochitl 46 *OR*
Coconut Curry Chicken Soup 48

Strawberry Rhubarb Crisp 196

FAMILY HOMECOMING SUPPER
Genoa Shrimp over Focaccia 17

Lemon Lamb Shanks 140 *OR*
Soft Shell Crabs Meunière 84
Horseradish Potatoes 208
Italian Chard 206

Cocoa Profiteroles
with Espresso Sauce 181

HEAVY HOR D'OEUVRES/ OPEN HOUSE
Mother's Buffet Crab Meat 14
Tangy Shrimp Mold 17
Mushroom Croustades 25
Cucumber Dip with raw vegetables 26
Spinach Feta Bits 27
Roasted Beef Tenderloins
with a Mustard Sauce 131

Aunt Pauline's White
Chocolate Coconut Cake 173
Intense Chocolate Cake 180
Cranberry Buttermilk Cake 168
Grand Marnier Fruit 185

HOLIDAY DINNER
Latin Seviche 15

Fillet Mignon with Herb Crust 132 *OR*
Grilled Quail with Shallot Sauce 135
Creamed Chestnuts 208
Oyster Pie in a Potato Chip Crust 202
Sautéed Green Beans with Pecans
and Fresh Tarragon 206
Madeira Carrots 203

Steamed Cranberry Pudding 189 *OR*
Rummed Wreath Cake 170
Old-Fashioned Egg Nog 211

4TH OF JULY
Savory Blue Cheese & Vidalias 22

Lamb Shish Kebabs 106
Asian Noodle Salad 54
Green Salad with
Strawberry-Basil Dressing 210

Sarah's Double Chocolate Cookies 179

TEENAGE POOLSIDE PARTY
Grilled Chicken Havarti Sandwiches
with Red Onion Tomato Relish 103
Squash and Potato Skewers 207
Overnight Layered Spinach Salad 61

Vanilla Eclairs with
a Chocolate Glaze 189

DINNER WITH FRIENDS
Polenta Stars with Wilted Spinach
and Gorgonzola 21

Peppery Scallops 82 *OR*
Capered Sea Bass in Black Butter 79
Strawberry-Asparagus Salad 59
Herb Biscuits 165

Greek Coconut Lemon Cake 172

GRILLING OUT
Basil Blue and Smoked Salmon Pizzas
on the Grill 100

Tangy Tandoori Chicken 101 *OR*
Flank Steak Teriyaki 104
Curried Basmati Rice 203
Far East Cucumber Salad 54

Blackberry Cobbler 196
with Golden Honey Ice Cream 197

BRUNCH
Libba's Shrimp and Cheddar Grits 77
Santa Fe Salad 54
Bread Basket featuring
Banana Nut Bread 155
Cornmeal Angel Biscuits 164

PRE-CONCERT PICNIC
Marinated Flank Steak Sandwich 69
Patty Sue's Rice Salad with Shrimp 75

Zucchini Brownies 174

POTLUCK SUPPER
Chicken Tetrazzini 123
Cherry Pecan Salad 59
Marinated Cauliflower Salad 60

Dried Plum Spice Cake 171

AN *AL FRESCO* TEA
Inspired by The Garden Parasol
by Frederick Carl Frieseke

Finger Sandwiches featuring
Pennsylvania Brown Bread 163
with Maple Walnut Butter and
Black Walnut Bread 163
with Gingered Orange Spread
Frances Fresh Garden Spread 65
on Sourdough Rounds
Lemon Berry Trifles 185

QUICK WEEKDAY SUPPER
Evie's Poached Fish 78
Fancy Succotash 205
Sarah's Herb Bread 155

Banana Rum Sundae 198

FOOTBALL TAILGATE
Hoisin Ribs 105
Spring Vegetable Orzo Salad 55
Winesap Slaw 57

Southern Comfort Cake 170

BOOK CLUB LUNCHEON
Chilled Avocado Soup 41

Barbecue Chicken with Grilled Corn
and Cilantro rolled in tortillas 150
Grilled and Chilled Vegetable Salad 203

Macadamia Raspberry Shortbread 175

ART INDEX

Several featured paintings have been shown in detail only; a thumbnail of the entire painting has been included for reference.

Pompeo Girolamo Batoni (Italian)
The Triumph of Venice, 1737, pp. 166-167
Oil on canvas; 65⅝ x 112⅝ inches
Gift of the Samuel H. Kress Foundation

Gerrit Adrianesz. Berckheyde (Dutch)
*The Fish Market and the Grote Kerk at
Haarlem,* c. 1675-80, p. 77
Oil on panel;
17¾ x 16¾ inches
Gift of the Samuel H. Kress Foundation

Pierre Bonnard (French)
The Lessons, 1898, p. 29
Oil on board;
20¼ x 13¼ inches
Purchased with funds from the State of N.C.

Lucas Cranach the Elder (German)
Madonna and Child in a Landscape, c. 1518, p. 1
Oil on panel; 16½ x 10¼ inches
Partial gift of Cornelia and Marianne Hainisch in
tribute to their great-uncle Philipp von Gomperz, and
partial purchase with funds from the State of N.C.,
Mrs. George Khuner, Howard Young, Hirschl & Adler
Galleries, D.H. Cavat (in memory of W.R. Valentiner),
and Ernest V. Horvath, by exchange; Thomas S.
Kenan III; and various other donors, by exchange

Marsden Hartley (American)
Indian Fantasy, 1914, p. 81
Oil on canvas; 46¹¹⁄₁₆ x 39⁵⁄₁₆ inches
Purchased with funds from the State of N.C.

Winslow Homer (American)
Weaning the Calf, 1875, pp. 124-125
Oil on canvas; 24 x 38 inches
Purchased with funds from the State of N.C.

Pieter de Hooch (Dutch)
The Fireside, c. 1670-75, p. 41
Oil on canvas; 25½ x 30¼ inches
Purchased with funds from the State of N.C.

Claude Howell (American)
Beach Umbrellas, 1954, pp. 98-99
Oil on canvas; 20 x 40 inches
Purchased with funds from the N.C.
Art Society (Robert F. Phifer Bequest)

Claude Monet (French)
The Cliff, Etretat, Sunset, 1883, pp. 12-13
Oil on canvas; 21¾ x 31¾ inches
Purchased with funds from the State of N.C.

Pieter Cornelisz. van Rijck (Dutch)
Still Life with Two Figures, 1622, pp. 200-201
Oil on canvas; 49¾ x 58½ inches
Purchased with funds from the State of N.C.

David Salle (American)
The Emperor, 2000, p. 64
Oil and acrylic on canvas and linen
84 x 147 inches
Purchased with funds from the N.C.
Art Society (Robert F. Phifer Bequest)
©David Salle

Neil Welliver (American)
Breached Beaver Dam, 1975, p. 89
Oil on canvas; 95¹⁵⁄₁₆ x 96⅛ inches
Gift of Lee and Dona Bronson in honor of
Edwin Gill

Pieter Aertsen (Netherlandish)
A Meat Stall with the Holy Family Giving Alms, 1551, p. 136
Oil on oak panel; 45½ x 66½ inches
Purchased with funds from Wendell and Linda Murphy and various
donors, by exchange

African, Nigeria, Yoruba
Ceremonial Dish in the Form of a Rooster, 20th century, p. 49
Wood and paint; 16 x 6⅝ x 21½ inches
Gift of Edward H. Merrin

Anonymous, Spanish
A Man Scraping Chocolate, c. 1680-1780, p. 178
Oil on canvas; 41 x 28 inches
Gift of Mr. and Mrs. Benjamin Cone

Balthasar van der Ast (Dutch)
Still Life with Basket of Fruit, 1622, p. 209
Oil on panel; 19½ x 32 inches
Purchased with funds from the State of N.C.

Sir William Beechey (British)
The Oddie Children, 1789, p. 188
Oil on canvas; 72 x 71⅞ inches
Purchased with funds from the State of N.C.

John Beerman (American)
Three Trees, Two Clouds, 1990, p. 71
Oil on linen; 77 x 77 inches
Purchased with funds from Thomas S. Kenan, III
and the National Endowment for the Arts
©John Beerman

Ben Berns (Dutch)
Swamp Mallows, 1995, p. 110
Oil on canvas; 52¹⁄₁₆ x 90¹⁄₁₆ inches
Purchased in memory of William Luther Staton
(1871-1944) and
Mattie Worsley Staton (1882-1963) with funds
from their daughter Mary Lois Staton

Albert Bierstadt (American)
Bridal Veil Falls, Yosemite, c. 1871-73, p. 143
Oil on canvas; 36⅛ x 26⅜ inches
Purchased with funds from the N.C. Art Society
(Robert F. Phifer Bequest) and various donors,
by exchange

Jan Brueghel the Elder (Netherlandish)
*Harbor Scene with St. Paul's Departure from
Caesarea*, 1596, p. 85
Oil on copper; 14¼ x 21½ inches
Purchased with funds from the State of N.C.

Giacomo Antonio Melchiorre Ceruti (Italian)
The Card Game, c. 1738-50, p. 23
Oil on canvas 28½ x 40¾ inches
Gift of the Samuel H. Kress Foundation

Jean Siméon Chardin (French)
*Still Life with Ray and Basket of
Onions*, 1731, p. 45
Oil on canvas; 16 x 12⅝ inches
Purchased with funds from the State of N.C.

John Singleton Copley (American)
*Sir William Pepperrell and
His Family*, 1778, p. 34
Oil on canvas; 90 x 108 inches
Purchased with funds from the State of N.C.

Darius Painter Workshop, South Italian, Apulian
Rhyton, c. 360-340 B.C., p. 135
Red-figure ceramic with added white paint
L. 7¾ inches
Purchased with funds from various donors,
by exchange

Lena Bulluck Davis (American)
Kissed by the Gods, c. 1948, pp. 52-53
Oil on canvas; 18¼ x 24¼ inches
Purchased with funds from the N.C. Art Society
(Robert F. Phifer Bequest)

Egyptian, Late Period, Dynasty XXII-XXXIII,
c. 945-712 B.C.
Mummy Case of Amonred, p. 24
Wood with gesso and polychrome; H. 71 inches
Gift of the James G. Hanes Memorial Fund

European, Central
Spice Container in the Form of an Egg,
19th century, p. 37
Silver, cast, repoussé, chased; wood, carved;
H. 6⅛ inches
Gift of Elizabeth F. Gervais-Gruen in honor of
David Jonathan Gruen

Frederick Carl Frieseke (American)
The Garden Parasol, 1910, p. 187
Oil on canvas; 57⅛ x 77 inches
Purchased with funds from the State of N.C.

Ghislandi, Fra Vittore (Giuseppe) (Italian)
Portrait of a Young Man with a Turban,
c. 1720-30, p. 214
Oil on canvas; 55 x 39¾ inches
Gift of the Samuel H. Kress Foundation

Gilbert and George (British)
Cabbage Worship, 1982, p. 92
Gelatin silver-print black and white photographs,
hand-colored; mounted and framed in 30 parts,
(overall) 118¾ x 120 inches
Purchased with funds from the Madeleine
Johnson Heidrick Bequest
©Gilbert and George

Guatemala, Mayan
Cylinder Vase, ca. 700-800, p. 120
Terracotta with paint and slip; H. 7 inches
Gift of John B. Fulling

George Inness (American)
Under the Greenwood, 1881, p. 102
Oil on canvas; 36½ x 29¼ inches
Purchased with funds from the State of N.C.

Jan Lievens (Dutch)
The Feast of Esther, c. 1625-26, p. 116
Oil on canvas; 53 x 65 inches
Purchased with funds from the State of N.C.

Frank London (American)
Song Silenced, 1938, p. 72
Oil on canvas; 58¼ x 48⅜ inches
Gift of Mrs. Frank M. London and
Mr. Marsden London

Master of the Latour d'Auvergne Triptych
(French)
The Annunciation with Saints and Donors, called
The Latour d'Auvergne Triptych, c. 1497, p. 146
Tempera on panel; (overall) 26¹¹⁄₁₆ x 38⅝ inches
Gift of the Samuel H. Kress Foundation

Christian Mayr (American)
Kitchen Ball at White Sulphur Springs, Virginia,
1838, pp. 112-113
Oil on canvas; 24 x 29½ inches
Purchased with funds from the State of N.C.

After Luis Egidio Meléndez (Spanish)
Still Life with Bread, a Jug, and a Napkin, after
c. 1830, p. 154
Oil on canvas; 17½ x 13 inches
Purchased with funds from the N.C. Art Society
(Robert F. Phifer Bequest)

Oceanic, Micronesian, Caroline Islands
Coconut grater, 20th century, p. 183
Wood, mother-of-pearl (nacre), twine
15⅛ x 11 x 24⅜ inches
Gift of Mr. and Mrs. Gordon Hanes

Anthonie Palamedesz. (Dutch)
Merry Company, 1632, p. 122
Oil on panel; 18⅛ x 27⅞ inches
Gift of Mrs. George Khuner

Primrose McPherson Paschal (American)
Beulah's Baby, 1948, p. 162
Oil on canvas; 30 x 25 inches
Purchased with funds from the N.C. Art Society
(Robert F. Phifer Bequest)

Severin Roesen (American)
Still Life With Fruit, c. 1855-60, p. 58
Oil on canvas, 30¼ x 25 inches
Gift of the N.C. Art Society (Robert F. Phifer
Bequest), in honor of Mr. and Mrs. Charles Lee
Smith, Jr.

Juan Bautista Romero (Spanish)
Still Life with Strawberries and Chocolate,
c. 1775-90, p. 191
Oil on panel; 17 x 23 inches
Purchased with funds from the N.C. Art Society
(Robert F. Phifer Bequest)

Thomas Sayre (American)
Gyre, 1999, p. 145
Concrete, colored with iron oxide, reinforced
with steel, and mottled with dirt residue from
earth casting; (overall) 24 feet, 6 inches x
22 feet x 150 feet
Gift of Artsplosure, City of Raleigh, NC
©Thomas Sayre

Ilya Schor (American)
Passover Seder Plate, c. 1952-55, p. 206
Silver; Diam. 17 inches
Gift of Drs. Abram and Frances Pascher Kanof

Jan Steen (Dutch)
The Worship of the Golden Calf,
c. 1671-72, p. 130
Oil on canvas ; 70¼ x 61¼ inches
Purchased with funds from the State of N.C.

David Teniers the Younger (Flemish)
Dancers at a Village Inn, c. 1650, p. 20
Oil on canvas; 65¾ x 94⅞ inches
Purchased with funds from the State of N.C.

Jan Jansz. den Uyl (Dutch)
Vanitas Banquet Piece, c. 1635, p. 16
Oil on panel; 31⅜ x 37 inches
Purchased with funds from the State of N.C.

ACKNOWLEDGMENTS

In addition to photographing food at the North Carolina Museum of Art, the crew also spent four days on location at the home of Nancy and Monty White *in Raleigh, North Carolina. Our thanks for both their hospitality and willingness to share their beautiful property.*

Our thanks to the following businesses who contributed props for An Appetite for Art:

ETCETERA of Raleigh
Bent Tree Plaza
7901-109 Falls of Neuse Road
Raleigh, NC 27615
(919) 870-5757
Fax: (919) 870-5724

NORTH CAROLINA
MUSEUM OF ART STORE
2110 Blue Ridge Road
Raleigh, NC 27607
(919) 839-6262, Ext. 2153
Fax: (919) 715-8311
Web: www.ncartmuseum.org
E-mail: mshop@ncmamail.dcr.state.nc.us

VIETRI, Inc.
343 Elizabeth Brady Road
Hillsborough, NC 27278
(800) 277-5933
Web: www.vietri.com
E-mail: vietri@vietri.com

ZEST CAFÉ AND HOME ART
Six Forks Station
8831 Six Forks Road
Raleigh, NC 27615
(919) 848-4792
Fax: (919) 848-4794

RECIPE CONTRIBUTORS

PEGGY ALLGOOD
SARAH ALMBLAD
MARIAN ARETAKIS
KARLA ARUNDEL
VERONESE ATKINS
YVETTE BAINI
GEORGANNE C. BINGHAM
BILL BLAAUW
MARY M. BLAKE
CAROLYN R. BOOTH
EMILY S. BOWEN
MARTA BREWER
HELEN BARNES CHAMBLISS
MARIAN B. CHASE
REBECCA CLAYTON
JOAN NEWMAN COHEN
DELORES (DEE) COOK
JOANNA S. DALLDORF
JUDITH DICKEY
KRISTA DOROSHENKO
EVELYN (EVIE) DURBIN
RITA ELLIOTT
FRANCES M. EMORY
LIBBA EVANS
MRS. JAMES FICKLEN, JR.
JOYCE FITZPATRICK
DORIS FREEMAN
MAZIE FROELICH
MRS. FORREST GETZEN
GERRY GILBERT
BETTY GINN
LIZ GOTTLIEB
NANCY GREGG
AURORA K. GREGORY
SALLY HALLIDAY
MICHAEL HAYNES
SUE HENDRIX
CAROLYN HERGENROTHER
CLAIRE C. HESTER
VICKY TEMPLE HUBAND
MRS. CHARLES M. JOHNSON, JR.
MARY ALICE JACKSON
PEGGY JO KIRBY
DEAN WASIL KLEMUSHIN, SR.
JEAN LADD
EMILY LAMBETH
BARBARA SISK LANDON
SALLY LAZAR
IRENE LEJMAN
ELIZABETH K. LEVINE
HEATHER LOONEY

ADAM DAVID LOPEZ
CHERYL MAUPIN
LILLIAN MAXWELL
GILDA MCKINNEY
HEYWARD H. MCKINNEY, JR.
SUSAN MCVEIGH
PAULA MEHLHOP
ASSAD MEYMANDI
MARTHA MICHAELS
JEAN-MARIE MILLER
CHARLOTTE NEWBY
BETSY A. NIZICH
DOROTHY O'CONNELL
BETH CUMMINGS PASHAL
ELIZABETH WHITE PERRY
GLORIA B. PERRY
DALE PIXLEY
CONNIE POPE
JANET C. RAND
DELLAINE RISLEY
SHARON ROHRBACH
EMILY S. ROSEN
INGEBORG SAGAN
MRS. JAMES RALPH SCALES
HERIETA SCHENKEWITZ
HANNAH SCOGGIN
SUSIE SHARP
CONNIE C. SHERTZ
KAY SHIPMAN SCHOELLHORN
KAREL SHULTZ
JANET SIEGFRIED
GAB SMITH
JANE PARKER SMITH
SCOTTY STEELE
BERTI STEVENS
CAROLYN STIDHAM
LOUISE WOOTEN TALLEY
MRS. FEREBEE TAYLOR
FRANCES TAYLOR
MARY LIB TRENT
JOHN TURNER
NANCIE A. WAGNER
SARAH J. WARDEN
NANCY WAY
MRS. ZOË S. WEBSTER
ALICE M. WELSH
LAWRENCE J. WHEELER
GUINEVERE D. WILSON
JUANITA B. WILSON
MARILYN WOLBERG
ROSEMARY WYCHE